CHU HSI AND HIS MASTERS

AMS PRESS
NEW YORK

CHU HSI AND HIS MASTERS

AN INTRODUCTION TO CHU HSI AND THE
SUNG SCHOOL OF CHINESE PHILOSOPHY

BY

J. PERCY BRUCE, M.A., D.Lit.

THESIS APPROVED FOR THE DEGREE OF DOCTOR OF
LITERATURE IN THE UNIVERSITY OF LONDON

PROBSTHAIN & CO.,
41 GREAT RUSSELL STREET, LONDON, W.C.
1923.

Library of Congress Cataloging in Publication Data

Bruce, Joseph Percy, 1861-
    Chu Hsi and his masters.

    Originally presented as the author's thesis, London.
    Original ed. issued as v. 11 of Probsthain's
Oriental series.
    Bibliography: p.
    1. Chu, Hsi, 1130-1200. 2. Philosophy, Chinese.
I. Series: Probsthain's Oriental series, v. 11.
B128.C54B78 1973   181'.11 [B]   78-38050
ISBN 0-404-56904-8

Reprinted from an original copy in the collections
of the College of the City of New York

From the edition of 1923, London
First AMS edition published in 1973
Manufactured in the United States of America

AMS PRESS INC.
NEW YORK, N. Y.

TO THE MEMORY

OF

SAMUEL VINCENT

THE REVERED FRIEND AND TEACHER

WHO DIRECTED MY EARLIEST

STUDIES IN ORIENTAL THOUGHT

THIS BOOK IS AFFECTIONATELY

DEDICATED

CONTENTS

INDEX

PREFACE

THIS volume has grown out of what in its inception was intended to be an Introduction to my translation of the *Philosophy of Human Nature* by Chu Hsi. It was found necessary, however, to include a large amount of material which might have been omitted but for the almost entire absence of literature accessible to English readers bearing on the subject. The " Introduction " thus grew to such proportions, and was so widened in its scope, that it became advisable to publish it as a separate work complete in itself.

With regard to its aim and scope, it has long been felt that in our sinological literature there is need for a work, or works, which will focus the philosophical conceptions of the Chinese people, as distinguished from the ethical teachings found in the Classics on the one hand, and from the religious beliefs and folk-lore of the country on the other. The importance of the Sung School from this point of view is shown in the following pages. As I have pointed out in the companion volume referred to above, to those who have lived in China it is of no small interest to find, when they study the writings of these philosophers, that on almost every page are modes of thought and expression which to this day are to be observed among all classes of the people. Present-day Confucianism—that is, the system of ethical and metaphysical

conceptions current in China for the last seven hundred years—
is rather Chu Hsi's philosophy than that of Confucius. This
has recently been recognized by P. Doré in his term
" Tchouhisme ", and is acknowledged by all sinologues.

No apology, then, is needed for attempting this work, unless
it be that it called for abler hands than mine. Of its imperfections no one can be more keenly conscious than I am myself.
But I may at least plead that such imperfections are in no
way due to lack of interest. The more I have studied the
writings of this school, and particularly those of Chu Hsi,
the more my interest has deepened, both because of the
intellectual power they reveal and of the high ethical tone
of the teachings they embody.

As indicated in the title, the scope of the work embraces
the teachings of the Sung School as a whole. It must be
pointed out, however, that, while each of the great philosophers
whose names are closely associated with the school made his
own special contribution to its stream of thought, it is as that
stream passed through the channel created by the last of the
famous Five—Chu Hsi himself—that it assumed its final
trend. The philosophy of Chu Hsi is the philosophy of the
Sung School. In the title, therefore, and in the headings of
the several parts, I have expressly used the name of Chu Hsi
as the one in particular I am endeavouring to expound ; and,
while I have drawn attention to the contribution made by each
of the founders of the school, the system as a whole which is
here presented must be understood to be that of Chu Hsi so
far as I have been able to interpret him.

My obligations to various authors from whose works I have
received much help is duly acknowledged in the body of the

book. Here, however, I must gratefully express my indebtedness to my former tutor, Professor S. W. Green, M.A., of Regent's Park College, University of London, and to my colleagues in the Shantung Christian University, the Rev. E. W. Burt, M.A., the Rev. George Fisk, B.A., B.D., and the Rev. J. C. Keyte, M.A., for many helpful criticisms and suggestions.

J. PERCY BRUCE.

TSINGCHOWFU,
  SHANTUNG, CHINA.
    January, 1923.

BIBLIOGRAPHY

The following are the most important of the Chinese works consulted in the preparation of this volume, together with the abbreviations used in the case of those most frequently quoted:—

Abbreviation.

The Analects of Confucius	Analects.
The Great Learning	G.L.
The Doctrine of the Mean	D.M.
The Works of Mencius.	Mencius.
The Historical Records	Shu Ching.
The Odes	Odes.

[The figures in the footnotes where the above are quoted refer to Legge's *Chinese Classics*, the Hongkong edition.]

The Canon of Changes	Yi Ching.
The Book of Rites	Li Chi.

[The figures in the footnotes where the above two works are quoted refer to the *Sacred Books of the East*, vol. xvi in the one case and vols. xxvii and xxviii in the other.]

The Philosophy of Human Nature, by Chu Hsi, translated by J. Percy Bruce . . . . P.H.N.

朱子年譜	The Annals of the Life of Chu Hsi.	
歷代名臣言行錄	The Lives of Celebrated Men.	
尙友錄	A Biographical Dictionary.	
子書二十三種	The Works of Twenty-three Philosophers.	
朱子語類	Chu Tzǔ's Conversations . . .	語類
近思錄	Modern Thought, by Chu Hsi.	

Abbreviation.

御纂朱子全書　The Complete Works of Chu Hsi, Imperial 全書
　　　　　　　Edition.

正誼堂全書　　The Chêng I T'ang Library (including the
　　　　　　　lives and works of most of the philosophers
　　　　　　　of the Sung period).

宋元學案　　　The Literature of the Sung and Yüan Dynasties 學案

二程全書　　　The Complete Works of the Two Ch'êngs,
　　　　　　　including :—

二程遺書　　　　The Literary Remains of the Two Ch'êngs 遺書

二程外書　　　　The Additional Remains of the Two Ch'êngs 外書

二程粹言　　　　The Selected Writings of the Two Ch'êngs 粹言

御製性理大全　A Symposium of Philosophy, Imperial Edition 大全

御纂性理精義　A Digest of Philosophy, Imperial Edition　.　精義

理學宗傳　　　An Epitome of Philosophy　.　.　.　.　宗傳

ADDENDA AND CORRIGENDA

Page 5, line 8. For "difference" read "differences".

7, 10. Omit comma after "himself".

15. For 孑 read 子. Note: The expression 五子 was used before Chu Hsi's time and then included Shao Yung with the four earlier scholars. In later times, however, it has been commonly used as referring to the scholars enumerated in the text.

8, 10, 26. For "Tai" read "T'ai". So also on pp. 9, 12, and 39.

12, 13. For "Po" read "P'o".

29, 18. For "solicitude" read "solitude".

31, 3. See note above.

32, 3. For "Kun" read "Kung".

46, 23. Insert "capable" after "heart".

48, note 1. For "248" read "246".

52, line 24. Note: *The Right Discipline for Youth* is the rendering adopted by Dr. W. A. P. Martin. The meaning, however, is rather: *The Correction of the Unenlightened*.

53, 26. For "abeyed" read "obeyed".

56. Note: Chu Hsi had two *styles*, Yüan Hui (元 晦) and Chung Hui (仲 晦). Other sobriquets were Hui An (晦 菴), Hui Wêng (晦 翁), Tun Wêng (遯 翁), Yün Ku Lao Jên (雲 谷 老 人), Ch'ên Lang (沈 郎), Chi Yen (季 延). He was canonized as Wên (文).

11. For 1131 read 1130.

65, 23. Omit "two".

67, 5. For 乎 read 平.

73, 16. For 人 read 八.

76, note 1. For 52 read 56. Note 2, for 63 read 66. Note 5, for 宗 read 案.

Page 89, line 23.   Insert reference figure [1] after *Ultimate*.

101,   14.   For " cosmology " read " cosmogony ".

105,   4.   For " or " read " of ".

106,   5.   For " conversation " read " conservation ".

128, note 1.   For 善 read 義.

135,   3.   Add : See ibid., f. 4.

137.   Transpose the Chinese characters in note 1 with those in note 3.

139, line 5.   Read as one paragraph with the preceding.

149, note 1.   For 127 read 130.

152,   3.   For 132 read 129.

169, line 3.   For " casual " read " causal ".

6.   Insert " the " before " Non-existent ".

172,   28.   For " Ultima " read " Ultimata ".

181,   7.   Read as one paragraph with the preceding.

182,   27.   For " fathering " read " gathering ".

196,   14.   Cf. pp. 113–14 on this whole subject.

201, note 2.   Transfer to p. 202 as a note to lines 4–8.

211, line 27.   For " bird " read " birds ".

220,   10.   For " established " read " establishes ".

224,   16.   For " out of " read " cut off ".

229,   10.   For " psychical " read " physical ".

10, 12.   Insert quotation marks (" ") before " he " and after " earth ".

234,   10.   For " word " read " work ".

note 3.   For " whom " read " which ".

250, line 1.   Insert " man's " before " mind ".

251,   12.   For " suscultation " read " auscultation ".

262,   21.   Read " of " for " if " and omit comma after " who ".

267,   17.   Omit " in " before " discriminating ".

287, note 1.   For 55 read 59. Note 3, for 378 read 387.

292, line 12.   For (— —) read (—).

298,   8.   For " namely, that " read " that, as you say ".

304, 10–12.   Cf. pp. 294–6.

305,   21.   For " Pantheistic " read " Naturalistic ".

306,   24.   For " Buddhistic " read " naturalistic ".

PART I

THE FIVE PHILOSOPHERS

CHAPTER I

PRELIMINARY OBSERVATIONS

Hsing Li (性 理), the Chinese term for Philosophy, literally means " The Principles of the Nature ", the word *Li* referring to the four ethical principles of which man's nature is believed to consist. The term is said to have been first used by Ch'ên Ch'un (1151–1216),[1] the author of a small glossary of philosophical terms to which he gave the title *Hsing Li Tzǔ I* (性 理 字 義). Later, it was used by Hsiung Kang Ta, the author of a work entitled *Hsing Li Ch'ün Shu* (性 理 羣 書), or *A Library of Philosophy*. From that time the term has been universally accepted by scholars and used by them in their writings.[2]

The word Nature refers primarily to the nature of man, so that in its narrower and more specialized sense the true meaning of *Hsing Li* is " The philosophy of Human Nature ". There is, however, only one nature in the universe : the nature of man is the nature of heaven and earth ; he possesses it in common with birds and beasts. In fact, the unity of the Nature is a doctrine which constitutes the very warp and woof of Chu Hsi's philosophy and that of his school. For them man and the universe are one.

The term *Hsing Li*, therefore, has a double application. On the one hand, like the ancient term " philosophy " in the

---

[1] A native of Fuhkien, and a favourite disciple of Chu Hsi ; see *Philosophy of Human Nature*, by Chu Hsi, translated by J. P. Bruce, p. 196, n. 2.

[2] See Wylie's *Notes on Chinese Literature* (1867), p. 69.

West, it is comprehensive in its scope : it includes the consideration of all things physical and metaphysical. On the other hand, the philosopher studies the phenomena of the universe chiefly as throwing light on the problems concerning man : and, while all things come within his purview, the original standpoint is never lost : human nature is the underlying theme whatever the topic immediately under discussion may be.[1] It is very important that the reader of Chinese works on Philosophy should keep this twofold aspect continually in mind. When reading of Law and Matter, for example, or of the Supreme Ultimate, we must remember that the writer is treating of these from the point of view of human nature ; and, perhaps in some passage where it is least expected, he is referring to them as inherent in man, and as explaining the constitution of man's being. And, vice versa, when reading of man's nature or mind, we must keep before us the wide cosmic outlook if we are to keep in touch with the writer's thought. Only thus can we obtain a true perspective for the study of Chinese Philosophy.

THE RISE OF THE SUNG SCHOOL

Chinese philosophy—so far at least as it is indigenous to China—takes its rise in the Chinese Classics.[2] None but

[1] In the famous *Symposium of Philosophy* the *Hsing Li Ta Ch'üan* (性 理 大 全), we have an instance of this double application of the term. The expression *Hsing Li* occurs as the special title of nine books, in which the discussion is strictly confined to the nature of man ; but, as the central theme, it gives its title to the entire work of seventy books, including treatises on Cosmogony, Biography, Education, and other subjects.

[2] The chief of these are : *The Historical Records, The Odes, The Canon of Changes, The Book of Rites,* and *The Four Books.* The last named consist of *The Analects, The Great Learning, The Doctrine of the Mean,* and *The Works of Mencius.*

Buddhists, Taoists, and other thinkers, who are regarded by the Confucianists as heretics and whose theories are deemed subversive of the very foundations of society—none but these would dream of going beyond the sacred canon for the springs of their philosophic thought. Even the heterodox—for a distinction may be allowed between the heterodox and the heretic—appeal to the sacred text with reverence unsurpassed by their orthodox opponents. The difference between opposing camps resolve themselves largely into questions concerning the interpretation of sacred writings accepted on both sides as the final court of appeal.

While this is true, however, philosophy in the Classics from the nature of the case is scattered and fragmentary. Even in those parts of *Mencius*, which may be regarded as exceptions to this statement, the philosophy propounded is unsystematized ; while in the *Canon of Changes*—the ultimate source to which is traced the theory of the universe with which we shall be most concerned—the thought itself eludes the most patient and concentrated search. There was room, therefore, for the philosopher—as distinguished from the sage—who, in the reflective quiet of his study, concentrating his thought on the fundamental problems of the world and man from their intellectual side, endeavoured to gather up and unfold the meaning of those pregnant sayings in the Classics which touch on the ultimate realities of things.

It must also be recognized that, so far at any rate as the philosophers of the Sung School were concerned, they owed much—more perhaps than they themselves realized—to both Buddhism and Taoism. Not only were the theories of the orthodox philosophers modified in no small degree by the

arguments of their opponents, but some of their conceptions
are directly traceable to such sources ; and famous representatives of the School—notably Chu Hsi himself—at one
time or another were devotees of one or both of the above-
named religions. While, therefore, the springs of the Sung
Philosophy are to be found in the Classics, the stream was
fed by affluents of widely different origin.

Of speculative thinkers China presents no unworthy roll.
We need not dwell upon Lao Tzǔ, a man of towering intellect,
the contemporary of Confucius—if we may accept the verdict
of tradition—and, not only the founder of the Taoist sect, but,
one might almost say, the originator of speculative philosophy
in China. Nor need we speak of Mencius, the sage, reformer,
and philosopher. Apart from the sages, in the centuries
following Confucius there appeared an almost unbroken line
of great writers of all shades of opinion. Among them we find
rank heretics, provoking controversy and stimulating thought,
such as Kao Tzǔ, notorious as the opponent of Mencius, as
well as vehement defenders of the ancient faith like Han Yü,
whose writings to this day are regarded as a model of pure,
flowing literary style. They include the pessimist Hsün Tzǔ,
the egoist Yang Chu, and the altruist Mo Ti, or Micius, famous
as the apostle of universal love. Nor must we omit the famous
mystic Chuang Tzǔ, the follower and interpreter of Lao Tzǔ.

All these have their place among the vigorous thinkers, not
of China only, but of the world. The majority, however,
were more or less tainted with heresy, and through the whole
of the period in which they flourished there was no such marked
development of philosophic doctrine as we find in the West.
It was not till the eleventh century A.D., in the dark and

turbulent days of the Sung dynasty, that, within orthodoxy itself, the mine of Chinese metaphysical thought yielded its richest harvest. Then, in the literary renaissance of Chinese history, a galaxy of thinkers arose, forming what is known as the Sung School of Confucianism (宋 儒), whose writings crystallized the thoughts of ages into a system which has dominated the Chinese mind ever since, colouring the mental outlook of the most ignorant peasant not less really than that of the erudite scholar.

It was in this age that Chu Hsi appeared, not himself, the founder of the school, but the one who did most to create for it its all powerful influence. This great thinker, and his predecessors whom he loved to call his Masters, formed a group generally known as "The Five Philosophers" (五 子). Their names, in order of their appearance, were Chou Tun I, the two brothers Ch'êng Hao and Ch'êng I, their uncle Chang Tsai,[1] and Chu Hsi. Chou Tun I, the founder of the school, was born in the early part of the eleventh century (A.D. 1017), rather more than a hundred years before Chu Hsi (A.D. 1130), while the whole period from the birth of Chou Tun I to the death of Chu Hsi in A.D. 1200, extended through nearly two centuries.

POLITICAL EVENTS OF THE SUNG PERIOD

The two centuries covered by the lives of the Five Philosophers fell wholly within the term of the Sung dynasty, which lasted from the latter part of the tenth century till towards the end of the thirteenth, and was characterized by two outstanding events—the struggle with the Chins and the

[1] Chang Tsai was older than the two Ch'êngs, but his appearance as a representative of this school was later ; see p. 50.

career of the socialist scholar Wang An Shih.[1] A brief glance
at these is necessary in order intelligently to estimate the
influence of the Sung School.

The Sung dynasty was preceded by a long period of internal
division and weakness, ending in the Five Dynasties, which,
short-lived and insignificant, within the space of sixty years
followed one another in rapid succession. It is not a matter
for surprise that at such a time Chao Kuang Yin, a popular
general in the army, found no difficulty in inducing his
soldiers to proclaim him Emperor—under the name Tai Tsu—
and so became the founder of a new dynasty. This step was
followed by measures both politic and stern, which resulted
in a union and consolidation of the empire such as it had not
known for nearly eight centuries.

The dynasty thus auspiciously begun proved to be the
feeblest of the greater dynasties of China's history. This
weakness was owing to the growth in power of the border
tribes. From time immemorial the warlike races inhabiting
the regions to the north and west of China (the modern
Manchuria, Mongolia, and Thibet) had been a constant menace
to the sons of Han ; and in the century immediately preceding
the establishment of the Sung dynasty a tribe known as the
Chitans had been gaining in military prowess in the country
to the north-east, now known as the Liaotung Peninsula.
Considerable inroads had been made into Chinese territory
when Tai Tsu first assumed the Imperial power and dignity.
As was to be expected, the Emperor immediately took steps

---

[1] For a clear and informing account of the whole period see Boulger's
and Macgowan's *Histories of China*, from which most of the facts here given
are culled.

to meet this menace to his newly won empire. He made Peking—the city in which he was born—his capital, and from this stronghold, facing the frontier itself, he was able to check the power of the invaders. His brother and successor Tai Tsung completed the work, so far as the Chitans were concerned, by driving them out altogether from Chinese territory.

Allied to the Chitans, however, and occupying the territory to the north and north-west of them was a tribe which, having separated themselves from the main body of the Chitans, rapidly became their rivals for power. To this tribe Akouta their chief gave the name of Chin, signifying " Gold ", in contrast to a name signifying " Iron " by which the Chitans had styled themselves. The Chins, under their powerful chief, set themselves to the conquest of the Chitan tribes, and the Chinese Emperor Hui Tsung offered to join them in an alliance with this end in view. The proposal aroused the keenest controversy among Chinese statesmen. The weak court party were for joining with this new power against their ancient foes. The sturdy patriot party with far-seeing vision fiercely opposed the alliance, urging that to aid the Chins in destroying the Chitans was to feed the tigers which would turn again and rend them. The counsels of wisdom and courage on the part of this latter party were rejected ; and many of the wisest of the Empire's statesmen, including several philosophers of the school we are considering, retired from public life rather than share in a policy which boded disaster for the nation. The two allies attacked the Chitans from the north and south respectively, with the result that, though the Chins were everywhere victorious, the Chinese suffered overwhelming defeats.

Having thus subdued the Chitans the Chins, as had been foreseen, now turned their attention to China. Their first demand was for the cession of all the territory north of the Yellow River; and this the Chinese Emperor Hui Tsung, with strange supineness, allowed them to take without offering any resistance. Not content with this humiliating evidence of weakness the Emperor abandoned his capital, which at this time was at Kaifêng in Honan, and retired to Nanking. Such acts of cowardice availed him nothing, however. He and his son Ch'in Tsung, in whose favour he abdicated, were taken prisoners by the Chins, and died in captivity. Another son was placed upon the throne as Kao Tsung, who with a more courageous policy succeeded in stemming the tide of invasion. The Capital, nevertheless, was again removed, this time to Hangchow. Eventually, the Chins remained in possession of the northern half of China and the Sungs of the southern half, the two dynasties continuing as rival powers till both were overthrown by the Mongols. It should be noted that throughout this conflict the key province for which the greatest struggle was made was Honan, the home of three of the famous Five and of Shao Yung their most intimate associate.

The second outstanding event of the Sung period was the meteoric career of Wang An Shih. This famous socialist was born in A.D. 1021, four years after the birth of Chou Tun I. He was a native of Kiangsi, and from early years showed considerable intellectual power. In his young manhood he established a friendship with Chou Tun I, and later with the two Ch'êngs and Chang Tsai, though they were among the strongest opponents of his political schemes. After holding various offices in the provinces, he was called to the capital, and, in 1069, in the reign of Shên Tsung, he was appointed a member of the Council of State. In this position he rapidly gained the complete confidence of the Emperor ; to such an extent, indeed, that he soon became his favourite minister. Finding himself thus securely entrenched in power, he proceeded to carry into effect the theories, social and political, which he had long held. New laws, effecting reforms startling and revolutionary in their nature, were promulgated with bewildering rapidity, of which the most important were the nationalization of "commerce, industry, and agriculture", a system of conscription, and a radical change in the monetary system. The object of these measures was the equalization of wealth and the uplifting of the poor, who not only were relieved of all taxation but were also generously assisted by state loans. The interference with the currency resulted in a depletion of copper cash followed by financial panic, to meet which the nominal value of each coin was doubled by proclamation. These innovations were violently opposed by a large number of the metropolitan and provincial statesmen, and the conflicts in the Imperial Council Chamber were many and bitter. It says much for Wang An Shih's ability and force of character that standing alone in the face of such universal opposition he was able to carry through his schemes. But his power was short-lived. In little more than ten years his policy was completely reversed, while he himself was banished in disgrace from the Court and superseded by his ablest opponent, the famous historian, Ssŭ-Ma Kuang. Wang An Shih died in 1086 at the age of 65.

THE LITERATURE OF THE SUNG SCHOOL

It is an interesting fact that the periods in which the Chinese Empire has been politically weakest have produced her greatest thinkers and writers. Confucius and Mencius each appeared in an age when the Empire was broken up into petty states in perpetual feud with each other, while the Imperial power was little more than a nominal suzerainty ; and throughout the whole period of the Sungs, when the Empire was engaged in the fierce struggle with the Chins, making it in a political sense the most humiliating period in her history, there was witnessed a literary revival not unworthy to be compared with the Elizabethan period of English literature. It affected every branch of scholarship. Historians like Ssŭ-Ma Kuang, poets like Su Tung Po, and philosophers too numerous to be specified, all shared in the great movement.

It is to the credit of the Sung sovereigns that, amid all the distractions of continual war with formidable enemies, they did much by their patronage to promote this renaissance. Tai Tsung, the second emperor, revived the hereditary privileges of the descendant of Confucius, and thus re-established ethical teaching in the respect and honour of the people. The fourth emperor Jên Tsung restored ancient seats of learning, and founded new schools in every town and city throughout the land. One cannot escape the conviction, however, that the turbulence of the times and the political unrest contributed not a little to the intellectual power, and still more to the moral force, of the philosophers' teaching; national dangers constituted a challenge which called forth their loftiest aspirations both for themselves and for their race. But whatever the cause, through their high ethical doctrines the Five Philosophers and their associates exerted a widespread, uplifting influence on the social conditions of the people ; in the statesmanship of the Empire they earnestly and persistently contended for their principles ; and, though unable to control either foreign or domestic policy, they kept those principles alive in the heart of the nation till events proved their worth and paved the way for their ultimate triumph.

Chu Hsi was born just after the Sungs, fleeing before the inroads of the Chins, had abandoned their capital at Kaifêng for Nanking, and later for Hangchow ; so that the appearance of the great philosopher, the last of the Five, synchronized with the culmination of national disaster. It adds to the force of what has been said above that, notwithstanding the fact that politically the nation had reached its nadir, the spread of the new learning from this time onwards was phenomenally rapid. Among the Chinese themselves it has become a byword that " with the southern migration of the Sungs the revival of Philosophy began ".[1] This revival was as remarkable in its persistence as it was in its rise.

Chu Hsi's own disciples were numerous enough, but the movement did not end with them. Many had their own schools, through which the new ideas were handed on to others, and by these again transmitted, until the system became the established orthodox cult for the whole nation, as it has continued to be for the last 700 years.

As will be seen from the biographical sketches given in the next three chapters, each of the Five Philosophers

[1] 宋自南渡理學始盛.

contributed valuable works to the literature of the period, the most important of which are there enumerated. To these were added the writings of numerous contemporary and later philosophers.

In the fifteenth century the *Hsing Li Ta Ch'üan* (性 理 大 全), a Symposium of Philosophy in seventy books, was compiled under Imperial auspices, and published in the thirteenth year of Yang Ho (1415), one of the early emperors of the Ming dynasty. In this library, as it may well be called, were gathered together the writings and opinions of as many as a hundred and twenty representatives of this school. The first part consists of complete works by the earlier philosophers Chou, Chang, Shao Yung, and others, with commentaries and original works by Chu Hsi. The latter part consists of the symposium proper, containing selected passages from the writings of various authors, grouped under different subjects. By far the largest proportion of these selections is from the writings of Chu Hsi himself, who, if not the most original, was probably the most prolific, and certainly the most famous writer of them all. A digest of the Symposium under the title *Hsing Li Ching I* (性 理 精 義) was published in twelve parts in the eighteenth century (A.D. 1717) by an Imperial Commission appointed by K'ang Hsi, the great emperor of the Manchu dynasty period. Portions of this work were translated into French by M. de Harlez, and published in Brussels in 1890. The translation is now out of print.

It is a disadvantage that in the latter part of both the " Symposium " and the " Digest " the opinions of the various philosophers are quoted in detached paragraphs, not to say detached sentences, apart from their original connexion, and re-grouped in such a way that, though a certain classification of subject-matter is followed, the continuity of argument is almost wholly lost. Fortunately, within a few years of the appearance of the " Digest ", a complete edition of Chu Hsi's own works was published, in sixty-six books, in which this defect is considerably lessened ; for, though the volumes consist of selections from the Philosopher's writings and lectures re-grouped according to subject, each individual selection is nevertheless sufficiently complete in itself to afford some idea of the course of the argument. In this way the advantage of classification is obtained at not too great a cost. This work was also produced under Imperial auspices. A commission for the purpose was appointed by K'ang Hsi in 1712, just five years before the appointment of the commission to prepare the above-mentioned " Digest ".

Of the Imperial edition of Chu Hsi's works, Books xlii to xlviii are devoted to the Philosophy of Human Nature and constitute a work complete in itself with its own special title of *Hsing Li* (性 理). Two other parts, Books xlix and l, treat of the Theory of the Universe under the title of *Li Ch'i* (理 氣), *Law and Matter*. Of these two parts on the Theory of the Universe, the first was translated into English by the late Canon McClatchie in 1874, and published under the title of *Confucian Cosmogony*, with full Introduction and Notes. Twenty years later, the same work was translated into French by le Père Stanislas le Gall with a discursus on the teachings and influence of the author Chu Hsi.[1] The

---

[1] *Le Philosophe Tchou Hi, Sa Doctrine, Son Influence*, par le P. Stanislas Le Gall, S.J.

former, as the title indicates, is a study in cosmogony rather than in philosophy. In his Introduction and Notes, however, the author has given an exhaustive comparison between Chinese conceptions and those of the ancient Greeks and Romans. Père Le Gall's translation is more successful than that of the Canon in expressing the thought of the Philosopher, and his introductory matter is considerably wider in its scope. Part I, which gives a historical survey of the Sung School and its literature, is specially helpful.

The seven books of Chu Hsi's works which treat of the Philosophy of Human Nature, a translation of which is published in a companion volume of this series, are the authoritative exposition of human nature as understood and interpreted by the Sung School. The work begins with a very full discussion of the nature of man from what perhaps may be called the metaphysical point of view, answering such questions as " What is it ? " " Is it good ? " and " What is its relation to the material element in man's constitution ? " (Books I and II). The more psychological point of view is next taken up, and the place of mind in man's constitution, together with its relation on the one hand to the Nature, and on the other to the external world, is fully treated (Books III and IV). This is followed by a discussion in Book V on the all-comprehensive Moral Law and its relation to concrete Virtue, forming a transition section leading up to the concluding portions (Books VI and VII), which treat of purely ethical subjects. In these, the last two books, the cardinal and subsidiary virtues are expounded in considerable detail, the greater portion of the space being devoted to the premier virtue Love.

CHAPTER II

CHOU TUN I AND SHAO YUNG

Chinese biography and Chinese history alike present considerable difficulty to the western reader. Apart from the question of their historicity, which in the nature of the case is not easy to determine, there is the added difficulty of the monotonous character of the records. The difficulty is somewhat analogous to that of the western traveller in some parts of the Flowery Land itself. As he journeys through the country he finds every village the exact counterpart of every other village, every city four-square, and, even to its gates and streets, its houses and shops, the facsimile of every other city ; so that it is difficult even to recognize places with which he would expect to be familiar, while the flowers, which the name of the country would lead him to look for to brighten and relieve the monotony of the landscape, are rarely seen. So it is with Chinese history. Consisting of chronicles of events more or less disconnected and at the same time similar in their essential features, the records of one dynasty differ little from those of the preceding—with the single exception of the last, the Manchu Dynasty, when the rude West intruded itself upon the scene—while they lack just those features which we most desire to know. In Chinese biography, again, the same or similar incidents, mostly prosaic, or if not prosaic, then fantastic, appear and reappear with monotonous repetition under different names ; and when the subjects of the biographies belong to one class, as in the case of the famous Five, this characteristic becomes still more marked. It should be said, however, that the source of the difficulty lies in the chroniclers rather than in their subjects. The patient perusal of the records furnishes sufficient indication of the character and influence of the men whose deeds they relate to make us wish we could know more of them, not simply as they appeared in the public eye, but as they were in their homes and among their friends.

CHOU TUN I

Chou Tun I (周 敦 頤),[1] the first of the Five Philosophers, was born in the year A.D. 1017 at Lien Hsi in Ying Tao, a district of Tao Chou, in Hunan province. His style[2] was Mao Shu (茂 叔), but he came to be best known by his literary name Lien Hsi (濂 溪),[3] the name of his native village, and taken from a brook in the immediate neighbourhood. It was here that as a young man the Philosopher spent his hours of recreation, either wandering along the banks of the stream, or in music in a kiosk on one of its bridges, or angling in the stream itself.

Chou Lien Hsi, to call him by his more popular name, was the son of Chou Fu Ch'êng, sometime magistrate of

---

[1] His name was originally Tun Shih. To avoid disrespect to the Emperor Ying Tsung, who had the same name, it was changed to Tun I.

[2] The Chinese custom is to have more than one name in addition to the surname. The first is the *ming* (名), which may be called the " clan " or " birth " name. It is given by the elder of the clan, and can never be changed. The second name, the *tzŭ* (字), translated by Giles as " style ", is a complimentary name by which its owner is addressed by his intimate friends. A third name is the *hao* (號), which in the case of our philosophers may be regarded as the " literary name ".

[3] Meaning " The Stream of the Waterfalls." *Hsi* is also read *ch'i*.

Kuei Ling, a district in Huo Chou, a sub-prefecture of Kuang Hsi. Though deprived of parental guidance and counsel by the premature death of his father, the boy, we are told, in early years developed a love for what was good and true. As a man he was actuated by high ideals, possessed of wide learning, strong and resolute in action, kind-hearted and generous to those in need. In office he was skilful in affairs, precise in his habits, showing in his judicial decisions a happy combination of severity and leniency. In a word, according to his biographers, he was not unworthy to be ranked with the ancient sages.

In the year 1036, through the influence of his uncle, a sub-chancellor of the Grand Secretariat, Lien Hsi obtained his first appointment in a Government Department at the Capital. Later he became Keeper of the Records—an office which carried with it the position of assistant Magistrate—at Fên Ning in Kiangsi. At this place almost his first official act was to settle a suit which had long baffled the efforts of his predecessors, with the result that he immediately became famous, and, in the eyes of the people, outstripped men of much longer experience.

From Fên Ning he was moved to Nan An, in the southern part of the same province. Here his sense of justice and faithfulness to conscience were as marked as his skill had been at Fên Ning. As an instance of this, the story is related of a man convicted of crime, but not legally liable to the death sentence. Lien Hsi's superior officer, the Salt Comptroller, was intent on the extreme penalty, and rejected the strong report of his subordinate, which was in a contrary sense. Whereupon Lien Hsi sent in his resignation, exclaiming:

" How can I continue in office under such conditions ? To take a man's life in order to curry favour with those in power is a thing I cannot do." The result was that the Comptroller's eyes were opened to the true facts of the case, and the convict's life was saved.

Lien Hsi's next appointment was to the magistracy of Kuei Yang, where his reputation for beneficent rule was still further enhanced. Here he won the admiration of his superior, the Prefect Li Ch'u P'ing ; one of the results of whose friendship was that the latter became desirous of studying philosophy, and accordingly sought Lien Hsi's advice. Lien Hsi, with characteristic frankness, told him that he was too old to study by private reading, but himself offered to teach him orally. The offer was accepted as simply as it was made, and for two years the tuition was continued with gratifying success. When Li died his young children were generously cared for by his friend, who made the necessary arrangements for the funeral, and managed all their family affairs for them.

From Kuei Yang, Lien Hsi was promoted to be Prefect of Nan Ch'ang, where the news of the appointment was received by the people with great delight. The fame of the Fên Ning case had already reached them, with the result that there was widespread expectation on the part of the victims of injustice that they would now be able to plead their cause in a just court ; while among the wealthy and those of the official classes, many of whom were both young and dissolute, there was great consternation at the unpopularity which they foresaw they would incur if in any way they obstructed the young officer's beneficent rule.

Later, while Judge at Ho Chou, through misrepresentations from various quarters, the Philosopher came under the displeasure of Chao Pien, a minister of one of the Imperial Departments in the Capital. He continued, however, to act as before, unperturbed by the Minister's attitude of manifest antagonism, until, Lien Hsi having moved to a post in Ch'ien Chou, Chao Pien had the opportunity of watching him more closely, and thus was able to form a truer estimate of his character. With striking frankness he took him by the hand, saying, " I had almost missed a noble man for my friend ; henceforth I shall know Chou Mao Shu."

In 1068, the first year of the Emperor Shên Tsung, Lien Hsi was Prefect of Pin Chou, but, through the recommendation of Chao Pien, was promoted again to be Judge in the Kuang Tung Transport Administration. Here, as elsewhere, he combined mercy with justice, seeking above all else to redress wrong wherever he went on his circuit, and sparing himself no toil or hardship if he could accomplish this end.

It is not surprising that such a strenuous life was a comparatively short one. On account of illness, brought on doubtless by strain and overwork, he applied for a post at Nan K'ang, which enabled him to reside among the Lu mountains. The spot chosen for his residence was at the foot of the Lien Hua Peak (Lotus Flower Peak), not more than 2 miles distant from the grave to which some years earlier his mother's remains had been removed from their original resting place. It is pathetic to notice how in these last months of his life he seemed to look back wistfully to the scenes of his boyhood. Flowing at the foot of the mountain was a tributary of the P'ên River, and this he named " Lien Hsi " from the brook at his old home in Ying Tao.

Chao Pien, who had now become general of the Ssŭ Ch'uan Army, was anxious to obtain the services of his friend ; but before the appointment could be made, the great philosopher died, on the seventh day of the sixth month in the year 1073, at the comparatively early age of 57. He was buried by the side of his mother in the village of Tê Hua on the slope of a low-lying hill about 4 miles south-east of the modern Kiukiang. Both the house and the monuments at the tomb were destroyed by the Taiping rebels. In the reign of Hsien Fêng, about the year 1866, the tomb was restored by an Imperial general, and again in the reign of Kuang Hsü, about the year 1884, by a high official of the court. Since that time it has been kept in a fair state of preservation under the care of the Sage's direct descendants, of whom at the present time there are representatives of the twenty-fourth and twenty-fifth generations.

The graves are all covered by one mound, and in front of the mound are five stone tablets, the centre three of which are to the memory of the Sage's mother, the Sage himself, and his two wives. The position of the graves is indicated by that of the tablets. The mother lies in the centre, her son on her left, and the son's two wives on her right. On the outermost tablet, next to that of the Sage, is engraved his portrait, copied from a similar tablet in the ancestral home at Tao Chou in Honan. On the tablet at the other end of the line is a picture of a boy and girl gathering lotus flowers for the Sage, who regarded them as the most beautiful of all flowers, and as typical of the noblest virtues.[1]

Behind the mound are three other tablets. On the centre one of these is inscribed a eulogy of the Sage by the general who restored the tomb. The tablet to the right, like one of those in front, but belonging to a more ancient period, is to the memory of the Sage. The one to the left is the most ancient of all, and by far the most interesting feature of the shrine. On it is engraved the famous " Diagram of the Supreme Ultimate " (T'ai Chi T'u), with its accompanying monograph, which formed the basis of the Sage's philosophy and that of the Sung School.

The tomb lies in the dense shade of noble, widespreading trees, enclosed by a wall on three sides, the hill against which the mound rests forming the fourth boundary of the enclosure. As the enclosure is entered, in the foreground is a pool, crossed by a miniature bridge, and beyond the pool, on the hillside, is the mound with its monuments, approached by two flights of steps.

The location is one of the most beautiful which could be found for such a purpose, and peculiarly appropriate to the personality of the Sage. Lying in a valley encircled by green-clad hills, the shrine faces the Lu Mountains, some of

---

[1] There is still extant what might be called a prose sonnet, entitled *Ai Lien Shuo* (愛 蓮 說), written by Chou Tzǔ in praise of the Lotus as compared with the Peony, with its profusion of display, and the Chrysanthemum, which to him was suggestive of excessive modesty and reserve. See 周 濂 溪 先 生 全 集, pt. viii, f. 1. Local scholars tell us that the boy and girl are guides to departed spirits in crossing the Bridge of Fate. The special connexion of this explanation with the Sage, however, is not very apparent.

which tower to a height of several thousand feet, while winding through the rice-fields which fill the valley is the inconspicuous " brook " which the philosopher loved. In such surroundings were the remains of Chou Lien Hsi laid to their rest. The shrine has now become a sacred resort for pilgrims, a worthy object of reverence for all who realize the debt they owe to the noble man who did so much to conserve the moral life of a great people.

Of Chou Tzŭ's literary works the two most noted have fortunately been preserved. They are the *T'ai Chi T'u Shuo* (太 極 圖 說), referred to above, and the *Yi T'ung Shu* (易 通 書), more generally known by its abbreviated title of *T'ung Shu* (通 書), both of which were edited and published after the author's death by his pupils Ch'êng Hao and Ch'êng I. *The T'ai Chi T'u Shuo*, or *The Diagram of the Supreme Ultimate Explained*, is of such importance that a complete translation is given in Chapter VI, where its teaching is fully discussed in connexion with Chu Hsi's theory of the Final Cause. It is not necessary, therefore, at this stage to do more than indicate its place in Chou Tzŭ's contribution to the thought of his age. It takes its title from a passage in the *Yi Ching*, or *Canon of Changes*, in which the eight diagrams symbolizing the phenomena of the universe are said to have their origin in the *T'ai Chi*. Chou Tzŭ seized upon this statement, and from it elaborated a theory of the universe, the fundamental thesis of which is the twofold assertion of the unity of the Great Source from which all things proceed and the essentially ethical character of that Source. This theory he set forth in his monograph. In its opening sentence, the One Source to which all things are traced is

described as " Infinite ! And also the Supreme Ultimate ! "
by which the author meant to predicate infinity of the First
Cause, not in the bare negative sense of the absence of all
limitation, but with the positive connotation of an ethical
Being, the absolute Truth, immanent in the universe as the
source from which all things spring, and at the same time
transcending time and space and all material existences.[1] As
has just been said, the fuller consideration of the significance
of this doctrine must be left for a later chapter, but the reader
may here be reminded that the great achievement of the Sung
School was to rescue the ethical teaching of the Classics from
its threatened oblivion by bringing that teaching into close
relationship with a reasoned theory of the universe, which in
comparison with that of Buddhism or Taoism may at least
be called a sane philosophy ; and the accomplishment of this
was largely owing to Chou Tzǔ's doctrine of the Supreme
Ultimate as set forth in this monograph.

It should be stated that Lu Hsiang Shan,[2] one of Chu Hsi's
contemporaries, throws doubt on the tradition which attributes
this treatise to our philosopher, maintaining that it could not
have proceeded from the same author as the *T'ung Shu*. A
long discussion between Lu Hsiang Shan and Chu Hsi mainly
turns on the word " Infinite " (Wu Chi) with which the treatise
begins. Lu's contention was that no such expression occurs
in the *T'ung Shu*, and therefore if the *T'ai Chi T'u Shuo* was
not by a different author, the expression must have been
either an interpolation from some other source which was
mistaken by later writers for Chou Tzǔ's own, or the monograph itself must have been the work of the Philosopher's

[1] See p. 135.   [2] See p. 74.

earlier years, and by the time he wrote the *T'ung Shu* he had come to recognize it as erroneous. The literary argument was really a pretext covering the objector's antagonism to the doctrine taught by the expression in dispute ; and Chu Hsi's answer, given at great length, is directed to this objection, showing the truth of Chou Tzǔ's statement and the place it has in his philosophy.[1] For us it is important to remember that Chou Tzǔ's works were published by the two brothers Ch'êng Hao and Ch'êng I, who were themselves his most intimate pupils ; that the interval between Ch'êng I's death and Chu Hsi's birth was not more than twenty-three years ; and that Chu Hsi's father was a contemporary, and indeed a pupil, of Yang Kuei Shan, who, in his turn, was a pupil of the two Ch'êngs.

The close relationship between the ethical teaching of the Sung School and their theory of the universe is strikingly illustrated in the *Yi T'ung Shu* (or *T'ung Shu*), the *Complete Interpretation of the Yi*. The theme of this later work is mainly ethical. As such it is complementary to the earlier treatise, and must be regarded as an integral part of the author's philosophical system. It contains forty chapters, consisting of terse, pregnant sentences, evidently constructed with great care. As some of the chapters are hardly more than paragraphs the book is not large. In the opening chapter the author explains what is the foundation of all good, namely TRUTH. The word is the same as that used in modern colloquial for sincerity, but its meaning is deeper and wider than is ordinarily conveyed by that word. It is truth in

---

[1] See 學 案, pt. xii, f. 4 ff.

one's whole being, the absolute TRUTH which pervades all nature. It is, in fact, another word for the Absolute itself, which the author in his earlier treatise terms the T'ai Chi, or Supreme Ultimate. This absolute Truth is the root of all goodness, whether in the Saint (聖 人), the highest type of goodness known to men, or in the Sage (賢 人), or in the Noble Man (君 子). These are the three grades of goodness which in this book, as in the Classics, are presented for men's aspiration. The Saint aspires to the Heavenly, the Sage aspires to Sainthood, and the Noble Man to the wisdom of the Sage.

From the consideration of Truth the author passes to the praise of Moral Law as manifested in the five cardinal principles of man's moral nature, and cherished in their perfection by the saints. To observe this law is the highest honour, to practise it the truest blessedness. Thence, by an easy gradation, we are led to the necessary qualifications of the teacher, on whom, above all others, depends the maintenance and spread of virtue among the people. Be he saint, or be he one in common life who fights the battle of the right against the wrong, the teacher must be just, straightforward, and firm, and at the same time kindly, lenient, and conciliatory. He must avoid evil, lest his good qualities be converted into cruelty, obstinacy, and weakness. With such teachers good men will multiply, and the whole nation, from the Throne downwards, will be virtuous. The greatest calamity for a people, the author maintains, is to be destitute of conscience, for it is conscience that makes men teachable.

In later chapters, the principles of government, the place of Thought, Love, Reverence, Friendship, and Music, in the inculcation and growth of virtue, and the relation of all these to the will of Heaven and the nature of man are treated, with examples of saintly attainments in Yi Yin the minister of T'ang and Yen Yüan the disciple of Confucius.

It is interesting to note that, in contrast to the sages, Lien Hsi in his public work held comparatively obscure posts. He does not rank as one of China's statesmen. His title to fame is as a teacher, and as founder of a philosophical school. As teacher the impression he made on his contemporaries was remarkable. Ch'êng Hao tells us that when he first saw Chou Mao Shu he was so exhilarated that he could not refrain from singing all the way home. On one occasion a pupil of I Ch'uan with his thirst for philosophy unsatisfied visited Lien Hsi and confided to him his perplexities. The Master, receiving him affectionately, said, " We must talk these matters over together " ; and, detaining him as his guest, he held his interest enchained while for three days they discussed the problem. Kindling with enthusiasm the youth returned to I Ch'uan declaring that to look into the vistas of truth now revealed to him was like gazing at the heavens in their vast illimitableness ; and I Ch'uan replied significantly, " Yes, you have evidently been with Chou Mao Shu." It is stated that the famous Wang An Shih, while still a proud young scholar, after an interview with Chou, was so excited by the new realm of thought opened up to him that he could neither eat nor sleep.

> Then felt I like some watcher of the skies
> When a new planet swims into his ken ;
> Or like stout Cortez when with eagle eyes
> He stared at the Pacific—and all his men
> Looked at each other with a wild surmise—
> Silent, upon a peak in Darien.

From the encomiums of his biographers it would appear that the secret of this fascination lay as much in the personality of the teacher as in the subject-matter of his teaching ; and the index to his character furnished by the incidents of his life so far as they are recorded fully justifies this belief. The picture presented to us is that of a simple, straightforward and warm-hearted man, modest when praised, and steadfast in the face of blame. Though personally frugal and abstemious almost to the point of asceticism, he was charitable to the poor and generous to friends in need.[1] And not the least interesting is the fact that, meagre as are the materials for his biography, they reveal an ardent love of nature which probably contributed not a little to his interpretation of the riddle of the universe. The story goes that he refused to allow the grass in front of his window to be cut, because in its instinctive love of life he recognized its kinship with himself. In his choice of a final retreat he betrayed the same love of solicitude and communion with nature as was shown in his younger days when he found his solace in music to the accompaniment of the rippling brook, or in angling in its numerous cascades. In all this we recognize that sympathy with nature which showed him to be poet as well as philosopher and which, it may well be, had much to do with the influence he possessed over the minds of those who attached themselves to him.

But it is probably as founder of a school that the name of Chou Lien Hsi is most honoured in history. We do not know

---

[1] On one occasion, when he was ill, a friend, P'an Hsing Ssŭ, who visited him, found that his belongings could be packed into a single basket, whilst his money amounted to less than a hundred copper coins.

what it was specifically that kindled the enthusiasm of men like Ch'êng Hao and Wang An Shih, but we do know that the influence of his teaching upon the thought of his age was sufficient to justify his claim to be one of the creative thinkers of the world. His conception of the Supreme Ultimate was so far removed from that of the *Yi Ching* as to be new in all but name, and, while it was expanded by later philosophers and reinforced by other lines of thought which they initiated, it was Chou Tzŭ who created the conception, and made possible all that followed. It must be borne in mind that from the death of Mencius there had been a dearth of scholars in the orthodox school of thought, while of Chou Tzŭ's contemporaries, outside the school which he himself founded, those who pretended to scholarship were the slaves of tradition and literary pedantry. What intellectual life there was in the nation was to be found rather among Taoists and Buddhists than among the orthodox, with the natural result that orthodox philosophy itself had to borrow from these other schools, and as a consequence was in danger of becoming contaminated by loose thinking. It is not too much to say that Chou Lien Hsi, with all the intellectual vigour and independence that was possessed by the heretics, but with a sobriety which both fostered, and was fostered by, his reverence for the sages, succeeded in restoring the stream of philosophical, not to say religious, thought to healthier channels. Small wonder that his biographers exclaimed, " What great things he achieved ! "

Shao Yung

In the preceding chapter the names of five philosophers are given as the founders of the Sung School. There was, however, a sixth, Shao Yung (邵 雍), who, born six years before Chou Tun I, may be regarded as the forerunner of them all. His name is not included by Chinese writers in the general title, possibly because he held a place somewhat apart ; but his influence on the opinions of the School, notwithstanding his retired life, was hardly less powerful than that of Chou Tun I himself.

Shao Yung was born in the year 1011 of humble parents at Fan Yang in Chihli. His style was Yao Fu (堯 夫), but he is more generally known as K'ang Chieh (康 節), the name by which he was canonized. In his youth Shao Yung showed unusual ability as a pupil, and was as ardent as he was intelligent, eagerly absorbing everything in the way of literature that lay within his reach. From early years his cherished ambition was to attain to such excellence as was reached by the sages ; in pursuance of which ideal he lived a spartan life, and devoted himself to his studies with untiring zeal. His biographers tell us, perhaps somewhat hyperbolically, that " He neither lit a fire in winter, nor used a fan in summer ; he neither stretched himself on a mat, nor reclined his head on a pillow ".

While still a young man he moved with his father to Kung Ch'êng in An Hui, where he attracted the notice of Li Chih Ts'ai, the Magistrate, by his earnestness in the pursuit of learning. The youth received much wise counsel and teaching from his older friend, and became his devoted pupil, ministering to him with reverent affection.

After completing his education Shao Yung decided to travel. " The Ancients," said he, " are the friends of a thousand generations, and can I be satisfied when as yet I have not

gone beyond the boundaries of my own home ? " He visited
Ch'i, Lu, Hsiang, Chin, and other northern provinces.
Returning to Kun Ch'êng, he settled at a place called Pai Yüan
(Hundred Springs), from which his school received its name of
the Pai Yüan School.

Subsequently he moved to Lo Yang (the modern Honanfu)
in Honan, choosing it partly because of its central position
in the Empire, and partly because it was both the home of
ancient sages and the favourite resort of modern scholars.
For a while he lived in a hut open on all sides to wind and rain,
but later his friend Ssŭ-Ma Kuang and others bought a cottage
and garden for him, which he named " The Nest of Peace and
Joy ". Here he lectured on the subjects dear to his heart,
and here he was visited by many from far and near, including
some of the most noted men of the day. One of these was
Ssŭ-Ma Kuang himself, who afterwards became famous as
historian, poet, and statesman. Chang Tsai and the Ch'êng
brothers were also among his most frequent visitors, and
doubtless owed much of their own philosophy to the Hermit's
teaching and inspiration. Others were Fu Pi, a distinguished
statesman, and Wên Yen Po, one of the ablest men of the
time, who established a club in which precedence was
determined by seniority in age. It was said that visitors to
Lo Yang might neglect to visit the grandees of the city but
did not fail to find their way to the Hermit's hut.

Shao Yung's influence in his own immediate neighbourhood
was not less than on those from afar. His simple goodness
shamed the wrong-doer. When, at intervals, he visited the
city, as soon as the sound of the barrow on which he rode
announced his approach, the people would rush to welcome

him, some even in their eagerness—so the tale goes—putting their shoes on the wrong feet; while the favourite name by which he was spoken of by many was " My Master ", so individual was the influence he exerted.

Although repeatedly recommended to the Throne, Shao Yung persistently declined office, and is the only one of those whose lives are here sketched who remained permanently in retirement. This did not mean that he took no interest in the political condition of his country; on the contrary, he had decided opinions, and was ready to give his advice to all who sought it. As already stated, it was a time of upheaval both from without and from within. Many consulted him about the problems by which they were confronted, particularly in the difficulties created by Wang An Shih's ultra-socialistic measures. Many in disgust were retiring from office, some even competing to be among the first to be cashiered. His urgent advice to such was to hold on. " This is the very time," he said, " when men of worth are needed to put forth all their strength. The new laws are severe ; but if in your administration you can relax their severity by only one-hundredth part, the people to that extent will be relieved. Why should you seek to be cashiered ? "

As a consequence of these laws many of the rich became poor and the poor poorer. Luxuries had to go. Shao Yung suffered with the rest, with the result that he had no wine even to offer to his guests. But poor as he was in material things, many felt themselves enriched by the new wine of his philosophy, and in their affection for him took care that his simple needs were supplied.

When 60 years old, pleading age and bodily weakness

D

as unfitting him for the ordinary affairs of life, he adopted the costume of the recluse and became more than ever rigid in his retirement. His intimate friends, however, did not cease to visit him. But the years that remained to him were few ; in the summer of 1077 he was attacked by a serious ailment which ended in his death. That he would not recover he himself seemed to realize from the first. " Life and death are but the common lot," he said to Ssŭ-Ma Kuang with a smile. Chang Tsai and Ch'êng I were with him in his last days. The former, himself versed in the mysteries of the Eight Diagrams, asked his friend if he might not reckon his destiny (*ming* 命) for him. The dying man replied, " If I already know Heaven's decree (*ming* 命) I do not need to know what the world calls destiny (*ming* 命)." Chang Tsai was silenced. " You do indeed know Heaven's decree," he said reverently, " what is there left for me to say ? " I Ch'uan asked if he had no last counsels to give now that he was to be separated from them. Extending both hands towards them the old man said : " Make the path before you broad, for if you make it narrow there will not be room enough even for yourselves ; how then can you help others along the road ? " Humour lighted up his face and words to the last. When I Ch'uan asked if all his learning now was as if it were nothing, he was too weak at the time to reply, but the next day he feebly whispered the answer: " If you were to tell me that yams grow on trees I would believe you." Whether or no his mental faculties were as weak as he whimsically described them to be may be questioned. In any case his physical senses were still alert, and his last words showed that there was no diminution in his love of country or of home. His friends had gathered together in the garden, at a little distance from the hut lest they should disturb the dying man, who naturally was the subject of sad and earnest conversation. To their surprise, however, he overheard all that passed. Calling his son to him, he said, "These friends are arranging for my funeral to be here in this neighbourhood. Tell them it is my wish to be buried with my own people in my own home." Later he heard someone speak of important news having been received, and eagerly inquired what the news might be. "Ah!" he exclaimed when he was told, "I had hoped it was that Yu Chou had been re-taken from the Chins!"

On the fourth day of the seventh month, the chronicler informs us, in the year 1077, the old hermit, quaint to the very end, composed his own epitaph :—

> In peace was I born,
> In peace now I die.
> You ask me my age ?
> I am threescore and seven.
> If I look up to Heaven
> Or out towards the world :
> Of intentional wrong
> I am conscious of none.

Shao Yung's chief literary works were the *Cosmological Diagrams* (經 世 衍 易 圖), *A Treatise on the Study of Phenomena* (觀 物), and *A Dialogue between a Fisherman and a Woodcutter* (漁 樵 問 對). These were edited and published in one work by the author's son, Shao Po Wên, under the title of *Huang Chi Ching Shih Shu* (皇 極 經 世 書). The *Cosmological Diagrams*, consisting of the first two parts of the complete work, contains an elaborate exposition of the theory of numbers with which the author's name is intimately associated. It was founded on the eight diagrams of the *Yi Ching*, the chief subject of his study. Starting from an assumed numerical value of the active and passive modes of matter a system of numbers was worked out by which all phenomena were explained. The main features of the system are given by Dr. Legge in the Introduction to his translation of the *Yi Ching*; and, in its relation to geomancy, it is explained in considerable detail by Dr. Eitel in his work on *Fêng Shui*. Following the treatise on Numbers is the *Study of Phenomena*, consisting of two parts, the first of which was composed by the Philosopher himself, and is of importance as presenting to us his application of the theory elaborated in the preceding treatise to the history of the world and man. The second is a more or less heterogeneous collection of sayings recorded by the Philosopher's pupils. The concluding part of this collection contains, besides some miscellaneous writings, the *Dialogue between a Fisherman and a Woodcutter*, a discussion of philosophical questions in conversational form.

In the collection of works above described the section on Numbers is manifestly the most important, and is generally regarded as the author's chief contribution to the philosophy of the period. Its outcome, however, has been for the most part a system of necromancy which has fostered superstition rather than developed healthy thought. The chief importance attaching to this philosopher's teaching from our point of view lies rather in a short passage of not more than four sentences occurring in the preface of a book which so far as we have been able to discover is not now extant. In the list of the

Philosopher's works given by his biographers, in addition to those mentioned above, is one entitled *Songs of the Soil from I Ch'uan* (伊 川 擊 壤 集). All we know of this work is its title, that it contained twenty books, and that it consisted of poems written by Shao Tzŭ in the later years of his life. The passage in the preface to which reference has been made contributed not a little to the Sung exposition of the doctrine of Human Nature. It reads : " The Nature is the concrete expression of Moral Law : the Mind is the *enceinte* of the Nature ; the body is the habitation of the Mind ; and the external world is the vehicle of the body." One of the problems which appears and reappears in the voluminous discussions of the period is the relation of the nature of man to the all-comprehensive *Tao*, the existence of which is assumed by all schools, though with varying interpretation of its meaning. Another problem, hardly less persistent in its demand for solution, is the relation of the Nature to the other elements in the constitution of man's own being. Shao Tzŭ's dictum helped to an explanation of both these problems. In his statement, " The Mind is the *enceinte* of the Nature," he teaches that the component principles of the Nature are contained in the Mind as the organ of their manifestation ; while in the opening sentence, not only does he assert what the Nature itself is, but he answers the question which for Chinese thinkers is the question of questions : " What is *Tao* ? " *Tao*, he says, is not unknowable, as Taoism teaches. Though invisible as to its substance, it finds its concrete expression in man's nature, the law of God written upon the heart. We shall find later that in Chu Hsi's time this question became the very pivot of controversy, and that Chu Hsi in

his cogent answer to Taoism owed more perhaps to Shao Tzŭ
than to any other of his teachers. As often in the storms
of controversy great minds have held tenaciousiy to some
single pregnant saying as vital to the whole fabric of truth,
so Chu Hsi and those who thought with him clung to this
dictum as to a sheet anchor amid the conflicting intellectual
currents of their time.

CHAPTER III

THE BROTHERS CH'ÊNG AND CHANG TSAI

While Chou Tzŭ was in office at Nan An a notable friendship was formed with a military officer of the same district, named Ch'êng Hsiang. At their first meeting Ch'êng Hsiang saw that Lien Hsi was no ordinary man, and, when he came to converse with him, recognized at once that he was a philosophical thinker. The acquaintance between them soon ripened into the closest intimacy. Ch'êng Hsiang sent his two sons, Ch'êng Hao and Ch'êng I, aged 14 and 13 respectively, to study under Lien Hsi; who early imbued them with deep reverence for the sages, especially for Confucius and Yen Tzŭ, urging them to pay special attention to what these two regarded as the chief good in life. Thus began a stream of influence destined to have far-reaching results in the ethical as well as the philosophical life of the nation.

Ch'êng Hsiang (程 珦) came from a family in Chung Shan, a small kingdom of the later Chou dynasty, but now a district, Wu Chi Hsien (無 極 縣), in the province of Honan. For three generations there had been members of the family in official life, the great-grandfather of Ch'êng Hsiang having held high provincial office in the reign of Tai Tsung. Ch'êng Hsiang was a man of high moral purpose, noted for his resolute independence and straightforwardness. Among the many incidents of his life recorded by his biographers two may be mentioned as indicative of his character. The first occurred during his term of office at K'ung Chou. A man named Ch'ü Hsi Fan, who belonged to some savage tribe, had been killed. It was spread abroad among the country people that Ch'ü's spirit had issued an order that they should erect a shrine to him at Nan Hai where they could meet with him. Ch'êng Hsiang sent to inquire into the matter, and was informed that the local magistrate had already tried to put an end to the superstition by ordering the sacrificial vessels to be thrown into the river, but that instead of sinking to the bottom they had floated, and even floated against the stream, with the result that the mischief was spreading more rapidly than ever. Ch'êng Hsiang peremptorily ordered the vessels to be thrown into the stream again. The order was obeyed, and, whatever may have been the case previously, this time they were washed away by the current, and the superstition with them. The other instance was on the occasion of a banquet in a Buddhist temple to which Ch'êng Hsiang was invited. When the wine-drinking was at its height a cry was suddenly raised that light was shining from the Buddha. Immediately there was a rush of guests trampling one upon the other in their eagerness to see the miracle. Ch'êng Hsiang, however, remained quietly seated, unaffected either by the superstition or by the turmoil.

The same spirit of independence marked his conduct in the larger matters of government. In the course of the revolution originated by Wang An Shih, many officials high and low, in dread of the all-powerful minister, promptly carried into effect the new laws as they were promulgated. Ch'êng Hsiang was among those who were strongly opposed to the new order of things, and, as a consequence, retired into private life. He died in the fifth year of Chê Tsung (1090), aged 85. He was accorded posthumous Imperial recognition of his high character, and his remains received a state funeral.

Ch‘êng Hao

The elder of Ch‘êng Hsiang's sons, Ch‘êng Hao (程 顥), style Po Ch‘un (伯 淳), is generally referred to by his literary name Ming Tao (明 道). He was born at Lo Yang in 1032, and, while still young, attained to considerable scholarship, obtaining the degree of Chin Shih at the age of 25. As already intimated, it was from Chou Lien Hsi that both he and his brother imbibed their love for philosophical study, and so became the channel through which Chou Tzŭ's conception of the universe was handed on to posterity.

Ming Tao's first appointment was as magistrate at Hu in Shansi, where he early distinguished himself by the manner in which he settled a family dispute concerning hidden treasure. A man, living in a house which he had borrowed from his brother, found a hoard of coins buried in the ground. The owner of the house having died before the discovery of the treasure, his son claimed the money, alleging that it had been buried by his father. Ming Tao asked, " When was it buried ? " The reply was, " Forty years ago." " When was the property loaned ? " " Twenty years ago." Some of the coins were then produced and found to be all of the same date, having been minted about sixty years prior to their discovery ; upon which Ming Tao said to the claimant, " Money does not take more than five or six years from the time it is minted to be circulated all over the empire, how comes it that these coins were not circulated in the same way, although, according to your own story, they were minted a score of years before they were buried here ? " The claimant had no answer to this conundrum, and the case collapsed.

Ming Tao's next appointment was at Shang Yüan, where he showed the same contempt for superstition as had characterized his father. Finding upon his arrival that the people were worshipping a huge variegated crocodile which had been in the neighbourhood for a long time, he immediately ordered the creature to be killed.

Later at Ch'in Ch'êng his tenure of office was marked by vigorous measures for the improvement of the morals of the people, of local government, and of education. He devoted a great part of his time to teaching those who visited the city, giving special attention to the inculcation of ethical principles. The system of local government was reorganized and a head man appointed for every five families, whose duties included such diversified matters as laying information against smugglers, the assistance of the poor and destitute, and the care of sick travellers. Education, however, called forth most of his reforming energy. Every village was provided with its school, in which none but efficient teachers were employed, while he himself spent much of his time in personally visiting those schools, conversing with the managers, and examining the scholars. On such occasions he seems to have taken delight in chatting familiarly with the country people, and especially in himself teaching a class of the most promising young scholars. It is not to be surprised at that, at the end of his three years' term of office, the people sorrowed as at the loss of a father.

In 1069, through the influence of Lü Kung Chü, the head of the Censorate, Ming Tao was recommended for appointment as Censor, and thus came under the notice of the Emperor Shên Tsung, who had but recently ascended the throne (1068). Ming Tao presented a courageous memorial in which he urged upon the Emperor the regulation of the mind, the control of the passions, and, in affairs of state, the promotion of the wise and talented. An audience having been granted, Ming Tao reiterated in person the most important points of his memorial. The Emperor seems to have been touched by the evident earnestness and sincerity of the memorialist. He bowed and said, " For your sake I will be careful."

It was in this very year, however, that Wang An Shih, already high in favour with the court, and appointed State Councillor, began to carry into effect his startling theories. Ming Tao's difficulties at such a time must have been very great, but his solution of them was the simple one of fearless and straightforward action. On one occasion, having been summoned by decree to the Council Chamber, he found Wang An Shih heated by a discussion in which he had just met the fierce opposition of his adversaries. Ming Tao, observing Wang's face as he greeted him to be still flushed with resentment, quietly reminded him that the government of the Empire was not the affair of one family alone, and urged him to control himself and listen to what the assembly had to say. Wang An Shih coloured at the rebuke but submitted to the advice. In the discussions which followed, Ming Tao frequently took part, fearlessly criticizing the new regime. In his final protest he said : " The wise man, like the fish in the sea, will avoid dangerous places. Never since the dawn of history has any one succeeded in the government of a people along lines condemned by all as contrary to reason and repugnant to virtue. To force measures by choking discussion, to promote the incompetent and unworthy, to side with the wrong against the right, is simply to court disaster."

As might be expected after such a protest, Ming Tao found it advisable to retire from the Court and the Capital. He accepted a provincial appointment as Judge at Hsien Shu Chên. The Yellow River having burst its banks at a place called Ts'ao Ts'un, Ming Tao approached the Prefect urging that the capital itself was endangered, that it was a minister's duty to sacrifice himself, if need be, for the state, and begged for troops to assist him in the work of stopping the breach. The assistance was given, and Ming Tao again distinguished himself by the skill and promptitude with which he averted the threatened disaster.

Appointed Magistrate at Fu Kou, Ming Tao found that the river at that place was infested with pirates, from ten to twenty junks being destroyed by them every year. Fortunately, he was able to secure the arrest of one of the robbers, and through him to seize the whole band ; but instead of inflicting severe punishment upon them, he compelled them to earn their living by towing junks under surveillance on the very river which they had previously terrorized. He was not allowed, however, to continue his beneficent administration. Impeached as one of the first to oppose the new regime, he was dismissed from office. Chê Tsung, on his accession in 1085, was anxious to bring the faithful minister into prominence once more ; but it was not to be : the Philosopher died in the same year at Lo Yang.

Ming Tao's biographers are full of his praises as a great and loyal statesman. They tell us that his face always wore a serene expression. His pupils and friends, who knew him through a long course of years, bore testimony that they never once saw him show temper. Whatever might be the business in hand, and however suddenly brought before him, he never became excited or lost control of himself. An earnest seeker after truth, he read widely the writings of philosophers of all schools. For ten years he studied deeply the doctrines of Taoism and Buddhism, but found his intellectual peace in the Classics. Anxious to pass on to others the inward satisfaction which he had experienced for himself, his writings are full of wise counsels to the learner. He urged that the mind of the student in his early years, when it is still alert but most easily swayed, should be steeped in the classics, and that he should not allow essay writing to make him the slave of literary form. Desire of any sort, he said, enslaves the will; and, while literary polish is desirable in the scholar, yet, if it be the one thing sought after, this ambition, like any other ambition, will destroy the will, and with it the moral sense.

Ch'êng I

Ch'êng I (程 頤), style Chêng Shu (正 叔), but best known by his literary name I Ch'uan (伊 川), was more famous in the literary world than his older brother, partly because his life was longer by twenty years, and partly because, for the greater part of his career, he elected to live in comparative retirement in order that he might devote himself to study and literary labours. It is probably for the latter reason also that his biographers have little to record of his life in other respects. In his youth he studied under Chou Lien Hsi and took his Doctor's degree at the age of 24, in the same year as his brother. When only 18 years old he had the temerity to memorialize the Emperor on the needs of the state.

During the reigns of Ying Tsung and Shên Tsung, though frequently recommended by high ministers, he steadily declined to take office. When Chê Tsung came to the Throne, Ssŭ-Ma Kuang and Lü Kung Chü together presented a memorial in praise of " The Honan scholar Ch'êng I " as a man who loved the ancients, was sincere and simple, was not a place-seeker, and ordered his life in accordance with the rules of decorum. Such a man, they urged, should be raised to high office. The Emperor, in accordance with this advice, offered I Ch'uan an appointment, but the offer was declined. Later, however, he accepted office as tutor to the Emperor.

Upon his arrival at Court, I Ch'uan lost no time in imbuing the youthful monarch with his principles. A small incident pleased him as showing that his teaching was not without result. Hearing that Chê Tsung on one occasion shrank from some ants which he found in his bath, he asked the Emperor if it was true. The Emperor acknowledged that it was so, and that his reason was that he feared he would destroy them. This to the Philosopher was significant of a heart of noble things.

In his public life I Ch'uan continued the family tradition of straightforwardness. He protested against any congratulations being paid to the young Emperor until after the funeral of his predecessor, and also against either music or banquet forming part of the funeral ceremonies. But his blunt speech, and perhaps haughty demeanour, made him many enemies in the Capital.   Among them was Su Tung P'o, the famous poet, whose opposition to I Ch'uan was strongly resented by the disciples of the latter.   In 1095 I Ch'uan was sent to Pei Chou, but was recalled to the court on the accession of Hui Tsung.   Not long after, however, he retired to Chung Ning, where he died in 1107.

The writings of the two brothers still extant are chiefly in the form of essays and letters.   They have been collected in compilations, the most important of which are entitled *The Literary Remains of the Two Ch'êngs* (二 程 遺 書),   *The Additional Remains of the Two Ch'êngs* (二 程 外 書), *The Collected Writings of Ming Tao* (明 道 文 集), *The Collected Writings of I Ch'uan* (伊 川 文 集), and *The Selected Utterances of the Two Ch'êngs* (二 程 粹 言).   Ming Tao seems not to have produced any large or distinctive work such as Chou Tzŭ's *T'ung Shu* or Chang Tsai's *Chêng Mêng*.   The *Ting Hsing Shu* (定 性 書), *A Treatise on the Steadfast Nature*, which is his one writing referred to by its title, is not more than a letter.   I Ch'uan wrote a commentary on the *Yi Ching* entitled *Chou Yi Chuan* (周 易 傳), which is often referred to, and seems to have had great influence in the development of the distinctive doctrines of the school.

The literary style of both writers was frequently commented upon by Chu Hsi.   Comparing the two he said, " I Ch'uan's method is to divide his matter clearly into sections.   Ming Tao generally favours continuous discourse, which seems at first to lack a governing unity, but when carefully studied reveals a connexion running through the entire work." [1]   " Ming

---

[1] 全 書, bk. xlv, f. 11 (*P.H.N.*, p. 248).

Tao's style," he says again, " is very comprehensive. Although at the first reading it is difficult to grasp his full meaning, with more careful study the divisions of the subject and their mutual relation become clear." [1] The reason for this characteristic seems to have been in the rush of his ideas ; his treatise on the Steadfast Nature, Chu Hsi says, " gushed out from his mind as if there were some force behind pushing the ideas out so rapidly that he could not express them all in writing." [2] Such a writer needs to be read carefully. His language, on the one hand, has qualities of genius ; it is " lofty, far-seeing, comprehensive, and broad ". On the other hand, and for this very reason, it could not be treated with the same precision as that of ordinary writers ; " the interpretation of it must not be restricted to its literal meaning."

If Chou Tzǔ's teaching is to be regarded as the source of the Sung philosophy and as having determined the direction of its current, it was the rush of thought flowing from the minds of the two Ch'êngs which gave volume to the stream. The greatness of their influence is evidenced by the extensive quotations from their writings by later philosophers, and the numerous discussions to which they gave rise. Perhaps their most conspicuous contribution was the doctrine of the Physical Nature, by which they clarified Mencius' doctrine of the goodness of the Nature, and laid to rest the long controversy which began with the discussions between that sage and Kao Tzǔ. But in other directions their influence was hardly less powerful. Chou Tzǔ's doctrine of the Supreme Ultimate was expanded

---

[1] Ibid., bk. xlv, f. 10 (*P.H.N.*, p. 248).   [2] Ibid.

and interpreted along lines suggestive of Plato and Aristotle. In a notable passage, much discussed, Ming Tao speaks of the Tao as " Void like the boundless desert, but filled with innumerable Forms like a dense forest ! " [1] The passage is quoted by Chu Hsi as explaining two sentences in Chou Tzŭ's monograph : " The statement, ' Infinite ! And also the Supreme Ultimate ! ' " he says, " means that latent in the Infinite are arrayed innumerable forms as in a dense forest ; . . . and, conversely, the statement that the Supreme Ultimate is essentially the Infinite means that the substance of the Supreme Ultimate is void like the boundless desert." [2]

To state all that the two brothers contributed to the Sung doctrine would be to anticipate a large part of what is discussed in subsequent chapters, but one other point must be mentioned, namely, the place of Love in their philosophical system. " The Principle of Origin of the Four Attributes," said Ming Tao, " corresponds to Love among the Five Cardinal Virtues ; in the narrow sense it is but one, in the comprehensive sense it includes the four." [3] The significance of this passage is that the principle of Origin pervading all things is what in man's nature we call Love, that it includes all those ethical principles which constitute man's being, and is the source of all laws by which the universe exists. It is of interest to note that the position thus given to Love in the universe and in man was one of the cardinal features of Chu Hsi's philosophy, and that he owed it largely to the teaching of his " Master the Philosopher Ch'êng ".

[1] Ibid., p. 297, n. 1.
[2] 精 義, bk. i, f. 9.
[3] 全 書, bk. xlviii, f. 17 (P.H.N., p. 417).

CHANG TSAI

The fourth of the famous Five was Chang Tsai (張 載), the uncle of the two brothers Ch'êng, to the elder of whom he was senior by not more than twelve years. He was born in A.D. 1020 at Ta Liang (大 梁) in Honan. Notwithstanding his seniority in age, and his earlier appearance as a philosophical teacher, his adherence to the doctrines of this school was later than that of his nephews to whom, indeed, he owed his own enlightenment. His *style* was Tzŭ Hou (子 厚), but he is more commonly referred to as Hêng Ch'ü (橫 渠), from the place in Honan where he spent his later years.

In his youth Chang Tsai manifested a keen enthusiasm for military affairs. He was even anxious to gather together a company and invade the country west of the Tao, a tributary of the Yellow River. When 21 years of age, however, he was entrusted with a letter to one named Fan Chung Yen,[1] who, recognizing in him a man of uncommon ability, asked him why he preferred a soldier's life to the superior delights of a literary career ; and induced him to begin by studying the *Doctrine of the Mean*. This book failing to satisfy his mind, Hêng Ch'ü applied himself to an exhaustive study of Buddhist and Taoist literature, but with no better success. With his thirst for truth still unsatisfied he returned to orthodox Confucianism.

He now began to give public lectures on the *Yi Ching*. The lectures soon attracted notice, and were attended by a large number of scholars in the Capital—the lecturer, so the

---

[1] A native of Kiangsu. He held high office under Jên Tsung, and was noted for his successful campaigns against the Tartars.

biographers tell us, sitting on a tiger's skin.[1] The eagerness
with which these seekers after truth gathered together to
listen to the young philosopher is a tempting theme for the
imagination to dwell upon. The writer well remembers one
evening, while strolling round a college compound in China,
coming upon a group of students sitting upon the ground, or
with a brick on end for a stool, and in the centre the old teacher
of the Classics discoursing from an open book on a form in
front of him. The book was a formality as useless as it was
unnecessary, for even the Oriental moonlight was hardly
sufficient to enable him to read. The exposition was but the
authorized and stereotyped exposition of nearly a millennium
of tradition, but it was given with sonorous voice and in
rounded periods, and excited keen enthusiasm in the almost
invisible listeners. To such enthusiasm add that which would
be kindled by a teacher who with creative touch makes the
old classic yield new truth like fresh gold from an ancient
mine, and little wonder that even the tiger's skin from which
Hêng Ch'ü discoursed is remembered as part of a vivid scene
indelibly stamped upon the minds of the listeners. Nor is it
surprising that the audience was large and varied. Young
men eager for knowledge, old men still seeking light upon
their beloved books, keen intellects braced for the courteous
debate : all would be there. Among them, it may be worth
while to note, was that same Ssŭ-Ma Kuang, already referred
to as the close friend of Shao Yung and the two Ch'êngs,
and at that time still a young man.

One evening in the year 1056, an evening which proved

---

[1] Said to be symbolical of the lecturer's office.

a turning point in the lecturer's career, his nephews, the two Ch'êng brothers, who had recently arrived at the capital, joined the circle and contributed their quota to the discussion. The next day Hêng Ch'ü told his audience that the two brothers' understanding of the *Yi* was superior to his own, and urged the class to make them their teachers. He discontinued his lectures, but had repeated discussions with his nephews on philosophic truth. Fresh from the powerful influence of Chou Lien Hsi, with their minds full of his teaching, and keen in their advocacy of his theories, the young men produced an impression on the mind of their uncle which was never afterwards effaced. He became an enthusiastic convert to their views, abandoning all lingering traces of his former Taoist and Buddhist speculations.

From this time Hêng Ch'ü's influence was exercised less directly by lectures to students and more by his books, the most important of which were the *Chêng Mêng* (正 蒙) and *Hsi Ming* (西 銘), both preserved for us in the *Hsing Li Ta Ch'üan* (性 理 大 全). The *Hsi Ming*—the *Western Inscriptions*—is mainly ethical. Its name is derived from the fact that its precepts were inscribed on the western wall of his library. Another of the writer's treatises was similarly named *Tung Ming* (東 銘), the *Eastern Inscriptions*.[1] The *Chêng Mêng—The Right Discipline for Youth*—is a more elaborate work. The opening chapter treats of the Great Harmony, which is Chang Tzŭ's equivalent for what the other philosophers understood by *Tao*, or the Moral Order. The

---

[1] It will be found in the *Li Hsüeh Tsung Chuan* (理 學 宗 傳), pt. iv, f. 7.

Great Harmony though identical with, is nevertheless distinguished from, the Great Void, which again is Chang Tzŭ's equivalent for the Supreme Ultimate of Chou Tzŭ. The one is the Ultimate Reality of the universe regarded as the all-comprehensive and all-pervading Moral Law ; the other is the same Reality regarded as the substance of Being, the Nature common to heaven, earth, man, and all forms of existence. In subsequent chapters the author treats of the Primordial Ether in its two modes, the active and passive ; of the Divine Immanence in the material universe ; and of spiritual agency in creative processes. From these cosmological questions he passes to the ethical. True intelligence with the necessity of importing the mind into the thing to be known ; and, as the pre-requisite of all true knowledge, a largeness of heart which recognizes the essential oneness of the ego with the external world [1]—these are subjects the consideration of which forms a natural transition to that of Virtue itself. The chapters on the last-named subject contain many lofty precepts for the guidance of the student in his moral culture, on which the author's teaching may be summed up in two noble sentences of his own : " To blame ourselves as we blame others is to fulfil the Moral Law. To love others as we love ourselves is to perfect Love." In the first of these aphorisms the writer's meaning is : If that moral sense which all possess and which is evidenced in the blame accorded to others, be listened to and abeyed in all its dictates concerning ourselves, we shall be on the highway of perfect

---

[1] A remarkable anticipation of Bergson's doctrine of intuitive sympathy as the means whereby " we get into the heart of things in the making " ; see *Eucken and Bergson*, by E. Hermann, pp. 149–52.

fulfilment of the Moral Law. In the second we have the author's explanation of Confucius' well-known negative version of the golden rule, to which, it will be noted, he here gives the positive form. The work closes with an exposition of the teaching of the *Canon of Changes*, and a discussion of the errors of Buddhism.

Of Hêng Ch'ü's life little remains to be recorded. After taking their degree of Chin Shih the paths of uncle and nephews lay in different directions. Ch'êng Hao was sent to Hu in Shansi ; his brother, preferring not to take office, returned to his native province of Honan ; while Chang Tsai was appointed to office at Ch'i Chou (邪 州) in Chih Li. While here, he instituted monthly lectures on ethical subjects to the district elders, on which occasions he would dine with them in person, so that in the freer intercourse of the table he might acquaint himself with their difficulties, and—a matter never far from his thought—advise them concerning the training of their youth.

Early in the reign of Shên Tsung, he was summoned to the Court, and there came into conflict with Wang An Shih, who asked his opinion about the new policy. The answer was as displeasing as it was candid. As the result, Chang Tsai returned to Hêng Ch'ü, where he devoted himself to his studies. These he pursued with his wonted ardour, often in the middle of the night, and always with notebook at hand. The methods he adopted he urged upon others, for with him the search for truth was a religion. He held that to flag in this would lead to flagging in virtue. He urged that study should be pursued at night, or at least in perfect quiet and alone ; and that the student should not be satisfied unless at each sitting he gained some new light.

Through the influence of Lü Ta Fang, Hêng Ch'ü was once more appointed to office, and accepted the post of Minister of Ceremonial ; but finding himself in disagreement with those in power, he again retired—in 1076. On his way home he was taken ill and died, at the early age of 56.

CHAPTER IV

CHU HSI

The philosopher Chu Hsi (朱 熹) came from a family with considerable literary reputation in Wu Yüan, a county in the prefecture of Sui An (the modern Hui Chou), in the province of An Hui. His father, Chu Sung (朱 松), more often called Wei Chai (韋 齋), in the course of his official career was appointed Magistrate of Yu Hsi, a county in the prefecture of Yen P'ing in Fuhkien. When subsequently he resigned this post, he settled for a time in the same county as tutor with a family named Chêng. It was in this home that Chu Hsi was born, on the 15th of the ninth month, in the fourth year of Kao Tsung (A.D. 1131).

Notwithstanding the fact that the birth of Chu Hsi was not till twenty-three years after the death of Ch'êng I, the latest survivor of the earlier representatives of the Sung School, there was a direct connexion between the great philosopher and his predecessors, which fully justified his association with them as one of the Five. Contemporary with the subjects of the preceding sketches was a scholar named Yang Shih (楊 時), a native of Fuhkien, more commonly known as Yang Kuei Shan (楊 龜 山). His name is more or less associated with that of the heterodox Hu School,[1] through his friendship for its founder, Hu An Kuo ; but he himself was untainted by the heresy of his friend. He was born in 1053, and died in 1135, when Chu Hsi was 5 years old and just beginning his education. In his early manhood, instead of following an official career, Yang Kuei Shan elected to devote himself to the pursuit of learning. Joining the school of the two Ch'êngs, he studied under Ming Tao, and afterwards under I Ch'uan. Eventually he himself became a teacher of the new philosophy. Of the many pupils who followed him, one was a native of the same province as himself, named Lo Ts'ung Yen (羅 從 彥), who, we are told, excelled all the rest as a man who could think deeply, act strongly, and carry heavy responsibility. Lo, in his turn, became a teacher of philosophy, with Chu Sung, the father of Chu Hsi, as one of his pupils. This was while Chu Sung was in Fuhkien, first in office and later in retirement. As Yang Kuei Shan at this time was still living, it is more than likely that Chu Sung met and conversed with the older philosopher as well as with his pupil ; a suggestion which, if true, adds considerable interest to Chu Hsi's frequent references in his writings to Yang Kuei Shan. It will be seen later that Chu Hsi received the personal instruction of his father for three years at his most impressionable age, so that Chu Sung himself was the intermediary through whom the teachings of the earlier philosophers were handed on to his son, and through him became the accepted tenets of the nation at large. To this must be added the further interesting fact that Li Yen P'ing, a fellow student of Chu Sung and pupil of Lo Ts'ung Yen, also became Chu Hsi's

[1] See p. 76.

teacher in later years, thus extending the direct connexion of Chu Hsi with his " Masters ". The following diagram will illustrate this connexion :—

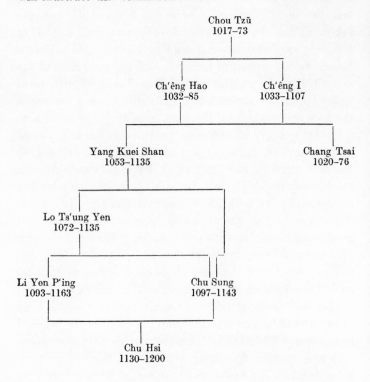

Chou Tzŭ
1017–73

Ch'êng Hao
1032–85

Ch'êng I
1033–1107

Yang Kuei Shan
1053–1135

Chang Tsai
1020–76

Lo Ts'ung Yen
1072–1135

Li Yen P'ing
1093–1163

Chu Sung
1097–1143

Chu Hsi
1130–1200

CHILDHOOD AND EDUCATION
(1130–50)

The biographers of Chu Hsi's childhood have the usual stories to tell of that precocity of genius which is supposed to characterize the tender years of all great men. When he was only four years old his father pointing to the sky said, " That is heaven." " What is there beyond heaven ? " the child asked, to the wonder of his parent. Whether the answer given to this question was too vague, or whether the father was too surprised to give any answer at all, it seems that the child was not satisfied ; for the philosopher himself tells us that when he was between 5 and 6 years old his mind was still exercised by the problem of what Heaven is in its essence, and what is the visible Heaven.

In 1135, in a letter to his wife's brother, the father announced with pride that the all-important step had been taken of sending the child, now 5 years old, to school. As in infancy, so at school, the boy appears to have manifested a marked difference in disposition from that of most children. While his schoolmates were playing, he would sit apart in dignified posture, as if absorbed in meditation. Once, the prodigy was observed to be writing mysterious symbols in the sand near where the other children were frolicking, which, when examined, were found to be the eight diagrams of the *Yi Ching* ! On his copy of the *Classic of Filial Piety* was found in his handwriting the words, " Not to conform to the teaching of this book is not to be a man ! "

Such, according to our authorities, was Chu Hsi as a child. How much of truth there is in these stories the reader himself will judge. The Philosopher, however, leaves us in no doubt as to the earnestness with which he applied himself to study in his earliest years. His reminiscence as to the problem concerning Heaven has been already cited. He also tells us how, as a boy 8 or 10 years old, he realized from his reading of Mencius that a student must above all things be diligent. But more important than his diligence were his moral earnestness and reverence for his teachers. He was particularly observant of, and stored up in his memory all that he learned from his elders : and even at this early age resolved not to fix his ambition on taking a degree, but to make the sages his model, keeping before him in all his study their high ideals. Doubtless he learned from later experience that some of his ideals were not so easy of attainment as they appeared to him when a boy. Indeed he himself tells us, " When in my teens I was overjoyed to read in Mencius that the sages were of the same flesh and blood as ourselves, for, thought I, if that be the case, then I, too, can be a sage. Now, however, I find it is hard."

Chu Sung appears to have been a wise and affectionate father, and especially solicitous about his son's education. In 1141, in consequence of his inflexible opposition to Ch'in Hui's policy of peace with the Tartar Chins, he resigned the office which he then held as Secretary to the Board of Civil Appointments. His retirement furnished the desired opportunity of becoming his son's teacher. For three years the father instilled into the boy's mind the high ethical principles of the sages, unfolded and clarified by the teachings which he had imbibed from the philosophers of his own school, and so laid the foundation for that massive scholarship, and helped to develop that clear incisive intellect, which have made Chu Hsi so powerful in his influence over his race for seven hundred years.

It was Chu Hsi's misfortune to lose his father when only 14 years old. Chu Sung died in 1143 at his home a little to the south of Chien Chou, in Fuhkien. But the same solicitude which he had shown in his personal education of his son was seen in the dispositions for that son's welfare which he made upon his death-bed. He committed his family affairs to Liu Shao Ch'uan, whom he appointed guardian, and entrusted his son's education to three friends, Hu Chi Hsi, Liu Pai Shui, and Liu P'ing Shan, the younger brother of Liu Shao Ch'uan. Admonishing the youth with all the solemnity and affection of a dying charge, he said, " These are my friends whom I revere for their profound learning. When I am gone I desire that you should serve and obey them as a son." After his father's death Chu Hsi was taken to the home of Liu Shao Ch'uan, continuing his education under the guidance of the three scholars named. He subsequently married the daughter of Liu Pai Shui.

The years immediately following his bereavement Chu Hsi devoted wholly to study, taking his degree of Chin Shih (D.Litt.) when he was 19 years old. Of this period he often spoke in his autobiographical reminiscences. From 15 to 16 he worked at the *Analects* the study of which appears to have so intensified his passion for learning that he became more than ever indefatigable in its pursuit. In later life, referring to this time, he says, " Even now I cannot claim to be satisfied in my search for truth, but I certainly suffered much hardship in my student days. My whole strength and determination were concentrated on study." His diligence was accompanied by increasing intelligence as to method. He tells us, for example, that though in his early study of *Mencius* he was satisfied with understanding the text sentence by sentence, without reference to its connexion, he learned later to recognize a thread running through an entire book ; and once having realized this unity, he studied each passage in its relation to the whole, with the result that he had a better understanding of the book, and more enjoyment in his work. There can be no doubt that it was the mental habit thus acquired that in later years gave him his constructive power ; so that he, chief among the Chinese philosophers, expounded philosophy as a system which, in his own mind at any rate, was consistent in all its parts. It is perhaps not surprising that our young zealot should be omnivorous in the subjects of his study. There was nothing that he did not seek to know, from things military, on the one hand, to the quietism of the Buddhist on the other. But this he came to realize was a mistake : it was impossible for one man to be expert in every branch of knowledge ; and the necessity was forced upon him of more and more restricting his studies to narrower channels.

Perhaps the most interesting stage in Chu Hsi's intellectual development was the period of his Buddhist and Taoist studies. That the creator of orthodoxy should himself have begun his career as a heretic is in itself an interesting fact, and hardly less so are the questions suggested by it. To what extent was he immersed in these philosophies ? And to what influences were his plunges into their speculations due ? It can scarcely be doubted that they must in part be attributed to his own hunger for knowledge, to which reference has been made in the preceding paragraph. The chief cause, however, was the influence of his early instructors. One of these, Hu Chi Hsi, finding that the doctrines of his namesake Hu An Kuo,[1]

---

[1] See p. 76.

excellent as he considered them to be in their teaching on Government, were unsatisfying from the religious point of view, turned to Buddhism and Taoism, hoping that in them he might find spiritual rest. Though still not fully satisfied, and though finally he returned to orthodox Confucianism, he was, nevertheless, profoundly impressed by their philosophy. Liu P'ing Shan, another of Chu Hsi's guardians and teachers, while in office at Fu T'ien, also came under the influence of a Buddhist priest, from whom he leared the secret of the meditation trance as the means by which he might attain to pure intelligence. He, too, in his old age returned to the study of Confucian literature, not because he had abandoned his Buddhist views, but because he had learned to look upon both systems as not necessarily inconsistent. Under such teachers, it was natural that Chu Hsi not only acquired a love for profound mataphysical study but also became tainted to some considerable extent with Buddhist and Taoist heresies. His biographers tell us, indeed, that he drank deeply of those streams of thought. Le Gall quotes evidence implying, as he thinks, that Chu Hsi even went so far as to become a Buddhist bonze ; [1] but that is by no means certain. Nevertheless, it is indisputable that at this period both Taoist and Buddhist ideas were prevalent and exerted a strong influence upon the minds of the leaders of thought ; and there can be little doubt that much of the freshness and originality in the writings of our school, not least in those of Chu Hsi himself, was due to the stimulus received from these two systems.

[1] *Le Philosophe Tchou Hi, Sa Doctrine, Son Influence,* p. 9.

OFFICE AT T'UNG AN
(1151–7)

In the year 1151, at the age of 22, Chu Hsi received his first official appointment. He was sent to T'ung An, a county in the prefecture of Ch'üan Chou in Fuhkien, as Keeper of the Records. This office, including as it did the superintendence of the education of the district, must have been peculiarly congenial to one who had already manifested keen literary tastes, and he entered upon its duties with ardour and enthusiasm. Upon his arrival at the city, in the autumn of 1153, his first care was the college, which he reorganized on a new basis. The most promising young men were selected as students, and the co-operation of well-known learned men was invited that they might assist the students with their experience and scholarship. At first the students resented the new regime with its earnest pursuit of solid learning and its strict rules of conduct. They wished regretfully that they might return to the lax rule of Chu Hsi's predecessor, when they rose at eight and finished at noon. But Chu Hsi patiently persisted in his reform. He delivered specially prepared lectures on the importance of study in youth, and the need of strenuousness if success was to be achieved and true scholarship attained.

Allied to the reform of the college, another matter that early claimed his energies was the establishment of a library of classical and historical works for the use of students. A large number of books lying unused in the store-rooms of his own department were collected together. Cases of books were discovered in the old college which had been stowed away for a long period. They were found to be in great disorder, worn and dilapidated, and with no catalogue : but all that were readable, to the number of about two hundred, were selected and added to the rest. These again were supplemented by a few volumes obtained from private libraries by a special appeal to the generosity of the public. In this way by the spring of the year 1155 the college was provided with a modest but useful library of some twelve hundred volumes.

Two other matters, though less congenial, were not less urgent. The collection of the taxes and the registration of land were in a chaotic condition ; the system itself was such as fostered corruption on the part of the tax-collectors and oppression of the poor by the rich. All this was corrected by substituting simple for complex methods of registration, by clearer instructions as to dates for the collection of taxes, and similar reforms. In the summer of 1153 measures were taken for the protection of the city from robbers ; in which measures Chu Hsi took a prominent part, accepting with the Salt Comptroller the joint responsibility for the north-western portion of the city.

Temples, religious rites, and marriages, also claimed the attention of the young reformer. He found the ceremonial observed at the sacrificial offerings in hopeless confusion ; and, discovering that there were no two copies of the Confucian *Guide to Ritual* to be obtained, he prepared a work of his own in which he gave a full description of ancient and modern ceremonies. This work was illustrated by charts which were hung on the college walls so that visitors joining with the students in the sacrificial rites might be familiarized with the different ceremonies to be observed. The marriage customs were so lax as to corrupt the morals of the people, rich and

poor, in city and in village. Realizing the supreme importance
to the state of a right relation between the sexes he devised
effective measures for the proper performance of the marriage
rite, and provided the people with clear rules for their guidance.

In 1156, acting on instructions to remove to another
district, he relinquished his office ; but owing to the sickness
and death of his intended successor, he was compelled to return
to T'ung An for a short period. The interval was spent in the
home of a physician Ch'ên Liang Chieh, where he invited his
students to join him and pursue their studies. After several
months, during which he conducted four examinations, he
finally retired in 1157. The assiduous attention which the
Philosopher had given to all that contributed to the happiness
and well-being of the people reaped its reward in their appreciation and respect. The inhabitants of the city, including the
students who had received his instruction, built a temple in
the college he had founded, in grateful recognition of his
beneficent administration.

STUDY UNDER LI YEN P'ING
(1158–63)

When Chu Hsi retired from office at T'ung An it was with
the strong determination to devote himself to literary pursuits,
both as a student and teacher. With this end in view he
sought and obtained a sinecure appointment as Guardian of
the Nan Yo Temple on a sacred mountain named Hêng Shan
near T'an Chou, the modern Ch'ang Sha, in Hunan. It was
at this time that he succeeded in throwing off the meshes of
Buddhist and Taoist heresies in which he had been involved
by his earlier education. His emancipation was due to the

influence of a teacher to whom he owed more than to any other, with the single exception of his own father, and whom he had now learned to regard with filial affection.

Li T'ung (李 侗), style Yüan Chung (愿 中), the teacher referred to, is better known as Yen P'ing (延 平), the name of his native prefecture in Fuhkien. As already stated, he was a fellow-student of Chu Hsi's father Chu Sung, both having studied under Lo Ts'ung Yen. Li Yen P'ing was recognized by his fellow-students to be *facile princeps* among them all. One of his admirers said of him, "Yüan Chung was like sparkling ice in a bowl of water, or like the harvest-moon : clear and pure, without spot or stain," an encomium which was repeatedly quoted by Chu Sung in the hearing of his son.

It was natural that on his way to his first appointment at T'ung An, when he found himself not far from the home of his father's friend, Chu Hsi made a point of visiting him. At this, the very first interview, the older scholar asserted his intellectual authority over the young student. Chu Hsi, in the youthful enthusiasm of his not inconsiderable scholarship, discoursed at length on his views of philosophy, especially on the profound teachings of Buddhism and Taoism. " Sir, how is it," asked Yen P'ing, " that you have such a deep understanding of these empty theories, while you are unable to grasp the most obvious truths of everyday life ? *Tao* is not a far-off mystery ; it is in the earnest practice of it day by day that you will gain a true understanding of it."

Chu Hsi was abashed, and though not wholly convinced by the stern dogmatism of his father's friend, he was so far impressed that he laid aside his Buddhist books, and set himself to an earnest and persevering study of the orthodox

classics. By patient daily perusal of the latter, reading them
many times over from beginning to end, he began to see the
errors and fallacies of his former position. But the four years
spent at T'ung An were years of severe mental struggle. At
intervals he visited his new-found teacher ; and he tells us
that while with him he was inclined to dispute his teachings,
but when, on his return to T'ung An, and in the quietude of
his own room, he pondered the whole subject of their discussion
together, he realized that the truth lay with his friend. The
bias in favour of his earlier views was strong, but the power
of the master mind was stronger, and in the end proved
victor.

It was not till later, however, that he arrived at full conviction. About a year after his retirement from T'ung An he
again visited his friend and remained with him for some
months. In a retired spot hidden away in the mountains, to
use his own words, " he ministered to his father and pursued
his studies." Here he was joined by one Hu Chang, also
fired by an ardent thirst for knowledge. They spent each
day in reading, and in the evening and early morning compared
notes, correcting and criticizing the results of each other's
labours. Of these days Chu Hsi wrote enthusiastically to
one of his friends : " Though poor in material things, we were
rich in joys that satisfy the heart."

Of Chu Hsi, the Master Li Yen P'ing spoke in terms of
highest praise. Severe as he was in condemnation of the ardent
young student's intellectual heresies, he recognized in him one
of no ordinary calibre. Combined with an unusually fine
character was incomparable ability ; with a power of con-
centration which his teacher characterized as " terrific ",

he was able in any problem to probe the difficulty to the bottom. Yen P'ing congratulated himself on his having received his own mental training from such a teacher as Lo Ts'ung Yen, for otherwise he would have felt himself unable to cope with the strong and nimble intellect of his pupil.

Two years later, the visit was repeated, and several months were again spent with the aged scholar, this time in a place called the " Western Park " belonging to a literary friend. This seems to have been the period of Chu Hsi's final conversion from Buddhism to the orthodox cult ; his lingering doubts were dispelled, and he realized once for all that his former teachings were " empty vapourings void of any real value for men ". The central thought of Li Yen P'ing's philosophy, and that which most impressed Chu Hsi, was the reconciliation of Unity with Plurality in the doctrine of the one Law with its infinite variety of operation. This became the favourite theme of Chu Hsi's own teaching.

After another two years' interval—early in 1162—Chu Hsi again visited his beloved teacher, apparently for the last time. Li Yen P'ing was staying with his younger son, Li Hsin Fu, who was in office at Chien An as Keeper of the Records. Here he was joined by Chu Hsi, who subsequently returned with him to his home at Yen P'ing. Once again they spent several months in the " Western Park ". This time Chu Hsi's advance in learning was phenomenal, and his teacher found great happiness in the thought of the career that he foresaw would be his pupil's. For Chu Hsi in his after memories these months must have held a sacred place as the last he was able to spend with one whom he regarded with the affection of a son. In the following year the Master died, in the 70th year

of his age, and Chu Hsi's next visit was made in 1164, in order
to weep at his tomb.

LITERARY PURSUITS

(1163–78)

The years that intervened between the death of Li Yen
P'ing and Chu Hsi's appointment to Nan K'ang, the young
philosopher devoted to the literary labours for which he had
been preparing from his youth. In his achievements in this
direction, this was the golden period of his life. Many of his
most important works were completed at this time. His
appointment as Guardian of the Nan Yo Temple in 1158 was
repeatedly renewed, and so furnished him the necessary
leisure, which he enjoyed with some interruptions until the
year 1176.

Before the death of his " Master " he had already begun his
career as an author with a work on the *Sayings of Shang
Ts'ai* (上 蔡 語 錄). This work was completed in 1159.
It was followed in 1163 by two works on the *Analects, The
Teachings of the Analects* (論 語 耍 義), and *Oral Lessons
on the Analects for Young People* (論 語 訓 蒙 口 義);
and in 1163 by a collection of Essays which he entitled *Toil in
Study and Fear in Listening* (困 學 恐 聞), in twofold
allusion to the name he had given to the room in which he
studied, and the saying in the *Analects* concerning Tzŭ-Lu
that when he " heard anything, if he had not yet carried it
into practice, he was only afraid lest he should hear something else ".[1]

---

[1] *Analects*, v, 12, p. 42.

The "toil in study" was not allowed to remain long unbroken. For nearly six years Chu Hsi's desire for retirement had been acceded to, but not without repeated efforts to secure his services for the State. In the autumn of 1159, the year following the retirement from T'ung An, a summons had been received to appear at Court. The Philosopher was by this time immersed in his studies with Li Yen P'ing, and, unwilling to leave these "joys" for those of court life, he declined the invitation. The summons, however, was repeated more than once, and at last was obeyed. In 1163 Chu Hsi presented himself at the Court and was granted an audience in the Ch'ui Kung Palace. He presented three memorials, on which he had consulted with Li Yen P'ing but a short while before that philosopher's death. The first memorial urged the importance of the study of the Classics, the second was in criticism of the foreign policy of the Emperor's ministers, and the third was on the necessity for a pure court. In a letter to a friend, Chu Hsi said that on presenting the first of these memorials the Divine Countenance was mild and serene, but after the second and third the sacred lips no longer deigned to speak.

Whether because of the unwelcome nature of these memorials, or because of Chu Hsi's persistence in refusing office is not clear, but, doubtless to his great joy, he was allowed to return to his books. Four years later, however, his literary labours were again interrupted by calamities in the neighbourhood of his birthplace. In the year 1167 there were devastating floods, followed as a natural consequence by severe famine in the following year. Chu Hsi's sympathetic nature was shown by the ardour with which he engaged in the work of mitigating the distress caused by these disasters. Negotiating a loan, he was able to purchase a supply of rice for distribution among the most destitute. A large surplus which still remained after the famine was over was utilized some years later (1172) for a similar beneficent purpose. The plan adopted on the latter occasion was to loan the rice to the people, to be repaid with interest in better times, and so while saving life the evil of pauperizing those benefited was avoided.

Chu Hsi's career differed from those of his predecessors of the Sung School in the matter of literary friendships. The first four were contemporaries, and one of the most charming pictures we have is that of the "Nest of Peace and Joy", where Chang Tsai and his two nephews, with Ssŭ-Ma Kuang and others, would gather together with the old hermit for rich intellectual feasts. For Chu Hsi there were few such delights. Though he had many students, and some literary friends, Li Yen P'ing was his only peer in intellect. One of the friendships formed, however, is of special interest. During his residence as Guardian at the Nan Yo Temple, there was living in retirement at T'an Chou at the foot of the mountain, a scholar who became one of his closest intimates, though a representative of an opposing school. Chang Ch'ih (張 栻), *style* Ching Fu (敬 夫), but better known by his literary name Nan Hsien (南 軒), was the son of a famous general, the Duke of I (益). He studied under Hu Hung (Wu Fêng), the son of Hu An Kuo, the founder of the Hu school.[1] In the autumn of 1167 Chu Hsi called upon him, and thus began an acquaintanceship which continued unbroken till the death of

[1] See p. 76.

Nan Hsien in 1181. On a later occasion, three months after
the first interview, when Chu Hsi again visited him, they spent
three days and three nights in an argument concerning the
Doctrine of the Mean, but were unable to come to an agreement. It would seem as if neither could surrender the hope
of convincing his friend, for they both ascended the Hêng
Mountain together, and went on some miles further to a place
called Hêng Chou, where at length they parted, and Chu Hsi
returned to his temple.

From this time his literary labours proceeded more rapidly
than ever. In 1168 the *Literary Remains of the Two Ch'êngs*
(二 程 遺 書), a work of twenty-five chapters, was completed; in 1172 the four works, *An Exposition of the Analects
and Mencius* (論 孟 精 義), *Outlines of General History*
(通 鑑 綱 目), *Memoirs of the Illustrious Ministers of Eight
Dynasties* (八 朝 名 臣 言 行 錄), and a commentary on
Chang Tsai's work, the *Western Inscriptions* (西 銘 解 義),
were all brought to a conclusion; and in 1173 he finished his
commentaries on Chou Tzŭ's works, *The Diagram of the
Supreme Ultimate Explained* (太 極 圖 說), and *The Complete Treatise* (通 書). In the same year he edited the
students' notes of lectures delivered by the brothers Ch'êng
under the title of *The Additional Remains of the Two Ch'êngs*
(二 程 外 書); and completed in the year following a work
on *Domestic Ritual, Ancient and Modern* (古 今 家 祭 禮).

In the year 1175 Chu Hsi formed a new friendship, out of
which grew one of his most important literary works. Early
in the summer of that year Lü Tsu Ch'ien (呂 祖 謙), *style*
Po Kung (伯 恭), with the literary name Tung Lai (東 萊),
came from a place called Tung Yang (東 陽) to visit our

philosopher. He stayed about ten days, and together they studied the works of Chou Tzŭ, Chang Tzŭ, and the two Ch'êngs. Comparing their experiences, both lamented the difficulty students must have in beginning their study of these voluminous and heterogeneous works without any clue to guide them. Together they selected all the passages that were closely connected with the main theme or with practical everyday conduct, and classified them in 632 sections and fourteen chapters. So unremitting was their work that before they separated they finished the first draft of their joint compilation, which they entitled *Modern Thought* (近 思 錄).[1] After Lü Tung Lai's return home, Chu Hsi continued the work by himself ; recasting some parts, and altering the order of one or two of the chapters. He consulted with his friend, however, by letter, at each stage, and induced Lü Tung Lai himself to add one or two sections.

When Lü Tung Lai left, Chu Hsi, at his visitor's instance, accompanied him as far as Hsin Chou, and in the "Goose Lake" Temple met Lu Tzŭ Shou, Lu Tzŭ Ching,[2] both of Chin Ch'i (金 谿) in Fuhkien, and others whom Lü Tung Lai had invited to confer on philosophical subjects. The interview ended in a sustained argument in which neither side was able to convince the other, and they separated without coming to an agreement. Subsequently, Tzŭ Shou's attitude changed and he came round to Chu Hsi's views, but Tzŭ Ching maintained his position to the end. In a letter to Chang Nan Hsien describing this interview, Chu Hsi wrote in terms

---

[1] 近 思 錄 是 近 來 人 話 便 較 功, v. *Chu Tzŭ Nien P'u*, pt. ii, f. 2.

[2] Also named Hsiang Shan.

of high praise of Lu Tzŭ Shou as a man, but criticized his views in regard to subjective introspection and meditation. Some years later both scholars visited Chu Hsi at different times : Tzŭ Shou in 1179 and Tzŭ Ching in 1181. On the latter occasion Chu Hsi was at Nan K'ang. When Tzŭ Ching arrived with a party of his pupils Chu Hsi invited him to the College of the " White Deer Grotto ",[1] and assembled the students to hear a lecture which his guest had consented to deliver. Chu Hsi was so pleased with the practical value to the student of what the lecturer urged that he induced him to leave it in writing for his permanent use.

The experiences of the year following the meeting of the savants at the " Goose Lake Temple " were varied and troubled. In the early part of the year the Philosopher visited his ancestral home at Wu Yüan, where he repaired the family tombs and performed sacrificial rites to the manes of his ancestors. In the summer he was offered the post of Keeper of the Secret Archives, but declined ; and in the autumn, when the offer was repeated, he again declined. He applied for the guardianship of a temple, which being granted he was sent to the Ch'ung Yu Kuan on the Wu I Mountain. In the winter of the same year his wife died,[2] and was buried in a valley of Chien Yang, her own home.[3]

Chu Hsi returned once more to his books, and in the year after his wife's death completed three of his works : *A Commentary on the Odes* (詩 集 傳), *The Essential Meaning of the I of Chou* (周 易 本 義), and *A Catechism on the Collected Commentaries on the Analects and Mencius* (論 孟 集 註 咸 問). The last named was a combination of his two earlier

[1] See p. 79.　　　[2] See p. 61.　　　[3] Cf. p. 91.

works on the *Analects* and *Mencius*, from both of which he
had selected portions for the use of students. These had been
circulated privately and copied one from another by various
students, with the result that many discrepancies existed.
He now revised them himself, and completed what was henceforth the authorized edition.

It may be well to refer here to the heterodox schools,
the controversies with which filled a large place in Chu Hsi's
philosophic labours. Of these the most important were the
Hu and Su Schools. The former was founded by Hu An Kuo
(胡 安 國), who was born in 1074 at Ch'ung An in Fuhkien,
and held high office in Hunan and Ssŭ Ch'uan. He is often
referred to as Wên Ting (文 定) the name by which he was
canonized. He was an intimate friend of Yang Kuei Shan.[1]
Hu An Kuo's son, Hu Hung (胡 宏), a pupil of Yang Kuei
Shan, lived a hermit life on the Hêng Mountain, where later
Chu Hsi spent several years of his period of retirement.[2]
He was the author of an essay entitled *Chih Yen* (知 言),
Words of Wisdom,[3] which was severely criticized and controverted by Chu Hsi in a critique entitled *Chih Yen I I*
(知 言 疑 義).[4] It has already been stated that Chang
Nan Hsien, Chu Hsi's personal friend, was a pupil of Hu Hung.
His daughter married Hu Hung's son Hu Chi Sui (胡 季 隨),
also a contemporary of Chu Hsi. Another of the same school
was Hu Yin (胡 寅), whose literary name was Chih T'ang
(致 堂), a nephew of Hu An Kuo.[5]

---

[1] See p. 52.   [2] See p. 63.
[3] 學 案, pt. xlii, f. 2.   [4] Ibid., f. 4.
[5] See 學 宗, pt. xxxiv, f. 1, 2 ; pt. xlii, f. 21 ; pt. lxxi, f. 1 ; 宗 傳,
pt. xvi.

Second only in importance to the Hu School was the Su School, founded by Su Hsün (蘇 洵), whose literary name was Lao Ch'üan (老 泉). Su Hsün had two sons, Su Shih (蘇 軾), better known as the famous poet Su Tung P'o (蘇 東 坡), and Su Chê (蘇 轍), both of whom were contemporaries of the Ch'êng Brothers and with them were strongly opposed to the policy of Wang An Shih. The father and two sons came to be familiarly referred to as " The Three Su-s ", and were differentiated as the " Venerable Su " (Su Hsün), the " Elder Su " (Su Shih), and the " Younger Su " (Su Chê).[1] The writings of the " Venerable Su " were collected and published as the *Lao Ch'üan Wên Chi* (老 泉 文 集) and the *Lao Ch'üan Chiang Yu* (老 泉 講 友). The writings of Su Shih, which were numerous and varied, were published as the *Tung P'o Ch'üan Chi* (東 坡 全 集).[2]

A third school originated with Hsieh Liang Tso (謝 良 佐), whose literary name was Shang Ts'ai (上 蔡), the name of the place in Honan where he was born. He was a pupil of both the Ch'êngs, but exaggerating a statement by Ch'êng Hao on the interpretation of *Jên* (仁), Love, he became the founder of the school known as the Shang Ts'ai School. Its tenets were frequently controverted by Chu Hsi, whose earliest literary labour, as already stated, was the editing of *The Sayings of Shang Ts'ai*.[3] [4]

---

[1] 老 蘇 大 蘇 小 蘇.

[2] 學 案, pt. xcix.

[3] See p. 70 ; also 宗 傳, pt. xv.

[4] The tenets of all three schools are referred to at length in Chu Hsi's work on Human Nature as well as in later chapters of the present work.

NAN K'ANG AND SHAO HSING

(1179–83)

For some years the Ministers at Court had vainly endeavoured to induce Chu Hsi to emerge from his retirement. In 1178 he was definitely appointed to Nan K'ang but declined the office, and persisted in the refusal notwithstanding that his declinature was disallowed by the Emperor. At length his friends Lü Tung Lai and Chang Nan Hsien became alarmed at the possible consequences of a confirmed unwillingness to serve the state. Lü Tung Lai wrote several letters begging him to accede to the Imperial command; and Chang Nan Hsien urged that, in the highest interests of the teaching he had done so much to promote, he ought to accept the appointment, lest he should give cause to the Court Ministers to say that scholars were lacking in patriotism. Chu Hsi could not resist these remonstrances. He accepted the appointment, and at once, in the first month of 1179, started on his journey. He halted at Hsin Chou, waiting for the necessary imperial documents, and while there was visited by Lu Tzŭ Shou with whom he had had his memorable argument at the Goose Lake Temple. In the third month he arrived at Nan K'ang.

His administration of the prefecture was on the same high ethical plane as that which characterized his office at T'ung An. The burdens of taxation were lightened; the elders, scholars, and priests were exhorted to report on abuses and make recommendations concerning desirable reforms; meetings were organized to promote the virtues of filial piety, loyalty, and fidelity among the young; the elders were instructed to select studious youths, and the teachers were assembled in summer schools that their progress in scholarship and teaching ability might be furthered.

Equally characteristic was the interest manifested from the first in the College itself. He selected the worthiest and most eminent men as governors, and personally visited the College every four or five days to lecture to the students. It would be expected that, reluctant though he was to accept office, it was none the less with peculiar interest that our philosopher found himself in the place where the founder of his own school of philosophy had formerly lived. That this was the case is shown by the fact that within a month of his arrival he erected shrines, or sacrificial halls, within the precincts of the College, to the memory of this and other famous philosophers. The principle shrine was in honour of Chou Lien Hsi himself; it was flanked by two lesser shrines in honour of the brothers Ch'êng; and a fourth was erected in honour of five others, and named " The Hall of the Five Worthies ".

Towards the close of the year he began the restoration of the college at the " White Deer Grotto ", situated in a nook by the side of a rivulet in a valley called " The Vale of the White Deer ". The college is very ancient; it originated with a hermit of the T'ang dynasty, named Li P'o (李 渤), who made the cave his home and to whom students flocked in large numbers to receive his teaching. According to tradition Li P'o had a tame white deer which accompanied him in his walks and which, when returning from the market, he employed to carry his provisions by slinging them on its horns; hence he was called " Pai Lu Hsien Shêng " (The

White Deer Gentleman) and the cave "Pai Lu Tung" (The White Deer Grotto). In the grotto itself there is at the present time the image of a deer hewn out of stone, said to have been placed there in the fourteenth century. The College thus founded was patronized by the Emperors T'ai Tsung (太 宗), 927–47, and Shêng Tsung (聖 宗), 963–1031, who each presented it with a copy of the Nine Classics. Some time during the period of the Five Dynasties it was endowed by the descendants of Li P'o with land for the support of its teachers. In the time of the nation's prosperity it was well supported and at one period rebuilt, but was subsequently neglected and became little better than a ruin.[1] Chu Hsi, with the help of the Literary Chancellor, Yang Ta Fa, and the Magistrate of Hsing Tzǔ, Wang Chung Chieh, restored it to something of its ancient glory. He obtained an edict of approval from the Emperor, and, raising funds by public subscription, brought his project to a satisfactory issue. Scholars by hundreds from all parts of the country visited the "Grotto", and before long it ranked as one of the four most famous colleges in the land.

The second year of office at Nan K'ang was marked by extreme distress among the people. Already, in the summer of the preceding year, a memorial had been presented to the Throne urging that taxes in the county of Hsing Tzǔ be remitted. In the following spring, in the second month of 1180, the memorial was repeated. Widespread drought was followed by terrible famine. As always in relief of distress, Chu Hsi displayed remarkable energy in the measures

---

[1] See *Sketches in China*, by Sir John Francis Davis, vol. ii, p. 62.

he took to meet the calamity. From funds which the Government placed at his disposal he procured large stores of rice for free distribution. He secured the prohibition of the export of the products of the distressed districts, and promoted the transportation of grain from more prosperous regions. In addition to these direct methods of alleviating the distress he organized relief-works, mainly in the repairing of the canal and river banks.

In the same year, in response to a public proclamation inviting memorials from the officials of the provinces, Chu Hsi submitted to the Throne a secret memorial which was probably the root of the troubles which overwhelmed him in later years. In this memorial he began by laying down the principle that the first duty of a prince was consideration for his people, by which alone the stability of the Throne could be secured. He then denounced in unmeasured terms the oppressive methods pursued by the Emperor's ministers in their government. The taxes, through the corruption and nepotism which honeycombed the army and the connivance of the high ministers of state, were out of all proportion to what would be a reasonable expenditure on the military defences. He very broadly hinted at " one or two " of those ministers on whom the chief blame should rest. The memorial was received with unmistakable anger on the part of the Emperor, which Chu Hsi described as " the rolling of thunder ".

To the sadness of public calamities was added that of personal sorrow caused by the death of the Philosopher's two friends Chang Nan Hsien and Lü Tung Lai. The former died in the year 1180, and the latter in the autumn of the following year. These two losses, following so closely the one upon the other, affected Chu Hsi very deeply ; and in each case when the news reached him he publicly observed the rites of mourning.

Little leisure, however, was afforded for indulging in grief. After the stormy reception which his sealed memorial received, Chu Hsi sent in his resignation, but received no reply. The Emperor, displeased though he was with his minister, was by no means disposed to dispense with that minister's services. He was advised that it would be the part of wisdom to retain such men in office, lest even the appearance of Imperial displeasure should increase their popularity. Moreover, the efficiency of Chu Hsi's administration at Nan K'ang—especially in his relief measures—was fully recognized. He was therefore appointed temporarily as the Comptroller of the Tea and Salt Revenues in Chekiang province, in the eastern part of which famine was now prevalent. At the end of the year he was summoned to the Court and received in audience in the Yen Ho Palace, when he presented seven memorials in which he urged drastic reforms in the Government. After the audience he was sent back to Chekiang as Prefect of Shao Hsing.

Upon his arrival at Shao Hsing early in 1183, he immediately put into execution the plans he had previously adopted at Nan K'ang. In the year 1183 he made an extended tour of the districts under his jurisdiction, unattended and carrying his own baggage, so that he might ascertain the real condition of the people and inspect the manner in which the magistrates carried out their instructions. He reported several cases of serious misdemeanour, especially those of oppression in the distribution of relief—including a case at Tai Chou of more than ordinary tyranny, which had occurred before his acceptance of office, and the difficulty of dealing with which was aggravated by the fact that the tyrant was highly connected.

In the autumn of this year he again resigned office and started for home. Repeated efforts were made to retain his services, but he adhered to his resignation, and finally obtained the guardianship of a temple, the Ch'ung Ta Kuan, at Tai Chou.

COURT ENEMIES
(1184–96)

Once more the ardent scholar was free to devote himself to his books and lectures. In the four years of leisure which were allowed to him he completed his *Elementary Guide to the Study of the Yi* (易 學 啟 蒙), *Corrected Edition of the Classic of Filial Piety* (孝 經 刊 誤), and the *Lesser Learning* (小 學). The intervals between his labours on these works were occupied with dialectic combats at different places.

In 1188 he was again summoned to the Court, and for the third time was received in audience, this time, as on the second occasion, in the Yen Ho Palace. On his way to the audience he was warned that to be exhorted " to make your heart true and your motives sincere " (正 心 誠 意) was the kind of advice that the Sovereign resented, and was urged to avoid such topics. Chu Hsi replied, " These four words represent the principles which have been my chief concern all through my life ; shall I suppress them now and deceive my Prince ? " The reception of his memorials, however, was kind and gracious. "It is long since I have seen my aged servant," said the Emperor. "I have watched your labours in Chekiang; it is only fitting that now you should receive an easier post, and be relieved from provincial administration."

The post of Vice-President of the Board of War was then offered to him, but a secretary of the Board named Lin Li, with whom Chu Hsi had a literary dispute only a few days earlier, sent in a memorial accusing Chu Hsi of plagiarizing the writings of Ch'êng Tzŭ and Chang Tzŭ, and of cherishing the ambition to influence the Sovereign and control the affairs of state, like Confucius and Mencius. The Emperor consulted his Prime Minister Chou Pi Ta, who advised conferring on Chu Hsi the office which was formerly offered to him, the Judgeship of Kiangsi. This Chu Hsi declined, and, with equal persistence, refused all other offers which were made to retain him at Court. The Emperor summoned him to another audience. He excused himself from personal attendance, but took the opportunity of sending in a sealed memorial, and then retired to his books.

Early in the following year, the Emperor Hsiao Tsung abdicated in favour of Kuang Tsung. The new Emperor offered Chu Hsi a post at the Court, and, upon that and other offices being declined, appointed him Prefect of Chang Chou. This time Chu Hsi, in view of the Emperor's recent accession, felt unable to refuse, and entered upon his office at the end of the year 1189. Although now 61 years of age he devoted himself energetically to his new duties. His first care was the reform of social abuses, which had become rife. He then memorialized the Throne urging that strong efforts be made for the suppression of bribery. In the course of a year he succeeded in inaugurating sweeping reforms similar to those which had been effected at Nan K'ang.

On the death of his eldest son Shu in 1192 at Wu Chou he again resigned, and this time retired to Chien Yang, sacred to him for its associations with his father's memory. He bought a residence amid beautiful surroundings at K'ao T'ing where he hoped he might pursue his labours. He was not allowed to remain long in retirement, however, but at the end of 1193 was appointed Governor at T'an Chou in Hunan, at the foot of the Hêng Mountain, where so many happy years had been spent in his literary labours.

In the autumn of 1194 Kuang Tsung abdicated and was succeeded by Ning Tsung with Chao Ju Yü as Prime Minister. One of the earliest acts of the new reign was to send for Chu Hsi, who had been strongly recommended to Kuang Tsung as the " first man in the Empire ". At first Chu Hsi declined, but his resistance being overcome he repaired to the Court, and was appointed Tutor to His Majesty.

Upon his settlement at the Capital the loyal patriot found to his grief that the young Emperor was exposed to serious danger from the machinations of an unscrupulous courtier fast rising to power. Han Ni Chou, a nephew of the Dowager Empress, made it his boast that it was his hand that had placed Ning Tsung on the Throne. Whether this was by forging the late Emperor's signature or by other means does not appear, but the obvious implication was that the man who could make could also unmake, and all lovers of their Emperor were concerned for the safety of his person. Chu Hsi repeatedly urged upon the Prime Minister promptly to dismiss the courtier, but without avail ; the Prime Minister with a fatuity that resulted in his downfall treated the danger with contempt, confident in his ability to crush his enemy if he ventured too far.

At first Chu Hsi was hopeful of the young Emperor's disposition. He appeared earnest in study and inclined to what is good. " If he obtains good men as counsellors," said the Tutor, " there is hope for the Empire." Encouraged by his Imperial pupil's responsiveness to his teaching he thought possibly that he might venture to do what Chao Ju Yü had refused to do and take measures for the overthrow of Han Ni Chou. Accordingly, it was arranged with a Vice-President of one of the Boards, P'ang Kuei Nien, that together they would seek audience and denounce the traitor. Unfortunately, P'ang was at this very time called away from the Court, and it fell to Chu Hsi to send in a memorial alone. This he followed by personal representations at the close of the lesson hour. The only result was that Han Ni Chou, roused to fury, threw off the last remnant of disguise and set himself to rid the Court of Chu Hsi and all his friends, including the Prime Minister.

He first attacked the Prime Minister, Chao Ju Yü, accusing him of gross maladministration. Chao, seeing that resistance was useless, fled to Yung Chou, where he remained till his death in what was virtually exile. Chu Hsi was filled with indignation, and impelled by a patriotic sense of his duty as a servant of the Emperor, prepared a lengthy memorial representing in vigorous terms the disaster to the state if the Emperor allowed himself to be deceived by traitors. His disciples, however, concerned at the danger he was incurring with no hope of benefiting his friend, entreated him to withhold the memorial. At first their entreaties were of no avail, but eventually Ts'ai Chi T'ung persuaded him to decide the matter by divination. The lot drawn indicated concealment as the course which should be followed. At this Chu Hsi was silent ; but, though contrary to the impulse both of patriotism and friendship, he did not venture to do other than abide by the result of the divination to which he had agreed. He kept up correspondence with his exiled friend from whose letters he learned that he was living in peace, and enduring his lot with fortitude.

The exile of Chao Ju Yü caused great consternation among the scholars of the Empire, and especially among the heads of colleges, with the result that many petitions were presented to the Emperor, to the no small anxiety of Han Ni Chou. Although his influence at Court and his power in the state had been greatly increased by the banishment of Chao, Han realized that the fact that the followers of Chao and the disciples of Chu Hsi were all scholars of repute boded ill for himself, and he determined to secure the discredit of the entire party. To accuse them one by one of individual crimes was obviously impossible, he therefore denounced the School as a whole, on the ground that it was propagating pernicious heresy which ought to be stamped out. Chu Hsi himself was charged with gross plagiarism of the writings of his predecessors, and other crimes. Han was assisted in his nefarious schemes by Hu Hung,[1] whom Chu Hsi had offended on a previous occasion when they had met at Chien An. Hu was now at the Court and himself wrote the memorial

---

[1] Not to be confused with Hu Hung, the philosopher.

which secured Chu Hsi's final disgrace. The Imperial document by which Chu Hsi was deprived of his office and of all his honours reached him while lecturing to his students in the first month of the year 1197. On receiving it, he glanced at it, then placed it on the table, and calmly proceeded with his lecture.

It may be of interest to add that Han Ni Chou, having secured the downfall of those who stood in his path, became increasingly powerful until his failure to withstand an invasion of the Chins furnished the only incentive needed to one of the numerous enemies he had made. " He was assassinated in a garden of the palace as he was passing in to an audience (1207)." [1]

CLOSING YEARS
(1197–1200)

Chu Hsi having been deprived of his office lost no time in retiring from the Court. He returned at once to the home he had prepared at K'ao T'ing in Chien Yang. Several hundreds of his friends and pupils escorted him for some distance on his way, parting from him at Ching An, where there was an affecting farewell at the temple in which he was to rest for the night. Here Ts'ai Chi T'ung joined him, and spent the night with him in affectionate converse, in which they plighted anew their covenant of friendship. It was their last meeting, for in the following year Ts'ai Chi T'ung died, deeply lamented by his Master.

On arrival at Chien Yang the aged philosopher again applied himself to lectures and literary work. Finding

---

[1] See Giles' *Biographical Dictionary*, p. 250.

that the number of his disciples had largely increased, he built a Lecture Hall on an islet in the river and named it " The House of Rest in the Bamboo Grove " (竹 林 精 舍). In 1199 he was again recognized by the Throne and to some extent reinstated, but he did not resume office, or take any further share in the responsibilities of the State.

In the spring of the year 1200 (on the 6th day of the 3rd month) he was taken seriously ill. The few days preceding had been full of activity. On the 3rd of the month two chapters of a Commentary on the *Shu Ching* were revised, and in the evening he lectured to his students. The next day was occupied in arranging for the building of a small kiosk just opposite the door of the Lecture Hall on the above-mentioned islet. Chu Hsi went to the river bank and watched a pupil Ch'ên Li Tao as he poured a libation of wine upon the foundations. As he stood there, the roaring of the wild beasts could be heard from the mountains toward the east. Some country people sitting on the ground near by remarked that whenever they could hear the wild beasts roar there was always a death in the neighbourhood, and their roaring had never been so loud as on this occasion. In the evening of the same day the Philosopher lectured on the *Doctrine of the Supreme Ultimate*; and the next evening on the *Western Inscriptions* and the *Essentials of Learning.*[1]

On the morning of the 5th the chapter on " Making the Thoughts Sincere " in the *Great Learning* was revised, and entrusted to a pupil Chan Ch'un to copy. In the afternoon a violent attack of dysentery set in, and the invalid went to

----

[1] Chap. VI.

his own home.   His last visit to his Lecture Hall, " The House of Rest," had been paid.   The next day he was much worse, and on the 8th he realized that his end was near.   The students from the " House of Rest " came to see him.   He sat up to receive them, deprecating their taking so much trouble, but recognizing their solicitude as characteristic of those engaged in religious studies.   After the students had left him he wrote three letters.   The first was to his son Tsai urging him to come quickly and collect his testamentary documents.   As he sealed up the letter he sighed and said, " Alas !   How many years it is since father and son were able to meet ! "   The second letter was to his disciple Huang Kan committing to him the task of revising and completing the manuscript of his work on Rites and Ceremonies ;   and the third was to Fan Nien Tê asking him to copy it.

The following morning he called into his bedroom his disciple Ts'ai Ch'ên, the son of Ts'ai Chi T'ung, who had been with him from the beginning of his illness, and who was bound to him by ties of deep affection.   The dying man was sitting up in bed and Ch'ên stood watching him.   The Master gently grasped his pupil's coat-sleeve and drawing him down to sit with him on the bed, said :   " If there is anything we wish to say to each other and do not say it now, it will be too late."   Just then the physician came in and forbade him to speak.   The dying man gave a sign that he wished the bed to be taken out into the central hall.   Later his students came again to see him, one of whom, Wei Tao, asked him a question as to the ceremony he would wish adopted in the event of his death.   He was now unable to speak, but gave his answer by signs.   Then he indicated a desire to write. A pen was put into his hand, and paper held in position for him. He held the pen with the old familiar grasp but was unable to move it in order to write. A little while after, with pen in hand, he fell back upon the pillow. With his hand he accidentally disarranged his cravat and motioned to Ch'ên to adjust it. His breathing now became gradually fainter, and in a few minutes, as two of his disciples watched him, Ch'ên at his head and another, Yi Chih, at his feet, the old Philosopher passed away, in the seventy-first year of his age.

He was buried at T'ang Shih, a village of Chien Yang, in a valley called the " Valley of the Great Forest ".[1] At the funeral there was a large concourse of people, numbering several thousands, described by the bitter chronicler of the contemporary hostile regime as a " gathering of heretics from all parts of the Empire to follow the Arch-Heretic to the grave ". A notable sight, in which we see this man taking his place side by side with the truly great in all ages, rejected and hated by men in power, but recognized and honoured by simple followers after goodness and truth !

Conclusion

So ended the life and work of the philosopher Chu Hsi. Even to record the closing scenes, and, throwing the mind back through the centuries, to watch the eyes opening with affectionate glance at the ministering disciples, and then closing in their last long sleep, is like watching the end of a dear friend. The study of his works and the perusal of

[1] Cf. p. 75.

the record of his life cannot fail to impress us with a sense
not only of his greatness but of his humanness. It was
doubtless this last quality combined with his intellectual
kingship which attracted so many to him.

Of his works the majority have been mentioned in the
preceding pages. To these should be added his *Tao T'ung*
(道 統), a biography of the sages, eminent scholars, and
statesmen. It should be mentioned that one of the most
important of his works was his commentary on the *Great
Learning* and *Doctrine of the Mean* included in the classic
entitled "Li Chi". There were also two posthumous works
of special importance, his *Conversations* and his *Collected
Writings*. The notes of the Philosopher's lectures and sayings
as recorded by his students were published in 140 parts by
Li Ching Tê (黎 靖 德) in A.D. 1270 under the title of
Chu Tzǔ's Conversations (朱 子 語 類). The work was
a combination of two earlier compilations, entitled *Yü Lu*
(語 錄), of which there were four different collections, and
Yü Lei (語 類), of which there were also four collections. The
Yü Lu were the *Ch'ih Chou Chu Tzǔ Yü Lu* (池 州 朱
子 語 綠), published in 1215, the *Jao Chou Chu Tzǔ Yü Hsü
Lu* (饒 州 朱 子 語 續 錄), 1238, the *Jao Chou Chu Tzǔ
Yü Hou Lu* (饒 州 朱 子 語 後 錄), 1249, and the
Chien An Chu Tzǔ Yü Pieh Lu (建 安 朱 子 語 別 錄),
1265. The *Yü Lei* were the *Chu Tzǔ Yü Lei* (朱 子 語 類),
1219, commonly known as the Ssǔ Ch'uan edition (蜀 本),
the *Mei Chou Chu Tzǔ Yü Lei* (眉 州 朱 子 語 類), 1222,
the *Hui Chou Chu Tzǔ Yü Lei* (徽 州 朱 子 語 類), 1252,
and the *Hui Chou Chu Tzǔ Yü Hsü Lei* (徽 州 朱 子 語
續 類), 1252. Similarly, the Philosopher's letters, essays,

monumental inscriptions, and other miscellaneous writings were collected in a work entitled *Chu Tzŭ's Collected Writings* (朱 子 文 集). The work now extant under this title was edited by Chang Pei Hsing, a littérateur who flourished at the close of the seventeenth century, in the reign of K'ang Hsi. It was based, however, on an earlier edition not now obtainable.

Voluminous as were the Philosopher's writings they were by no means superficial ; all were stamped by his keen incisive intellect, and any one, at least of his greater works, would have been sufficient to establish his reputation as a great thinker. The supremacy of his intellect was acknowledged by his contemporaries as well as by posterity. His disciples were two numerous to mention even by name. Wherever he went, in office or in retirement, he established a school, with the result that at the time of his death his followers were to be numbered by thousands, and were found in all parts of the Empire. Some of the more prominent of these have been referred to in the preceding pages. But so many were they that most are unknown to posterity, and of those who are mentioned in the biographies the majority are mere names to the present day scholar. It is not the number of his disciples, however, which it is here desired to emphasize, but rather the fact that the most celebrated littérateurs of his time acknowledged him as Master.

If it be asked what was the secret of this mastery over the intellects of his age, the answer surely must be that it lay in his marvellous dialectic power. His reasoning was clear, incisive, and cogent. It is true that it was mainly of the *a priori* sort which would have little weight with the modern

thinker in the West, but that was no demerit in the eyes of
Chu Hsi's compatriots, either in his own or in later ages. If
his conclusions are wrong, the error is in the premises
rather than in the processes of his reasoning. Whatever
inconsistencies there may appear to be in his system, there is
abundant evidence that in his own mind at all events they
had their solution. For his many questioners he always had an
answer ready, and for his disputants a courteous and good-
humoured retort. Surely no teacher was so catechized as this
man, and rarely one so little nonplussed. And yet, confident
and dogmatic as he was, he was intellectually sincere and
modest. He was a serious thinker. His mind dwelt on
realities and instinctively brushed away intellectual sophistries.
A seeker after truth for truth's sake, he criticized his own as
well as the arguments of others. If he erred, the acknow-
ledgment of his error was frank and spontaneous; if he was
baffled, he confessed his perplexity. And always he acknowledged his indebtedness to his Masters; in fact, his writings
were in large part in vindication of their teachings rather than
the assertion of his own theories.

Added to his intellectual power and sincerity was thoroughness of method both in study and interpretation. He scorned
all short-cuts. "Get at the real meaning of the passage or
book!" was his cry. "Read the passage over and over
again until absolute conviction as to its meaning has been
acquired." "Look at the connexion, and interpret the
phrase or sentence in the light of its context." A slavish
literalism was denounced as simply a form of intellectual
laziness that could rest content with something less than the
real thought of the writer. Clear and logical in his own

thinking he was no pedant and did not insist upon verbal consistency in the works of others. Alike in the teachings of the sages and in the writings of the philosophers who preceded him, he had a quick eye to detect apparent discrepancies, but also sufficient penetration to discern the essential unity of the underlying truth. With such mental habits it was but natural that he should insist upon the necessity of ridding the mind of preconceived ideas, and that in controversy he possessed a singular power of understanding the other's point of view.

To thoroughness of method was added lucidity of style. In Chu Hsi's dialectic there was none of the picturesqueness, or vehemence, or moral force, which we find in Mencius. His power lay in the cold, clear, and exact expression of keen, incisive reasoning. If in his works the sections from the *Collected Writings* and those from the *Conversations* be compared in the original, a marked difference will be observed between his written and oral style, showing that his writing was by no means careless or slipshod ; but there was no pedantic labouring at the letter, nor even that packed terseness which characterized the style of Chou Tzŭ and Chang Tsai. Clear and flowing, with phrasing smooth and varied, his language was the natural clothing of his thought, so that the testimony of one of his pupils was : " The Master's teaching is very ripe, he expresses himself easily, and always explains a subject thoroughly."

We have compared Chu Hsi's style with that of Mencius as having less of warmth and passion. So true is this of his writings that it would be easy to infer that he was lacking in emotional qualities. But this would be far from the truth and a grave injustice. The study of his life reveals a warm heart. His touching devotion to his adopted father Li Yen P'ing, his warm friendship for his opponent Chang Nan Hsien, his loyal solicitude for his Prince, all witness both to the depth and to the generosity of his affections. Wherever he went he attached men to himself by ties of love that nothing could quench. Such were Ch'ên An Ch'ing at Chang Chou, Ts'ai Chi T'ung at the Court, and Ts'ai Ch'ên at Chien Yang. His sympathy was always stirred by suffering. Reluctant as he was to take office, and restive as he was when away from his books, yet, even in retirement, he could not resist the call of the distressed. The sufferers from flood and famine found in him a ready helper.

Such was Chu Hsi. Not unworthily has he been held in honour by the nation as second only to the sages. For seven centuries his mind has dominated the intellect of China. Once and again his supremacy has been disputed, notably by Wang Yang Ming of the fifteenth century, who bids fair to be the most popular philosopher with the young China of to-day. But with these exceptions Chu Hsi and his philosophy have held their own, and, however much he may be displaced by others in the present age, his teaching must still form the background in any true perspective of Chinese thought.

CHAPTER V

LAW AND MATTER

" God is Light," said Saint John. " Heaven is Law," [1] says Chu Hsi. The two assertions differ in form, for one is the language of metaphor, and the other of plain statement. Needless to say, they differ also in the content of the terms " God " and " Heaven ". Altogether apart from " Term " [2] and other controversies, the idea of the Christianized Greek word θεὸς is immeasurably richer than that of the Chinese word T'ien (天). But looking solely at what is predicated in each case, the two statements are not far apart in meaning, for both assert that God in His essence is ethically perfect. The all-pervading, immanent Law of Chinese philosophy consists of the ethical principles Love, Righteousness, Reverence, and Wisdom, in absolute perfection and harmony.

Another great word which has come down to us from the inspired apostle is : " God is Love." The sentence, as it stands, does not occur in the writings of Chinese thinkers ; and *Jên* (仁), the Chinese word for love, though perfectly pure in its lofty altruism, contains none of that infinity of passion and self-sacrifice conveyed by the New Testament phrase. But with this understanding the phrase itself would be the most natural expression of Chinese

[1] 天 即 理 也
[2] The controversy as to the most fitting Chinese term for " God ".

philosophical teaching as we find it in the Sung School. For, according to this school, of the cardinal virtues enumerated above, Love is the parent of the rest; it is the originating principle of the universe, whence all things proceed; it is the first and all-inclusive attribute of Heaven; and, without exaggeration, may be said to be a synonym for the word Heaven itself.

These, then, are the two key-words to the understanding of Chinese thought: Law and Love, the foundation of all things. The ideas they embody, and their relation to other great words in the philosophical system, will be fully discussed in the course of this and the following chapters. Enough now to say that it is on these that the emphasis must be placed in any just appreciation of the school we are considering.

The best presentation of Chu Hsi's theory of the universe is to be found in Books xlix and l of his *Complete Works*, referred to in Chapter I. The title of the work contained in the two Books named is *Li Ch'i* (理 氣), which at once indicates the fundamental thesis of the system; namely, that the universe is a dualism, the two terms of which are *Li* and *Ch'i*. Our first inquiry, then, will be: What do these terms imply? After which we shall need further to consider the relation between the two, and ask: What is the nature of this Dualism? Is it ultimate, or does it resolve itself into Monism? And if the latter, what is the nature of the Monism?

MATTER

" The Plenum of the Universe," says Chang Tsai, " is the substance of my being, and the Pilot of the Universe is my Nature." [1] Chu Hsi, in his comment on this passage, says that the Plenum of the Universe is *ch'i* and the Pilot of the Universe is *li* ; he further tells us that the *ch'i* constitutes man's corporeity.[2] Here we have the two elements *ch'i* and *li* in sharp antithesis, and of the two, *ch'i* is represented as filling all space, and as constituting the substance of our physical existence. It is, in fact, the "plenum" of Western philosophers. Of what then does this plenum consist ?

The Chinese word *ch'i* (氣) in modern speech means "air ", "gas ", "vapour ", "breath ", "temper ". In its philosophical sense it has been variously translated. Giles gives it as "the vivifying principle or aura of Chinese Cosmology ". Wells Williams renders it "the ether, the aerial fluid, the vital force or fluid, the primordial aura ".

McClatchie, in his translation of the *Li Ch'i*, the work referred to above, takes *ch'i* to be "air ", and consistently all through his book boldly translates it by this word. He sees in it an evidence of the similarity between Chinese philosophy and that of Greece and Rome. To quote from his Introduction, "The Chinese philosophers hold the eternity of the Primordial Matter, which, in common with Anaximines, they consider to be air and a god." [3] McClatchie, however, hardly does justice to the word *ch'i* as used by the Chinese philosophers. Whatever it may be, it is not air such as surrounds us in our atmosphere. Any

---

[1] The passage occurs in the *Western Inscriptions* (西 銘). See 大 全, bk. iv, f. 2. See also *Hanlin Papers*, by W. A. P. Martin, pp. 38-9.

[2] See *P.H.N.*, p. 50, and n. 2 (全 書, bk. xlii, f. 22).

[3] *Confucian Cosmogony*, by Thos. McClatchie, Introd., p. viii.

Chinese scholar would negative the bare suggestion. It may be true that philologically the origin of the word is to be traced to some such idea held by Chinese as by other races in primitive times. Even this, however, is by no means clear; for the history of the ideograph suggests " vapour " rather than " air " as its original meaning. Dr. F. H. Chalfant, in his *Early Chinese Writing*, traces the character through several forms, and gives as its probable original 𡘋 , representing vapour produced by the heat of fire or sun.[1] But, in any case, we are dealing with the philosophy of Chu Hsi and his school, and by the time this system was developed, in the eleventh and twelfth centuries of our era, the word had acquired a very different meaning. To translate it, therefore, as " air " is misleading.

Le Gall in his work on the same subject translates *ch'i* as *matière*, which is nearer the mark, for *ch'i* undoubtedly represents the material element in the dual constitution of the universe, and often it is best represented by the English word " matter ". An important qualification, however, needs to be made, for, though there is nothing in the whole universe into which *ch'i* does not enter as one of the two ultimate elements of existence, *ch'i* is not confined to matter in the sense of being tangible and perceptible to the senses. There is another word, *chih* (質), which represents this form of matter,[2] and, though *chih* is a form of *ch'i*, *ch'i* is not always *chih*. Beyond the solid, or the liquid, or the gaseous, beyond and antecedent to the *chih*, there is

---

[1] *Early Chinese Writing*, by F. H. Chalfant, *Memoirs of the Carnegie Museum*, vol. iv, No. 1, pl. x.

[2] 氣 積 爲 質, see 全 書, bk. xlix, f. 1.

ch'i, the primordial substance or plenum, invisible and intangible, the source from which spring all phenomena, the basis, not only of all that we call matter, but of every form of existence, material or spiritual, physical or psychical. Where this aspect of *ch'i* is prominent, the word Ether is the more appropriate word to express its meaning.

The fact just stated needs to be emphasized. For while we shall find it increasingly apparent, as we proceed with our inquiry, that the significance of the physical aspect of *ch'i* in the Sung interpretation of the universe can hardly be overstated, we must nevertheless not lose sight of the fact that according to that interpretation *ch'i* is spirit as well as matter. This view is not without its modern counterpart in the West. The trend of thought with some advanced physicists to-day is to regard spirit and matter as a twofold manifestation of the one substance, Ether. One writer, referring to an emanation which, in addition to the alpha, beta, and gamma radiations, is emitted by radio-active bodies, says that this emanation, while it has many of the characteristics of gas, yet, unlike matter, at certain phases of its evolution it wholly disappears by transforming itself into electric particles. "Here, then," says this writer, "we have established the fact that nature before our very eyes is constantly changing the material into the immaterial and the ponderable into the imponderable. Startling as it may seem, this emanation is both matter and not matter, and similar substances might enter into the construction of those bodies which, for want of a better name, St. Paul once described as 'spiritual'." [1] The same writer also

[1] *Matter and some of its Dimensions*, by W. K. Carr, p. 22.

says, " Matter, then, is a projection from a spiritual plane, and since modern science tends to confirm that view, it must profoundly modify the conceptions of the religion and philosophy of the future." [1] Another well-known writer says : " To suppose that our experience of the necessary and fundamental connexion between the two things—the something which we know as mind, and the something which is now represented by matter—has no counterpart or enlargement in the actual scheme of the universe, as it really exists, is needlessly to postulate confusion and instrumental deception. Philosophers have been so impressed with this that they have conjectured that mind and matter are but aspects, or modes of perception, of one fundamental comprehensive unity : a unity which is neither exactly mind nor exactly matter as we conceive them, but is something fundamental and underlying both—as the ether is now thought of as sustaining, and in some sense constituting, all the phenomena of the universe." [2] On another page of the same work it is said : " It is incorrect to say that Ether is Matter. For there is a clear distinction between the part of the ether which is modified into electrons or atoms and the part which is not so affected ; and it is often also convenient to discriminate between the adjectives ' material ' and ' etherial '.[3] Nevertheless ether is material in the sense of belonging to the material or physical aspect of the Universe, as distinguished

[1] Ibid., p. 34.

[2] *Man and the Universe*, by Sir Oliver Lodge, pp. 278–9.

[3] The spelling " etherial " is adopted by Sir Oliver Lodge to distinguish the meaning of this word from the very different conception suggested by the word " ethereal ".

from the mental or physical aspect. It may have psychical functions to perform, but it does not itself belong to the psychical order of things. Its direct connexions appear to be with the world or matter, not with the world of spirit." [1]

It will be noted that in the latter part of the passage last cited there is a difference in the writer's account of Ether and Chu Hsi's account of *Ch'i* in that in the former case ether is said not to belong to the psychical order of things. With this exception, however, the ideas contained in the above passages come very near to those connoted by Chu Hsi's *ch'i*. In Chu Hsi's philosophy there is the same indefiniteness in the line of demarcation between matter and spirit as is suggested by some of these statements ; the *ch'i* in some of its manifestations is both matter and not matter; in its primordial form it is pure spirit, and of this primordial *ch'i* there is a part which is modified in one direction and properly called matter and a part which is not so affected, so that it may even be said that for our philosopher " matter is a projection from a spiritual plane " ; and it detracts nothing from the parallel that, like Sir Oliver Lodge, Chu Hsi tells us that *ch'i* belongs to the material, or, more literally, to the class of things which have form.[2]

For the Sung philosophers the first stage in the evolution of the material universe is the rotation of the *ch'i*, by which are produced its two modes, Energy and Inertia. This rotation of the *ch'i* corresponds to the vortex movement of the modern scientist, while the Two Modes are parallel

---

[1] *Man and the Universe*, by Sir Oliver Lodge, pp. 300–1.
[2] 全 書, bk. xlix, f. 3.

to what Sir Oliver Lodge refers to when he speaks of Matter and Energy as the two great entities with which Science has to do. " Perhaps," the same writer says, " Science may be induced in the long run to modify this form of statement, and to assert conversation and real existence of ether and motion (or perhaps only of ether in motion) rather than of matter and energy." [1] In either case, this stage of development corresponds to the " Two Modes " of Chu Hsi. Following this evolution of the Two Modes is the development of the Five Agents,[2] at which stage we come to what may certainly be called matter. But in both these stages we find the word *ch'i* still applied. The Two Modes are called the two *ch'i* and the Five Agents are called the five *ch'i*. *Ch'i*, in fact, is the underlying substance in all stages in the evolution of the cosmos, the ground of all phenomena both physical and psychical ; and, while it is not always, or necessarily, matter in the ordinary acceptation of the word, its most characteristic manifestation is matter.

Ch'i, then, must be interpreted in three senses. It is the primordial substance in which both spirit and matter originate ; it is that part of the primordial substance which becomes spirit, in contrast to *chih* the part which becomes solid matter ; and it is the general term which represents the material element in all the myriad transformations of the cosmos in contrast to the immaterial element *li*. Obviously, in the more general sense of the term, as the antithesis of *li*, its meaning is best expressed by the word matter ; while in

---

[1] *Man and the Universe*, by Sir Oliver Lodge, p. 172.

[2] 五 行, often translated " Five Elements ". For the " Two Modes " and " Five Agents " see Chap. VI.

its primordial sense, and in the sense in which it is contrasted with *chih*, the word ether is the more appropriate rendering. It must be borne in mind, however, that, notwithstanding the three different senses in which the word is used, *ch'i* is but one ; whether as the primordial substance, or as spirit, or as matter, it is the same *ch'i*. It must also be borne in mind that the dualism which we here find to be characteristic of *ch'i* runs through all stages in the evolution of the cosmos. There are two modes of the primordial ether, there are two modes of spiritual existence, and there are two modes of matter.

LAW

Li (理), the second term in the dualism, presents less difficulty to the student than does *ch'i*, but perhaps needs to be more carefully defined. Mr. Evan Morgan, in his dictionary of Chinese terms, says : " *Li* originally meant the trimming of precious stones. Its use was verbal. Hence it came to be applied generally to attention to any business. Gradually from putting things to rights it came to signify the truth in a thing." [1] In other words, from the idea of putting things to rights it came to mean the inherent rightness of a thing. Hence we get the meaning " principle " or " law ". McClatchie translates the word as " fate ", and, as in the case of *Ch'i*, so with *Li*, he is rigidly consistent throughout his book. Le Gall translates it as " forme ", or " formel principe ". How far these meanings are correct we shall see as we proceed.

The great problem of philosophy, in seeking to explain the phenomena of the universe, is to account for the contrasts,

---

[1] *Chinese New Terms and Expressions*, by Evan Morgan, p. 169.

and the apparently irreconcilable contradictions which present themselves. Of these the antithesis which has claimed most attention in the West is that between Matter and Mind. The account given by any particular school of the relation between these two elements is in itself sufficient to give the name to that school as expressive of its most important characteristic. When, therefore, we turn to Chinese philosophy and find that it, too, seeks to account for a dualism as the main problem by which it is confronted, and that that dualism is an antithesis between the material and the immaterial, we are at once tempted to ask whether we are not dealing with the same problem as is dealt with in Western philosophy, and whether *Ch'i* and *Li* are not our old friends Matter and Mind.

There are other antitheses in Western philosophy which will also suggest themselves. There is, for example, the antithesis mainly associated with the school of Herbert Spencer, and we might ask whether the dualism of Chinese philosophy is not that of Matter and Force. The question has also been raised whether we have not here a system similar to that of the Greek philosophers, and whether *Li* does not constitute the type of each individual thing or class of things, the norm to which it conforms, in such a way as to make it practically identical with Aristotle's " Form ".

The answers to these questions cannot in any case be wholly in the affirmative. Chinese mentality differs so widely from the Western that it is not surprising if categories seemingly inevitable to us do not wholly coincide with Chinese modes of thinking. A term such as *Li*, used to designate the fundamental immaterial element in the universe, cannot but have a wide and comprehensive connotation, whatever its root meaning may be. Much of that connotation corresponds to concepts with which we are familiar. Yet we must be prepared at any moment to find that *Li* has ceased to travel along the same road as the concept to which we had allied it. For this reason alone, apart from any other consideration, we shall not be surprised to find that *Li*, as explained and discussed by the Sung philosophers, while suggestive of some, if not all, of those conceptions of Western philosophers to which reference has been made, is, in the fundamental meaning of the term—the meaning, that is, from which it derives its name—essentially different from those conceptions.

As we shall learn later, there are other terms, such as *Tao*, *Hsing*, *T'ai Chi*, and *T'ien*, which are synonyms of *Li*, but each expressive of its own particular aspect of the one entity. Similarly there is one meaning specifically expressed by the term *Li*. That meaning, in accordance with its etymological derivation, is a " principle " or " law ". In the first paragraph of Chu Hsi's work on " Human Nature ", in a statement submitted to and endorsed by the Philosopher, it is said, " In the term *Li* the reference is to the fact that every event and thing has each its own rule of existence." [1] The statement is an allusion to an important passage in the *Odes* quoted by Mencius. The passage reads : " It is the ordinance of Heaven, in giving birth to the multitudes of the people, that inherent in every single thing there is its rule of existence. The people therefore hold within themselves a normal principle of good, and consequently approve this excellent virtue." [2] From this passage it will be seen that in the statement quoted above

[1] *P.H.N.*, p. 1.　　　　　　　　[2] *Odes*, p. 541.

the reference is to the fact that in every individual thing there is an ethical standard or rule of existence, and the assertion is that it is from this fact that *li* derives its name. The same idea of Law as the meaning of *li* was expressed by the Philosopher on another occasion in answer to the question : " What evidence is there that *li* is inherent in the Ether ? " The philosopher said : " The fact that the Active and Passive Modes and the Five Agents do not get tangled up and lose every thread of order is owing to *li*." [1]

Li, then, is Law. In everything, animate and inanimate, there is a standard, a rule of life, a principle of existence, to which it conforms as the law of its being. Search the universe, and you find it is the same. Everywhere are laws. Everywhere is law. Infinitely diversified, indeed, but with a unity pervading all, and a unity in this, if in nothing else, that all things, individually and collectively, are governed by law. This universal reign of law leads the Chinese philosopher to account for the cosmos as having its origin in law. Heaven itself, by whose decree all things are what they are, Heaven, the self-existent, is Law.

With this root meaning of the term we are considering clearly established in our minds, we may now proceed to compare it and its implications with those conceptions current in Western philosophy to which we have previously referred.

First, then, how far does *Li*, in the dualism of the Sung School, correspond to Spencer's " force " ? Le Gall apparently regards this as a prominent element in the Sung conception. " *Li*," he says, " est le principe d'activité, de mouvement,

---

[1] 全 書, bk. xlix, f. 2.

d'ordre dans la nature, ce que nos évolutionistes contemporains H. Spencer, Darwin, Haeckel, appellent une force de développement inhérente à la matière." [1] It must be admitted that some of Chu Hsi's statements seem to support this view. " The movement of matter is dependent upon *Li*," [2] he says. The Supreme Ultimate, which is *Li*, is also said to be the original substance of the energy which produces the positive mode, and of the inertia which produces the negative mode. In such statements *Li* suggests Spencer's " primordial element " inherent in both energy and inertia.[3] Possibly it is in this sense that we are to understand Chu Hsi's statement that *Li* has both motion and rest, which, he says, is the reason why the Ether has motion and rest.[4] On the other hand, Chu Hsi also says : " *Li* neither devises nor plans nor makes anything. *Li* is a pure, empty, and vast world, with no visible traces of its presence. It can form nothing." [5] In fact, in the philosopher's use of the word, generally, the idea of " force " is not prominent. While, in the ultimate, *Li* is the source both of energy and inertia, it is not this aspect of it which is to be regarded as its chief characteristic. It is thought of rather as a regulative principle than as a principle of activity.

The use of the expressions "*forme*" and "*formel principe*" by Le Gall suggests the further question whether *Li* corresponds to Aristotle's " form " or Plato's " idea ". The expression " rule of existence " in the passage cited on an

---

[1] *Tchou Hi, le Philosophe, sa Doctrine, son Influence*, p. 29.

[2] 全 書, bk. xlix, f. 2.　　　　　　　[3] Cf. p. 131.

[4] 全 書, bk. xlix, f. 14.　　　　　　[5] Ibid., f. 3.

earlier page might also be rendered " norm " and the passage read, " In the term *Li* the reference is to the fact that every event and thing has each its own norm." If, then, *Li* is inherent in each individual thing as the law of its being, the rule of existence, or norm, to which it conforms, does it constitute, as it were, the type of that thing ? The idea of myriad archetypal Forms corresponding to Things is strikingly suggested by a passage in the writings of Ch'êng Tzǔ to which attention was called in an earlier chapter. " Void like the boundless desert," he says, " but filled with innumerable forms like a dense forest ! " [1] This, indeed, approaches somewhat to Plato's doctrine of Ideas, or, as modified by Aristotle, of Substantial Forms. But the " rule of existence " or " norm " referred to in the passage quoted above is an ethical norm. *Li* is Love, Righteousness, Reverence, and Wisdom, and never anything else. It is not " norm ", then, in the Aristotelian sense of " form ". Moreover, in recognizing the Sung doctrine of Plurality we must not lose sight of the emphasis placed on Unity. In the very passage just quoted, in the first term of Ch'êng Tzǔ's paradox, this aspect of *Li* is expressed just as emphatically as that of innumerable forms in the second. As stated by Chu Hsi, " *Li* is one, its functions are diverse." [2] In other words, although the differences of form and function in the infinite variety of species are due in the ultimate to *Li* as the controlling and directing principle, by reason of which each thing assumes the form and fulfils the functions proper to it, Chu Hsi nevertheless insists that " permeating the universe there is but one *Li*

---

[1] See p. 49.   [2] 全 書, bk. xlix, f. 1.

as the absolute Reality, the pivot of creation and transformation, received alike by men and other creatures in all
ages ". [1] The differences between species and the differing
degrees in which the ethical principles of which *Li* is composed are embodied in different individuals, are attributed
to *Ch'i* rather than to *Li*. *Ch'i* is the manifesting medium and
differs in density and purity, and therefore *Li* differs in the
extent to which it is able to manifest itself, much the same as
the sun, shining through a mat shed, differs in the extent to
which it is obscured, or allowed free course, by the mat
medium.[2] Thus, while *Li* differs in its manifestation in the
myriad genera, it is not because, inherent in, or apart from,
the sensible thing or class, it constitutes a form-essence
differing from all other form-essences. It is the one ethical
standard to which all things conform in varying degrees
according to their individual capacity. *Li*, therefore, however
suggestive of Aristotle's " form ", is not identical with it.

Does the thought of the Chinese philosopher, then, in the
case of *Li*, as in the case of *Ch'i*, approach more nearly to the
speculations of later Western philosophy ? To quote Sir Oliver
Lodge once more, as a representative of modern scientific
philosophy on its speculative side : " All are animated,"
he says, speaking of the different forms of life, " by something
which does not belong to the realm of physics and chemistry,
but lies outside their province, though it interacts with the
material entities." This immaterial element the writer calls
life or soul, and goes on to say : " Life is not matter, nor is
it energy, it is a guiding and directing principle, and when

[1] 全 書, bk. xliv, f. 33 (*P.H.N.*, p. 220).
[2] Ibid., bk. xlii, f. 27 (*P.H.N.*, p. 61).

I

considered as incorporated in a certain organism, it, and all
that appertains to it, may well be called the soul, or
constructive and controlling element, in that organism.
The soul in this sense is related to the organism in somewhat
the same way as the Logos is related to the universe, it is that
without which it does not exist—that which vivifies and
constructs or composes and informs, the whole." [1]   All this
might be said of Chu Hsi's *Li*. It is neither matter nor energy.[2]
It is a guiding and directing principle. It is the controlling
element in the individual organism. It is related to that
organism much as *Tao* is related to the universe. Moreover,
Li is what constitutes the life of the individual organism. It is
its *hsing* (性), or nature, imparted by the *ming* (命) or decree
of Heaven. In common speech to-day the combination of
these two words *hsing ming* (性 命) means life. Ch'êng Tzŭ
even goes so far as categorically to affirm that life constitutes
the nature, which is a synonym for *Li*. Sir Oliver Lodge,
referring to the vast variety of organisms, asks : " What is
the controlling entity in each case, which causes each to have
its own form and not another, and preserves the form constant,
amid the widest diversity of particles ? "   And goes on to say :
" We call it life, we call it soul, we call it by various names,
and we do not know what it is. But common sense rebels
against its being nothing." [3]   In view of all that has been said
above, we are fully warranted in affirming that Chu Hsi calls
it *Li*, and we may add that Chu Hsi would not quarrel with
the statement that *Li* is the life of the individual organism.[4]

[1] *Man and the Universe*, by Sir Oliver Lodge, p. 166.
[2] Except as the ultimate source of both, cf. p. 111.
[3] *Man and the Universe*, pp. 164–5.
[4] See Chap. VIII.

A statement, already referred to, made by one of Chu Hsi's questioners, is specially important in this connexion. The whole passage is worth citing. It reads : " *Question* : In distinguishing between the four terms, Heaven and the Decree, the Nature and Li, would it be correct to say that in the term Heaven the reference is to Heaven's attribute of self-existence ; in the term Decree-to-its-all-pervading activity and immanence in the universe, in the term Nature to that complete substance by which all things have their life, and in the term *Li* to the fact that every event and thing has each its own rule of existence ; but that taking them together, Heaven is *Li*, the Decree is the Nature, and the Nature is *Li* ? *Answer* : Yes." [1] In this passage there are four terms, one of which is *Li*, left untranslated as the term under discussion. These four terms all refer to the same thing, but differ in their connotation according to the different aspects from which this same entity is regarded, and it will be seen that, according to this statement, all things owe their life to their possession of the Nature, and that the Nature is identical with *Li*. While, then, the idea of life is not that from which *Li* derives its name, it must be recognized that, according to Chu Hsi, *Li* constitutes the life of each individual organism.

We come back to the question with which we began. Does the dualism of Chinese philosophy represent the antithesis, familiar in the West, of mind and matter, and does *Li* correspond to Mind ? The answer is : It comes very near it, so near that to many, as to Dr. Martin, *Li* will seem to involve mind, and even personality ; for Love, Righteousness,

------

[1] 全 書, bk. xlii, f. 1 (*P.H.N.*, p. 3).

Reverence, and Wisdom, the component principles of *Li*, are, as Dr. Martin reminds us, attributes of mind. But the same writer, while he expresses the belief that Chinese thought will come to understand that law implies mind, and will proclaim that

" Conscious law is King of kings,"

nevertheless maintains that the word *Li* does not in itself mean mind. " With both Chu Hsi and the Taoist," he says, " this Reason (*Li*), if we may so call it, is rather a property of mind than mind itself. Each denies its personality, not perceiving that a property implies a substance, and that in this case the substance must be mind." [1] Chu Hsi, however, recognized that a substance is implied by *Li*. " *Li*, apart from mind," he says, " would have nothing in which to inhere," [2] and similarly he says, " If there were no ether *Li* would have nothing in which to inhere " ; [3] which is only another way of saying that *Li* is an attribute, and that mind in the one case and the ether in the other, is the substance. As is pointed out in a later chapter, the four component principles of *Li* are really the three phases of mind of Western psychologists, knowing, feeling, and willing, but with an ethical import. And so far *Li* is identical with mind. But for Chu Hsi these principles have no substantive existence apart from the Ether. *Li* is not conscious apart from its vehicle of manifestation. *Li*, therefore, is what makes mind to be mind, and, given the vehicle of manifestation, *Li*, or Law, *is* conscious.

---

[1] *Hanlin Papers*, by W. A. P. Martin, p. 38.

[2] 全 書, bk. xliv, f. 2 (*P.H.N.*, p. 159).

[3] 全 書, bk. xlix, f. 1.

It is important, then, to bear in mind that, while the idea of Law is what gives to *Li* its name, *Li* is yet much more than Law. From all that has been said, it will be apparent to the reader that *Li* is not merely a norm or standard to which all things conform : it is itself the principle, guiding and directing, which brings that conformity to pass. And, still more important, it is an ethical principle. Were it not so, we might be tempted to translate the word as " fate " as McClatchie has done. But *Li* is not arbitrary or colourless or blind, as the word fate would suggest. It is ethical. " *Li* is absolutely pure," we are told, " and perfectly good." [1] Moreover, just as the pencil of white light, when broken up into its constituent rays, is seen to be composed of red, blue, violet, and other colours, so we find that *Li*, when we come to analyse it, is distinguishable into four component principles, Love, Righteousness, Reverence, and Wisdom. A conception which can be defined in such terms as these cannot possibly be adequately represented by the word " fate ". The law which governs the universe is the law of Love, the law of Righteousness, the law of Reverence, the law of Wisdom.

It is here that we have the key to the true antithesis as it presents itself to the Chinese philosopher. Not matter and force, not inanimate matter and the principle of life, not matter and the principle which gives it form—antitheses such as these, which appeal so readily to the Western mind, may be and are more or less implied, but are not what confront the Chinese philosopher's mind as constituting the problem to be solved. Nor is the antithesis on which his thought fastens itself that of matter and mind, the contrast between

[1] Ibid., f. 8.

the physical and the psychical. In his view the immaterial element is never dissociated from its ethical character. The antithesis for him is between the material and the moral, between the physical and the ethical. This, and nothing less than this, must be held clearly in the mind if we are to estimate aright the contribution made to the thought of the nation by the Sung School; if we would appreciate in any adequate measure the lofty character and moral passion which characterized so markedly the life and work of Chu Hsi.

There is one other aspect of *Li* which will emerge more fully in later chapters, but which must be referred to here— though it can only be by a passing reference. *Li*, we have seen, derives its name from the fact that it constitutes the norm or rule of existence for each individual thing. But *Li* has a double application—to the individual and also to the universal, to the Many and to the One. " Law is one," we are told, " its functions are diverse." [1] It is repeatedly stated that in the universe as a whole there is only one Law, though each individual thing has within it its own individual law.[2] From the emphasis on Unity side by side with Plurality the transition is easy to the thought of Divine immanence and other theistic conceptions. The passage identifying *Li* with Heaven the self-existent and Heaven's decretive will has been cited on an earlier page. Its theistic import, however, must be reserved for a later chapter. Here, in connexion with our study of the ideas embodied in the term *Li*, it is the all-pervading, abiding unity, in contrast to plurality and transient individuality, to which attention is called. " Where was *Li* before man came to be ? " asked one of the philosopher's

[1] Ibid., f. 1. [2] Ibid.

disciples. " Even then it was here," was the reply. " It is like the water in the sea ; whether you fill one bucket with it, or a pair of buckets, or a single bowl, it is all the same water from the sea. But He is the host, I am the guest. He is eternal whereas I receive Him but for a little while." [1] That is to say, man and the individual thing are like the transient guests at the wayside inn—they come and go ; while *Li* is like the host who stays on through the months and years.

> The One remains, the many change and pass ;
>   Heaven's light for ever shines, earth's shadows fly ;
> Life, like a dome of many coloured glass,
>   Stains the white radiance of eternity,
>   Until Death tramples it to fragments.

The word Law, therefore, as the equivalent of *Li* must be understood in a wide sense. In the individual, it is the rule of existence for that individual, and it is from this aspect of it that it derives its name. But it is more. It is a principle, living and active, which directs and controls the development of the being in which it is inherent. It is a principle which pervades the universe ; with infinite variety of function, it is, nevertheless, one. It is an ethical principle : the essence of its life is ethical, the secret of its activity is ethical. And, finally, it is Divine. All-pervading, and immanent in every individual thing that exists, it is the ALL in ALL.

THE RELATION BETWEEN LAW AND MATTER

We are now in a position to consider the relation between the two terms of the dualism, Law and Matter. What is the nature of this dualism ? Is it ultimate ? If not, is it Materialism, or is it some form of Theism, or what is it ?

[1] Ibid., f. 2.

Canon McClatchie says that the system is a species of Monotheism combined with Pantheism ;[1] but he also says that primordial matter being eternal we have two gods, a first god and a second god, which may be described as deified Fate and deified Matter—in other words, a dualism. He further asserts that " there is no such thing as a personal God wholly separate from Matter to be found in the Confucian classics ", or in the teachings of Chu Hsi.[2] Le Gall is very severe in his condemnation of the Sung system and its most famous exponent. " Beau diseur," he says, " autant que philosophe détestable, cet homme est parvenu à imposer, depuis bientôt six siècles, à la masse de ses compatriotes une explication toute matérialiste des anciens livres." [3] Those who have studied Chinese Philosophy will not be surprised to find that Dualism, Materialism, Monotheism, and Pantheism are all asserted of it. We shall perhaps arrive at a truer understanding if we content ourselves with not labelling it at all, though careful comparison may serve the useful purpose of teaching us something of what it is by showing us what it is not. In this and the following chapters of Part II we shall confine ourselves as far as possible to the consideration of the subject from the point of view of the physical and moral order of the universe, reserving its discussion from the theistic point of view for Part IV, after our discussion of the Sung doctrine of human nature in Part III.

That Dualism of a sort characterizes the whole Chinese system is obvious to the most superficial reader. Indeed,

[1] *Confucian Cosmogony*, p. 126.
[2] Ibid., p. 146.
[3] *Tchou Hi, sa Doctrine, son Influence*, Preface, p. 1.

there is a twofold dualism. The two elements Law and Ether
constitute a dualism, and the Ether itself resolves into a
dualism—assuming two modes of existence, the active and
passive, or spirit and matter. Each of these again has its
active and passive modes. Moreover, in the dualism of Law
and Ether attributes are predicated of both elements which
are usually understood to imply deity. McClatchie and Le Gall
both agree that Chu Hsi taught that these principles are
co-eternal ; and, though not directly asserted, the doctrine is
perhaps implied in the statement that they are inseparable.
" In the whole universe," it is said, " there is no *ch'i* apart
from *li*, nor *li* apart from *ch'i*." [1] " *Li* is never separate
from *ch'i*." [2] We are told further that these two elements
are mutually necessary and interdependent. " If there were
no *ch'i*, *li* would have nothing in which to inhere." [3] " The
existence of *li* can only be perceived through *ch'i*." [4] And
still further, although Chu Hsi endorses the famous dictum
which forms the opening sentence of the *T'ai Chi T'u Shuo*
asserting the infinity of the Supreme Ultimate, he yet implies
that the Ether itself is infinite. In reply to the definite
question : " Law is infinite ; has the Ether limits ? " he said,
" As to limits, where can you assign limits ? " [5]

So, then, we have two elements in the universe mutually
dependent and inseparable. This would seem to be sufficient
to justify the term Dualism. Other important considerations,
however, must be taken into account. In the first place, the
Dualism, even if we call it Dualism, must be sharply

[1] 全 書, bk. xlix, f. 1. [2] Ibid.
[3] Ibid. [4] Ibid., f. 5.
[5] Ibid., f. 3.

differentiated from certain dualistic theories of the West. For example, in the Dualism of the Sung School there is nothing antagonistic in the component elements. On the contrary, they are interdependent and complementary to each other. Law pervades Matter as its directing principle, and Matter furnishes Law with its means of manifestation. It is true that in the dualism of Matter we have the two opposites of the *Yin* and the *Yang* or the Active and Passive Modes, translated by some as Light and Darkness. But even these opposites are complementary not antagonistic: the Two Modes follow each other in harmonious succession, and the governing factor in their alternation is goodness.[1]

Apart altogether from this consideration, however, a careful study of Chu Hsi's teaching as a whole shows that in his thought the two elements *li* and *ch'i*, coexistent and mutually dependent though they be, are not coequal; that the one is subordinate to the other, and is even derived from it. More than once the Philosopher was pressed with the question whether there is priority of Law over Ether. He would not commit himself to a categorical assertion that Law actually existed before Ether in the time sense; but he insisted upon the ontological priority of Law as well as its precedence in dignity. " If it be the case," said his questioner, " that when *li* exists *ch'i* also exists, does it not follow that there cannot be any precedence of one as compared with the other ? " " As a matter of fact," he replied, " *li* is antecedent, but we cannot say that to-day there is *li*, and to-morrow there will be *ch'i*. Precedence, however, there

---

[1] 一 陰 一 陽 之 謂 道 繼 之 者 善 也, a passage frequently cited from the *Yi Ching*, q.v., pp. 355-6.

certainly must be." [1]   Again the question is asked : " Does
li exist first or does *ch'i* ? "   And again the reply is : " *Li*
is never separate from *ch'i*, but *li* is incorporeal and *ch'i* is
corporeal ; from the point of view of corporeity, therefore,
how can it be otherwise than that there is priority ? " [2]   On
still another occasion the same question is asked, and the
answer is : " If we trace it back to the beginning of things
li is, as it were, antecedent, and *ch'i* subsequent." [3]   These
passages unmistakably assert a certain precedence of Law
over Matter.   But that is not all ; the superiority of Law
is not one of precedence merely, whether in time or in dignity.
Matter is subordinate to Law.   " Wherever *ch'i* accumulates,"
he says, " *li* is inherent in it, but *li* is the ultimate ruler." [4]
In another passage he paradoxically affirms that while
neither can be said to be antecedent to the other, and while
neither exists apart from the other, yet, if we trace them
to their origin, *li* is antecedent to *ch'i* ; by which is meant
that there is no priority in the time sense and both are
coexistent, but there is priority in respect of origin.[5]   Again,
he tells us that while the two are coexistent *li* is the root or
source ; [6]   so that the priority is because the source of *ch'i* is
in *li*.   In short, what the Chinese philosopher teaches is an
eternal generation of Matter by Law, and, in that sense, Law
is ultimate.

  To sum up, *li* and *ch'i* are coexistent and inseparable,
but *ch'i* is subordinate to *li*, as the source or root from which
it is derived.   Here, then, we have the answer to the question

[1] 全 書, bk. xlix, f. 3.   [2] Ibid., f. 1.
[3] Ibid., f. 3.   [4] Ibid., f. 7.
[5] Ibid., f. 1.   [6] Ibid.

with which we began.   Chu Hsi asserts the essential subordina-
tion of Matter to Law as its ultimate source, Chinese Dualism
resolves itself into Monism.

We have thus also answered the question suggested by
Le Gall's severe comment on Chu Hsi as a materialist. It is
obvious from all that has just been said that the Monism,
whatever it is, is not Materialism.   There are two very
important respects in which it differs from Materialism, at
least from certain familiar forms of Materialism.   In the
Materialism of the West, Matter is what one might well term
aggressively insubordinate. It is true it is absolutely obedient
to laws, but they are its own laws and unethical.   To the
Chinese philosopher the material is subject to the immaterial,
and the immaterial is the moral.   For, again, it must be
emphasized that the Law which we are discussing is ethical ;
it is Love, Righteousness, Reverence, and Wisdom.   This,
according to Chu Hsi, is the ultimate element in the universe.
Moral Law pervades all matter as the ruling and directing
principle.   Such a conception in itself is far removed from
Materialism.   It is in its moral sanctions that Materialism,
whether ancient or modern, most conspicuously fails.   In its
worst forms it is frankly sensual.   At its best it can appeal to
no higher sanction than self-interest.   A moral standard
imparted from above or without is to the materialist unthink-
able.   The contrary is the case with Chu Hsi.   Our nature is
imparted to us by Heaven ; it is recognized as the law of our
being ; it is the law of Love.   It is true that in man, as in all
creation, the ethically perfect nature appears soiled and
warped ;   the control of Law is limited.   This is frankly
recognized.   The difficulty of accounting for the ethical and

material elements is a real difficulty. It has baffled the ablest intellects. But the great merit of the Sung School is that the MORAL is recognized as fundamental. It teaches that the material universe which we see around us has an ethical basis which consists of those same ethical principles which we find embedded in our own hearts. Here, doubtless, lies the secret of its permanence. In the form which it received from Chu Hsi it has remained substantially the same through the seven centuries which have elapsed since his day, pure and lofty in its ethics, a conservative force in the nation, the very salt, indeed, which has preserved it from decay.

CHAPTER VI

THE FIRST CAUSE AND THE EVOLUTION OF THE COSMOS

We have seen that the dualism of Law and Matter resolves itself into Monism; that, though the two elements are coexistent and interdependent, one is nevertheless derived from and subordinate to the other; in other words, that Law is fundamental. In the present chapter we shall have under consideration the same fundamental element regarded from the point of view of causality and the evolution of the Cosmos.

THE DIAGRAM AND CHOU TSŬ'S CLASSIC

Chou Lien Hsi was the philosopher who first developed the Sung doctrine of the Supreme Being. Regarding Dualism in the ultimate as an impossible conception, and some kind of unity as necessary to thought, he conceived that the two elements, Law and Matter, must have a larger and more fundamental unity in which they unite as the Final Cause of all things. This he found in the *T'ai Chi*, or Supreme Ultimate, of the *Yi Ching*. The expression *T'ai Chi* occurs in the Third Appendix, and is there translated by Legge as the Grand Terminus, though in his Introduction he adopts the rendering Great Extreme. The whole paragraph refers to the famous diagrams of King Wên, and reads: " Therefore in the system of the *Yi* there is the Grand Terminus which produced the two elementary Forms. These two Forms produced the four

Symbols, which, again, produced the eight Trigrams, the eight Trigrams served to determine the good and evil issues of events, and from this determination was produced the success-ful prosecution of the great business of life." [1] On this passage Dr. Legge in his Introduction remarks : " Who will under-take to say what is meant by ' The Great Extreme ' which produced the two elementary Forms ? Nowhere else does the name occur in the old Confucian literature. I have no doubt myself that it found its way into this Appendix in the fifth (? or fourth) century B.C. from a Taoist source." [2]

How the elaborate doctrine of the Supreme Ultimate was ever evolved from the *Yi Ching* may well puzzle the Western student. Even this one single passage in which the expression occurs speaks of it merely as the basis of certain diagrams, while the term itself suddenly emerges from nothing-ness, without any apparent source in the argument preceding and without any after consequence. It must be remembered, however, that the diagrams are symbols, the mystical expression of the transformations of the universe. The theme of the whole work is " the *Yi* (易 change), the ever-changing phenomena of nature and experience." [3] These transformations are traced back to two modes of Matter represented in the symbols by the two *I* (儀), translated by Legge as Forms, which are the divided line, thus, — —, and the undivided line, thus ———. Here, for the writer of the *Yi*, is the starting point in the development of " the ever-changing phenomena " of the universe, as is clearly pointed out by Dr. Legge.[4] But

[1] *Yi Ching*, p. 373.
[2] Ibid., p. 12 ; cf. also Legge's note on pp. 365–6.
[3] Ibid., p. 44.
[4] Ibid., pp. 375–6 and note.

what lies beyond these ? Granted that they constitute the starting point of phenomena so far as we can trace them, what is the ultimate source whence these primary forms of Matter proceed ? Do the transformations consist of an endless chain of causes, or is there a Final Cause ? To this, the question of the ages, the author of the Third Appendix, or, if Dr. Legge's suggestion is correct, the author of the interpolation, gives his answer. There is a Final Cause. The finite cosmos with its ceaseless round of CHANGE, its endless FLUX, is born of the Infinite, the ultimate cause beyond which thought itself cannot reach, and which is therefore termed the *T'ai Chi*, or Supreme Ultimate.

From the seed-thought embedded in this solitary passage in the *Yi Ching* was evolved Chou Tzŭ's doctrine of the Supreme Ultimate, as represented in his famous diagram, called "The Diagram of the Supreme Ultimate", and expounded in what has proved to be an epoch-making classic, the *T'ai Chi T'u Shuo*, or *The Diagram of the Supreme Ultimate Explained*. This monograph, of which a full translation is here given, is one of the most terse and pregnant writings ever penned. In the *Symposium* it is accompanied by the Diagram itself, which is also here reproduced with the most important of Chu Hsi's notes explaining its construction.

THE DIAGRAM OF THE SUPREME ULTIMATE EXPLAINED [1]

Infinite ! And also the Supreme Ultimate !

The Supreme Ultimate by its energy produces the positive ether. Energy having reached its limit, inertia ensues. By

[1] The Chinese text is given in the 性 理 大 全 and 性 理 精 善.

THE DIAGRAM OF THE SUPREME ULTIMATE.

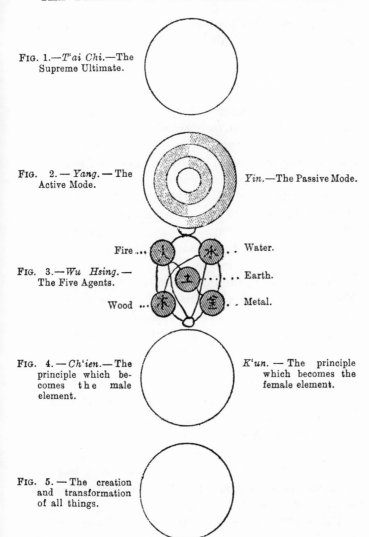

FIG. 1.—*T'ai Chi.*—The Supreme Ultimate.

FIG. 2.—*Yang.*—The Active Mode.

Yin.—The Passive Mode.

FIG. 3.—*Wu Hsing.*—The Five Agents.

Fire ... Water.

Earth.

Wood ... Metal.

FIG. 4.—*Ch'ien.*—The principle which becomes the male element.

K'un.—The principle which becomes the female element.

FIG. 5.—The creation and transformation of all things.

K

inertia the Supreme Ultimate produces the negative ether. When inertia reaches its limit, energy returns. Thus energy and inertia, in alternation, become each the source of the other : the distinction between the negative and positive ethers is determined ; and the Two Modes stand revealed.

By the transformation of the positive ether and the union therewith of the negative ether, Water, Fire, Wood, Metal, and Earth are produced. These five ethers are diffused in harmonious order, and so the Four Seasons proceed in their course.

The Five Agents are the one negative and the one positive ether ; the negative and positive ethers are the one Supreme Ultimate ; and the Supreme Ultimate is essentially the Infinite. The Five Agents at their birth are endued each with its own nature-principle.

The substance of the Infinite and the essence of the Two Modes and Five Agents uniting in mysterious union, consolidation ensues. The heavenly principle becomes the male element, and the earthly principle the female element. The two ethers by their interaction produce the ALL THINGS, and universal production and reproduction follow in an unending stream of transformations.

It is man alone, however, who receives the ethers in their highest excellence, and is therefore the most spiritual of all beings. When bodily form is produced and the spirit develops consciousness ; when the five nature-principles are affected by the external world and become active, there follows the distinction between good and evil and the myriad phenomena of conduct appear.

The saints ordered their lives by the Mean, by Truth,

by Love, and by Righteousness. They maintained an undisturbed calm, and thus created an ideal for mankind. Hence the virtue of the saints was one with that of Heaven and Earth; their brilliancy was equal to that of the sun and moon; they were in harmony with the course of the seasons; and their fortunes were propitious as those of spiritual beings. The good fortune of the noble man lies in cultivating the virtues of the saints, and the evil fortune of the ignoble man proceeds from the violation of them.

Therefore it is said: " In representing the law of heaven they used the terms ' negative ' and ' positive '; in representing the law of earth they used the terms ' weak ' and ' strong '; in representing the law of man they used the terms ' love ' and ' righteousness ' " ; and also, " If we trace things to their beginning and back again to their final issue we shall know the true meaning of life and death."

Great is the Canon of Changes ! Here [1] we have presented its fullest meaning.

NOTES BY CHU HSI EXPLANATORY OF THE DIAGRAM

Figure 1 represents that of which it is said: " Infinite ! And also the Supreme Ultimate ! " It is the original substance of that energy which originates the positive mode, and of the inertia which originates the negative mode. It should neither be regarded as separate from, nor confounded with, the Two Modes.

The concentric circles in Figure 2 represent the Supreme Ultimate inherent in the Two Modes, the complete circle in the centre representing the circle of Figure 1. The semi-

[1] That is, in the Diagram.

circles on the left show the energy of the positive mode, the operation of the Supreme Ultimate ; those on the right show the inertia of the negative mode, the substance of the Supreme Ultimate. Those on the right are the root from which those on the left are produced and vice versa, the negative mode producing the positive, and the positive the negative.

Figure 3 represents the transformation of the positive mode and the union therewith of the negative, by which union the Five Agents are produced. The former is represented by the curved line from left to right ⌄, and the latter by the curve in the opposite direction ⌒. Water is predominantly negative, and is therefore placed on the right. Fire is predominantly positive, and is therefore placed on the left. Wood and metal are respectively modifications of the positive and negative modes, and are therefore placed the one under Fire, and the other under Water. The order of their procession is indicated by the lines connecting the Five Agents, Water being followed by Wood, Wood by Fire, Fire by Earth, Earth by Metal, and Metal again by Water, in an endless circle. The crossing of the lines above Fire and Water represents the fact that the negative proceeds from the positive and the positive from the negative. The small circle below, connected by the four lines (♉) with the Agents above, indicates the Supreme Ultimate in which all—that is, the Two Modes and Five Agents—are united in one indissoluble unity.

Figure 4 represents the operations of the Ether in the two modes exhibited in the heavenly and earthly principles, *Ch'ien* and *K'un*, which become the male and female principles pervading the universe ; each having their own characteristics, but still modes of the one Supreme Ultimate, as indicated by the reproduction of the original circle.

Figure 5 represents the creation and transformation of all things in their innumerable sensible forms, each of which has its own characteristic. But, as indicated again by the reproduction of the original circle, the All Things are still the one Supreme Ultimate.

CHU HSI'S DOCTRINE OF THE SUPREME ULTIMATE

It will perhaps be well at the outset of our discussion to make clear the construction of the first sentence in the monograph. We are repeatedly told that the two terms are not to be regarded as the names of separate entities; still less are we to think of one as antecedent to the other. " When it is said, ' Infinite ! And also the Supreme Ultimate ! ' " says Chu Hsi, " and ' The Supreme Ultimate is essentially the Infinite,' it is not meant that subsequently to the Infinite the Supreme Ultimate is produced as another being, or that beyond and antecedent to the Supreme Ultimate there is the Infinite." [1] In other words, they are two terms for the one entity.

The term Supreme Ultimate in Chinese is *T'ai Chi* (太 極). It is translated by McClatchie and Le Gall as the " Great Extreme ", by Legge both as the " Great Extreme " and the " Grand Terminus ", and by Giles more freely as the " Absolute ". The word *Chi*, which is here translated " Ultimate ", literally means a pivot. It is the word for the primitive wooden pivot which takes the place of hinges on

[1] 精 義, pt. i, f. 9.

a Chinese door. It is further said to have the meaning of the root and ground of a thing. Thus the Supreme Ultimate derives its name from its being the Final Cause of the universe, the controlling pivot on which all things turn. It is also the word for pole in the terms North Pole and South Pole, in the sense of the northern limit and southern limit. Again, it means the roof ridge of a house, or the zenith of the heavens, and expresses the idea of the ultimate reach of thought beyond which even imagination cannot go. The same word (*chi*) with a negative prefixed forms the other great word in the sentence ; namely *Wu Chi* (lit. Without Limit), here translated Infinite, which is thus set in paradoxical contrast to the term Supreme Ultimate (or Supreme Limit). The meaning of the sentence as a whole is explained very clearly by Jao Lu, a member of the same school as Chu Hsi, from whose comments the following may be cited :—

" The term *T'ai Chi* is a term which expresses the dignity of Divine Law. The word *Chi* means extreme, or pivot, or root ; what is constantly spoken of as a pivot or root in common speech. The sages regarded the Two Modes of matter and the Five Agents as continuously alternating in opening and closing operations, and Law as the controlling factor in this opening and closing like the pivot of a door. Man and the Cosmos proceed in an endless succession of production and reproduction, and Law is the source of this production like the root of a tree. In the case of man, this Law is the Root whence all goodness is produced, and the Pivot by which all actions are determined. Hence the term *Chi*. The word *T'ai* means great, so that nothing can be added, and expresses the fact that it is the Great Pivot and the Great

Source of the Universe. Everything, however, that bears this name—such as the South Pole, the North Pole, the ridge of a house, the ' Capital of Shang ', [1] and the four points of the compass—has visible form and location to which we can point, but this *Chi* is without form and has no relation to space. For which reason Chou Tzŭ added the term *Wu Chi*, expressing the fact that it has not the *form* of a pivot or root, but none the less is really the Great Pivot and the Great Source of the universe." [2]

The *T'ai Chi*, therefore, is like the roof ridge of a house, the highest point that can be reached. It is like the zenith in the heavens beyond which even thought cannot pass. It is the Great Pivot of the Universe, the Source of all things visible and invisible, material and moral. In a word, it is the Ultimate Reality in the Cosmos, the Extreme Limit in the vast chain of causes, the Final Cause of all things. [3] And yet, as the closing words of the passage just quoted remind us, and as the first sentence in Chou Tzŭ's classic asserts, the Extreme Limit in the vast chain of causes is itself Illimitable, the Final Cause is Infinite. Such is the sublime conception embodied in the dictum which forms the opening sentence of this remarkable monograph. What, then, is the nature of this Supreme Ultimate or Final Cause ? The answer, as the

---

[1] The allusion is to a passage in the *Odes*, pt. iv, bk. iii, ode v, which speaks of the capital of Shang as the " model for all parts of the kingdom ". The word for " model " is *chi*, the word here translated " ultimate ".

[2] 精義, pt. i, f. 9.

[3] " The Original Ultimate obtains its name from the idea of a pivot. The sages termed it the Supreme Ultimate in respect of its being the First Cause of the universe."

Dictum itself would indicate, leads us into the region of paradox and calls for patient inquiry.

The first thing to note is the unmistakable clearness with which it is asserted that the Supreme Ultimate is the immaterial element in the universe. The very first sentence in the chapter under this title in Chu Hsi's works is : " The Supreme Ultimate is expressed in one word, Law."[1] And again, in the succeeding paragraph the Philosopher says : " The Supreme Ultimate is simply the Law of the Universe." Again, " There are but two elements (端) in the universe, namely, energy and inertia, in ceaseless alternation. But given energy and inertia, it follows that there must be the Law of energy and inertia, and this is what is termed the Supreme Ultimate."[2] Such statements abound all through the writings of this school. This, then, is clear ; for Chu Hsi the Supreme Ultimate, the Final Cause, is Law. It should be noted that the word " Infinite " in this connexion does not mean illimitableness only. In this narrower sense it is somewhat hesitatingly applied to Matter also. But in Chou Tzŭ's dictum it means much more. " It is called the Infinite because it has no relation to space or form. It is before all things, and yet did not cease when the world came into existence. It is above the Two Modes of Matter, and yet moves in them. It permeates the whole universe so that there is nowhere where it is not, and yet its sound is not heard ; it is invisible and cannot be perceived by any of the senses."[3] Moreover, although denoting the same

---

[1] 全 書, bk. xlix, f. 8.
[2] Ibid., f. 16.
[3] 精 義, pt. i, f. 4.

entity as does the word Law, the term Supreme Ultimate connotes more than simply Law. It is the source of all laws as well as of all things. Various terms are used to express this. The word ultimate itself is used in the sense that it is " the ultimate extreme of Law (理 之 極 至)." [1] It is " highest Law (至 理) ".[2] " Of the All Things," says a philosopher of the same school, " each has its law. These innumerable laws all proceed from one source, and this one source of all laws is the Supreme Ultimate." [3]

The next thing to note, however, is that, according to this school, this Supreme Ultimate as the Final Cause is inherent in matter, and that its identification with the Ether is so close that the name Supreme Ultimate is also applied to the Primordial Ether in which it is manifested. " All things," we are told, " The Four Seasons, the Five Agents, proceed from the Supreme Ultimate. The Supreme Ultimate is simply ether which divides itself unequally into the two Ethers ; of which the active mode is positive, and the passive mode is negative. Again, it divides itself into the Five Agents, and again, multiplying itself it becomes the All Things." [4] " The Supreme Ultimate is not a separate entity. It is the Two Modes, and it is in the Two Modes. It is the Five Agents, and it is in the Five Agents. It is All Things and it is in All Things." [5] And yet, to guard against mis-understanding of such bold statements, the Philosopher says in the same paragraph, in a sentence immediately following the one last quoted, " It is nothing else than Law."

---

[1] 精 義, bk. xlix, f. 13.
[2] Ibid., f. 14.
[3] 全 書, pt. i, f. 10.
[4] 全 書, bk. xlix, f. 9.
[5] Ibid.

The meaning of all this would appear to be : The phenomena of the Universe are traced back to their beginning in the Primordial Ether, an infinite mass of world stuff, if we may so term it, described by some writers as Chaos. From this primordial ether by its self-revolution are produced the two Modes of matter, energy and inertia, which, by their varying combinations produce the Five Agents, from which again all things in the universe are evolved. But inherent in this Ether is the immaterial principle Law, which is really the Supreme Ultimate properly so termed.

And the third thing to note is that the Supreme Ultimate is inherent in the Ether in its two modes as their creator, and as the director and controller of their evolution in all its stages ; while they in their turn constitute its material instrument, or vehicle of manifestation. " The Supreme Ultimate is the immaterial Law, the Two Modes are the material instruments." [1] " The Supreme Ultimate is the fundamental mystery, energy and inertia constitute the machinery it employs." [2] " The Supreme Ultimate produces the active and passive modes, and Law produces the Ether. Seeing that the Two Modes are thus produced the Supreme Ultimate is inherent in them, and Law is inherent in the Ether." [3]

Although, on the one hand, therefore, the identification of the Supreme Ultimate with its manifesting vehicle is so close that the name of the former is often used as though it applied equally to the latter ; we are, on the other hand, expressly warned against confusing the two. " Energy and

---

[1] 精 義, pt. i, f. 5.   [2] Ibid.   [3] Ibid., f. 6.

inertia, the positive and negative modes, belong to the material; but the energy is the energy of the Supreme Ultimate, the inertia is the inertia of the Supreme Ultimate, and yet energy and inertia are not the Supreme Ultimate." [1]

"The Supreme Ultimate is inherent in, and cannot be separated from, the Two Modes; but the Supreme Ultimate is the Supreme Ultimate, and the Two Modes are the Two Modes." [2] "The Supreme Ultimate is simply the uttermost extreme beyond which you cannot go; most high, most wonderful, most subtile, most spiritual, and all-surpassing. To guard against the idea that the Supreme Ultimate has material form, Lien Hsi designated it 'Infinite! And also the Supreme Ultimate!'". [3]

Once more, however, the statement must be guarded against misunderstanding. It must not be supposed that because the Supreme Ultimate produces the Two Modes it is therefore antecedent to them. "When it is said that the Five Agents are one negative and one positive mode, and that the Two Modes are one Supreme Ultimate, it is not meant that the Two Modes and the Five Agents are produced as additional entities subsequently to the Supreme Ultimate, or that beyond and antecedent to these is the Supreme Ultimate." [4] The immaterial Supreme Ultimate and the material Two Modes are coexistent; but the latter are subordinate to, and derive their existence from, the former.

We have now reached by a different road the same point as that at which we arrived in our discussion of the two elements

---

[1] 全 書, bk. xlix, f. 11.

[2] 精 義, pt. i, f. 6.

[3] 全 書, bk. xlix, f. 14.

[4] 精 義, pt. i, f. 9.

in the dualism of Law and Matter. As we saw with reference to Law, so now we see with reference to the Supreme Ultimate. The immaterial element is fundamental; it is the inherent source, director and controller of the material element. We find also that the term Supreme Ultimate connotes the additional thought of Law as the Final Cause of the material universe, and the One Source of its innumerable laws.

There are two other respects in which what we found to be true of Law is also true of the Supreme Ultimate. The first is its ethical perfection. " The Supreme Ultimate is the most excellent and supremely good ethical principle. Every man possesses a Supreme Ultimate. What Chou Tzŭ calls the Supreme Ultimate is the supremely excellent archetype of everything that is called good in heaven and earth and man and the all things." [1] Thus we find that the Supreme Ultimate is not only identified with *Li* (Law), but also with *Tao* (Moral Law). A questioner, referring to this and the parallel statement, " The Mind is called the Supreme Ultimate," asked whether " Moral Law " did not refer to the self-existent Law of the universe, and " the mind " to man's reception of this Law as the ruler of his entire being. To which Chu Hsi replied, " Certainly it is so, but bear in mind that the Supreme Ultimate is one and without compare." [2] Chu Hsi elsewhere also says explicitly : " The sentence, ' Infinite ! And also the Supreme Ultimate ! ' together with the chain-diagram, expresses the truth that Moral Law existed before all things, and is the true source of all things." [3]

---

[1] Ibid., i, 10.
[2] 全 書, bk. xlix, f. 14.
[3] 精 義, pt. i, f. 4.

So, then, the First Cause of the universe is identical with Moral Law ; and those principles which constitute that Moral Law, Love, Righteousness, Reverence, and Wisdom, are really attributes of the First Cause.

The second point to be observed is that just as we have found that Law—which derives its name from the fact that inherent in every individual thing there is its law or rule of existence—has its universal aspect as the one Law of the Universe, eternal and all-comprehensive, so conversely the Supreme Ultimate—which derives its name from the fact that it is the Final Cause of the universe—is yet immanent in all its parts. "The Supreme Ultimate is the law of the universe. It is immanent in heaven and earth, it is immanent in every individual of the All Things." [1] A statement similar to this evoked the question : " If all things share the essence of the one Law so that it becomes the substance of each, then each has its own Supreme Ultimate, in which case the Supreme Ultimate would be divided, would it not ? " To which the Philosopher replied : " There is but one Supreme Ultimate, which is received by each individual of the All Things ; but this one Supreme Ultimate is received by each individual in its entirety and undivided, just as in the case of the moon shining in the heavens, when it is reflected on river and lake and so is visible in every place we would not say that it is divided." [2] The Supreme Ultimate is All in All.

THE TWO MODES

As is shown by Suzuki in his *Early Chinese Philosophy*, the dualistic conception of the universe in China has its origin in

---

[1] 全 書, bk. xlix, f. 8.   [2] Ibid., f. 10.

the *Yi Ching*,[1] " Whatever we may call them (that is, the *Yin Yang*)," says this writer, " the strong and the weak, or the rigid and the tender, or the male and the female, or heaven and earth, or *yang* and *yin*, or *ch'ien* and *k'un*, there are, according to the *Yi Ching*, two independent principles, and their interplay, governed by certain fixed laws, constitutes the universe." [2]

Like the term *T'ai Chi*, the two terms *Yin* and *Yang* originated in the Third Appendix, or " Great Treatise ", of the *Yi Ching*. As in the case of the Supreme Ultimate, Dr. Legge denies that in that work they were intended to mean what they came to mean for the Sung philosophers. His statement is of such importance that we quote it at length. " Had the doctrine of a primary matter of an ethereal nature," he says, " now expanding and showing itself full of activity and power as *Yang*, now contracting and becoming weak and inactive as *Yin*—had this doctrine become matter of speculation when this Appendix was written ? The Chinese critics and commentators for the most part assume that it had. P. Regis, Dr. Medhurst, and other foreign Chinese scholars repeat their statements without question. I have sought in vain for proof of what is asserted. It took more than a thousand years after the closing of the *Yi* to fashion in the Confucian School the doctrine of a primary matter. We do not find it fully developed till the era of the Sung dynasty, and in our eleventh and twelfth centuries. To find it in the *Yi* is the logical, or rather illogical, error of putting ' the last first '. Neither creation nor cosmogony

[1] *A Brief History of Early Chinese Philosophy*, by D. T. Suzuki, p. 14.
[2] Ibid., pp. 17–18.

was before the mind of the author whose work I am analysing. His theme is the *Yi*—the ever-changing phenomena of nature and experience. There is nothing but this in the ' Great Treatise ' to task our powers !—nothing deeper or more abstruse." [1] Although to the names of P. Regis and Medhurst those of McClatchie and Le Gall must be added as opposed to Dr. Legge's views, it would seem, from the point of view of the Sung School as well as from that of the most natural interpretation of the Yi, that Dr. Legge's interpretation is in the main correct. Indeed, one great cause of the enthusiasm created by the Sung philosophers was the new interpretation they gave to the *Yi*. But the fact remains that the sources of the Sung philosophy are to be found in the *Yi* ; and it is to the *Yi* that we must go for the original meaning of the terms *Yin* and *Yang*. According to Legge's view, their explanation is not primarily as descriptive of two modes of the Ether. The ideographs are 陰 and 陽. They mean " the dark and the bright, the moon-like and the sun-like, for the sun is called the Great Brightness (太 陽), and the moon the Great Obscurity (太 陰) ".[2] They were originally applied to the light and dark circles in the legendary " map ", consisting of an arrangement of marks which a dragon-horse issuing from the Yellow River bore on its back, and from which Fu Hsi obtained his idea of the trigrams. The light and dark circles in the map became respectively the whole line (——) and the divided line (— —) in the trigrams, and to these the terms " light " and " dark " were applied.[3] By an easy transition the terms came to be

---

[1] *Yi Ching*, p. 44.   [2] Ibid., p. 16.   [3] Ibid., pp. 14–16.

applied also to the things symbolized. Similarly, the expression "Two Modes" (兩 儀), by which the whole and divided lines were known, came to be used of the two modes of the Ether.

Thus understood, it is obvious that thé use of the terms "light" and "dark" does not imply that these were the only qualities or even the fundamental qualities of the things they signified. In fact the terms "*kang*" and "*jou*", meaning "strong" and "weak", were used for the whole and divided lines as often as the terms "light" and "dark". Legge therefore says rightly, "We may use for these adjectives a variety of others, such as active and inactive, masculine and feminine, hot and cold, more or less analogous to them."[1] For these reasons to translate the terms uniformly as "light" and "darkness", and still more as "male" and "female", is to prejudice their meaning by limiting it to one of several pairs of qualities implied. It is better therefore as a rule to use a pair of terms such as "positive" and "negative" which, while suggesting the antithesis, are sufficiently wide to cover the various uses to which the original terms are applied.[2]

When we come to the philosophy of the Sung period we find that the most characteristic and fundamental qualities of the *Yang* and the *Yin* are energy and inertia. These are the properties attributed to them in Chou Tzŭ's monograph. It is important to note that they are not two substances but two *modes* of the one substance—Ether. As has been said already this primordial ether, taking its name from the

---

[1] Ibid., p. 43.

[2] But not, of course, exclusively. Other terms, like "active" and "passive", are more appropriate in some connexions.

immaterial element by which it is permeated, is often termed the Supreme Ultimate. Using the term in this sense Chu Hsi insists upon the real identity of the *Yin* and the *Yang* with the Supreme Ultimate, even while he maintains that they are distinct from it.[1] " Energy," he says, " is not the Supreme Ultimate, but it is the operation of the Supreme Ultimate. Inertia is not the Supreme Ultimate, but it is the substance of the Supreme Ultimate." [2] " The Supreme Ultimate is simply the Ether which divides itself unequally into the two ethers of which the active mode is positive and the passive mode is negative." [3]

This view of matter in two modes is by no means strange to Western philosophy. According to Herbert Spencer Matter and Motion are two modes of the one primordial element, Force. Thus :—

$$
\begin{array}{llll}
\text{MATTER} & \begin{cases} \text{Resistance} & = \text{Force Element} \\ \text{Extension} & = \text{Space Element} \end{cases} & \rbrace & \begin{cases} \text{The Primordial} \\ \text{Element.} \end{cases} \\
\text{MOTION} & \begin{cases} \text{Energy} & = \text{Force Element} \\ \text{Velocity} & = \text{Space and Time Element.} \end{cases}
\end{array}
$$

More recent theories assume some form of the vortex theory. " We are told that these electrons," says one writer referring to the electrons composing the atom, " are infinitely small stresses, or strains, or vortices, in the ether." Using the illustration of a mass of quivering jelly into which two knives have been plunged and twisted in opposite directions this writer says : " A strain, or stress, or torsion exists between

---

[1] 全書, bk. xlix, pp. 11–12 ; cf. p. 139.
[2] Ibid., f. 11.
[3] Ibid., f. 9.

the points of the knives. . . . Now move the stress around a central point in the mass of jelly, and a certain amount of bound jelly will be carried along with the stress, and the moving, bound jelly, because of the motion, will have weight, or mass, or inertia. . . . In like manner we may conceive an exceedingly small vortex moving in the ether. This moving vortex, or electron, will carry along with it a certain amount of bound ether." The writer then goes on to show how the vortex motion and the mass, or inertia, act and react upon each other.[1] The same writer in another connexion used the illustration of an absolutely transparent block of glass, which, so long as it remains at rest, is invisible to one supposed to be embedded in it, but which, as the result of a strain, or stress, "will be filled with exceedingly minute nodules, or points of fraction, which, of course, will be visible." [2]

For our purpose, the essential features of the theory thus illustrated are that Motion and Rest, or Energy and Inertia, are the result of a vortex movement in the Ether, that they interact the one upon the other, and that they are two modes of the one primordial Ether. These are precisely the points upon which Chu Hsi insists. The last of them he illustrates by a fan. " Wave it," he says, " and you have its operation, lay it down and you have its substance ; whether in motion or at rest it is the same fan ; " [3] just as, in the illustration given above, the transparent block of glass, whether at rest or disturbed by the strain, is the same block of glass.

[1] *Matter and some of its Dimensions,* by W. K. Carr, pp. 10–12.
[2] Ibid., p. 37.
[3] 全 書, bk. xlix, f. 12.

The *Yin* and *Yang*, then, represent Inertia and Energy, or, if we will, Matter and Energy, as the two modes of the Ether. But, according to the modern scientist, when we speak of the dualism of matter and energy we come very near to the dualism of matter and spirit, or extension and thought. " Try to divorce ' force ' from its psychical significance. You cannot do it," says Mr. Carr, "for men have always realized that force connotes a conscious Will, a sustained, directing, intelligent effort." [1] Such statements, of course, do not necessarily imply that force is in itself psychical. The " Conscious Will " may be behind and transcending the force. And for Chu Hsi, as we have seen already, distinct from the energy of the ether, but inherent in it and inseparable from it, there is *li*, the regulative, directing, and informing principle ; which principle as the *T'ai Chi* is transcendent and ultimate. But apart from this consideration, energy and spirit in Chu Hsi's system are intimately connected. The positive mode, which in the physical realm is energy as contrasted with inertia, is also spirit as contrasted with matter. It is like vapour in the process of distillation : bright, pure, and refined, expanding and ascending, invisible, intangible and penetrable ; while the negative mode is like the dregs : dull, turbid and gross, contracting and descending, consolidating into the visible, tangible and impenetrable. The one pertains to the world of spirit and the other to the world of matter. As categorically stated by Chu Hsi, " The spirit has its origin in the positive, and the body in the negative ether." [2] In two different connexions Chu Hsi

---

[1] *Matter and some of its Dimensions*, p. 34.

[2] *P.H.N.*, p. 196 (全 書, bk. xliv, f. 21).

defines spirit and mind alike as the Ether in its purity and brightness.[1] On an earlier page we saw that Chu Hsi, following his predecessor Chou Tzŭ, regarded the *Yin* and the *Yang* as two modes of the one primordial ether, the vehicle of manifestation of the *T'ai Chi* or Supreme Ultimate. We now find similarly that matter and spirit are affirmed to be two modes of the one substance ether. If, therefore, we would find in Western philosophy the nearest parallel to Chu Hsi's account of matter and spirit it would be in Spinoza's twofold distinction of matter and spirit, or extension and thought, in a higher synthesis. For Spinoza " that synthesis is God : the one principle having Thought and Extension as two eternal and infinite attributes, constituting its essence." [2] What, from the theistic point of view, the synthesis means for Chu Hsi will be discussed in later chapters. The point which concerns us now is that in this system spirit and matter are regarded as the dual manifestation of an underlying unity, Ether.

When we have distinguished the Two Modes as Energy and Inertia, it is only one step further to distinguish them as active and passive, acting and acted upon ; and this distinction is very prominent in the Sung philosophy. In short, as in the *T'ai Chi* we have Spinoza's conception of the " higher synthesis ", so in the *Yang* and the *Yin* we have his conception of *natura naturans* and *natura naturata*, expressed by Chou Tzŭ in the two terms which he borrowed from the *Yi Ching*, *Ch'ien* or the heavenly principle, and *K'un* or the earthly principle. These two, *Ch'ien* and *K'un*,

---

[1] Ibid., p. 159 (全 書, bk. xliv, f. 2) ; and 全 書, xlix, 41.

[2] *Lewes' History of Philosophy*, vol. ii, pp. 197–8.

says Chou Tzŭ, become respectively the male and female elements in the universe.[1]

The Yin and the Yang are produced by the rotation of the ether, and follow each other in endless succession. The diagram commonly used to illustrate their alternating movement consists of a circle divided by a double curve into two parts, light and dark, the former representing the positive and the latter the negative mode. Two things are indicated by the circle : the endlessness of the alternating movement, and the fact that the two modes are not merely derived from the Supreme Ultimate, but that they are the Supreme Ultimate—one and yet two, two and yet one.[2]

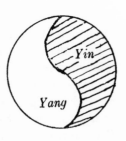

The unbroken succession of the Two Modes is due to a reciprocal causation : the cause of the *Yang* lies in the *Yin* and vice versa. But in the ultimate, as stated above, the energy of the *Yang* and the inertia of the *Yin* are the energy and inertia of the inherent Law, the Supreme Ultimate or Final Cause. In this connexion we are frequently referred to a statement in the *Yi Ching*, " The law of their succession is goodness," [3] which literally translated is, " That which succeeds it is goodness." The word " it " refers to the " *Tao* " of the preceding clause, while the words " that which

---

[1] See p. 127.   [2] 精 義, pt. i, f. 6.

[3] *Yi Ching*, pp. 355–6. The whole passage reads : " The alternation of the negative and positive modes is what is termed Moral Law ; the law of their succession is goodness ; their realization is the Nature." The first sentence literally is : " One *yin* one *yang* is what is termed *Tao*," which de Groot renders : " The universal *yin* and the universal *yang* are the

succeeds" refer to an efflux which follows upon the internal movement of the *Tao*. This efflux is "goodness", and the alternation itself is the expression of the same *Tao*, or Moral Order, as that which pervades the whole universe. Thus in the very beginning of things, in causation itself, there is an ethical principle at work which manifests itself in all the transformations of the Ether.

From the endless alternation of the *Yin* and the *Yang* the primordial ether, of which they are the two modes, receives the name of "*yi*" (易), signifying "change", or "flux", the word which appears in the title of the *Yi Ching*. Its meaning as it occurs in that classic is discussed in our study of Chu Hsi's doctrine of Mind (Chap. X), mind itself being defined as "*yi*". Its significance in connexion with our present subject is that it emphasizes the unity of the primordial element of which the *yin* and the *yang* are but the two modes. Law, the Supreme Ultimate, as inherent in the primordial ether, is termed the *T'ai I* (太 一), or Supreme Unity, the one fundamental existence ; and as manifested in the two modes this Supreme Unity is termed *Yi*, or Flux. To borrow the language of Professor Knight : " There is only one imperishable force which undergoes perpetual change—a ceaseless physical metempsychosis, or palingenesia. It appears, in a particular form or aspect, only to disappear, and to reappear trans-

---

Tao " (*Religion in China*, by J. J. M. de Groot, p. 10). But the phrase " one *yin* one *yang* " is a recognized idiom expressing alternation, and this is the meaning adopted by Legge. The same interpretation is given by Chu Hsi, who says : " If it said, ' *yin* and *yang* are what is termed *Tao*,' the meaning would be that the *yin* and the *yang* are the Tao ; but seeing that it says ' one *yin* and one *yang* ' the meaning is that the alternation to and fro of the *yin* and the *yang* in endless succession is *Tao*." 大 全, i, 18.

formed." [1] This "metempsychosis" which characterizes all phenomena has its source, according to Chu Hsi, in the alternation of the modes of the one primordial ether, which is therefore termed Flux.

THE FIVE AGENTS

In the introductory paragraphs of this chapter, attention was drawn to a passage in the Third Appendix of the *Yi Ching*, Legge's translation of which reads : " Therefore in the system of the *Yi* there is the Grand Terminus (Supreme Ultimate) which produced the two elementary Forms (Modes). These two Forms produced the four emblematic Symbols, which again produced the eight Trigrams." [2] We have seen that the Supreme Ultimate and the Two Modes of the Sung philosophy had their origin in this passage. Similarly, the Four Symbols, consisting of the different combinations of the " two elementary Forms ", became the basis of the theory of the Five Agents. The Five Agents are produced by the interaction, in differing degree, of the Two Modes, just as the Four Symbols consisted of the different combinations of the " two elementary Forms " : the whole and divided lines ; and again, just as the Four Symbols, when combined with the " two elementary Forms ", constitute the Eight Trigrams, so from the Five Agents, combining together in union with the Two Modes in infinitely varying degree, the innumerable phenomena of the universe are produced.

The Five Agents are Water, Fire, Wood, Metal, and Earth. We are, of course, irresistibly reminded of the four elements of the Ancients—Water, Fire, Earth, Air ; and for this reason

[1] *Aspects of Theism*, by William Knight, p. 77.

[2] *Yi Ching*, p. 373. The words in parentheses are the renderings adopted in the present work.

the Five Agents have frequently been termed elements. The
fact that three of the " elements " correspond is certainly
suggestive of some connexion in their origin. The Chinese
word *hsing* (行), however, is not " element ", its meaning is
" to go " or " to act ". We might call these entities the five
activities pervading the universe, a conception which seems
fairly well expressed by the word " agent ".[1] It is perhaps
unnecessary to say that we must disabuse our minds of any
confusion we may have with the literal substances called by
these names. The Five Agents are five ethers, all five of which
permeate every existing thing ; their names are given to them
as the best expression of their respective qualities. The
quality of the ether named Water is humidity, of that named
Fire caloric, of Wood softness, and of Metal hardness.[2]

In the cosmos evolved from the two modes and five agents
the Ether assumes two forms, the Ether properly so called,
constituting the celestial and spirit portion of the cosmos, and
the gross and tangible portion constituting the solid matter of
earth. Corresponding to these two forms, the Five Agents
are of two kinds, the Five Celestial and the Five Terrestrial
Agents. The order of their *production* (生) as Terrestrial
Agents is the order represented by their position in the
Diagram [3] : above are Water and Fire, the first to be produced
by the direct combination of the *yin* and the *yang*. From
these are produced Wood and Metal, but indirectly by way of
Earth. As Celestial Agents the order of their *procession* (行),
or pervading operation, is Wood, Fire, Earth, Metal, Water,
as exhibited in the order of the seasons. In this order also

---

[1] *Suzuki* calls them the " Five Forces "; *Early Chinese Philosophy*, p. 19.
[2] 全 書, bk. xlix, f. 41.   [3] See p. 132.

there is a causal relation which results in Fire following Wood and so on.

The differences in the properties of the respective Agents is due to the manner in which the active and passive modes unite and the predominance of one or the other in each case. Water is originally the humid ether of the active mode, but in its initial movement it becomes ensnared by the passive mode, and is impeded in its action, and so the passive mode prevails. Fire is originally the caloric ether of the passive mode, but in its initial movement it is submerged by the active mode and cannot emerge, so that in this Agent the active mode prevails. Wood is the humid ether of the active mode, which gradually increases and under the influence of the passive mode expands. Its substance is soft, its property warm. Metal is the caloric ether of the passive mode, which gradually increases and under the influence of the active mode contracts. Its substance is hard, its property cold. In Earth the two modes combine, each in its fullness. The Five Agents thus evolved enter into the constitution of the whole cosmos, permeating all things with their respective properties.[1]

Although it can hardly be expected that the Chinese conception of the Five Agents will have its counterpart in any theory held by modern physicists, it may be worth while to note in passing one or two features in which the coincidence is of some interest. Professor Carr, for example, to whose monograph reference has already been made, says : " Mathematicians tell us that a perfectly homogeneous substance, such as we have supposed Ether to be, could not withstand such a pressure as a cubic mile of granite and retain

[1] 精 義, pt. i, p. 7.

the exceeding slight density that the theory demands. They calculate, however, that a structural ether would satisfy the requirements. An ether made up of five other ethers of varying densities would, they assure us, be capable of withstanding such pressure, and still retain the density which the theory demands." [1] The suggestion here made contains two ideas in common with the theory of the Sung philosophers. The first is that the Ether of the universe is not one homogenous ether, but consists of a plurality of ethers of differing quality; and the second is that the differences between the five component ethers have a numerical basis. The Five Agents have different numerical values and different densities according to the different proportions of the Two Modes in their composition. Their numbers correspond to the order of their production : thus Water is represented by One, Fire by Two, Wood by Three, Metal by Four, and Earth by Five ; the odd numbers represent the positive, and the even numbers the negative mode ; and, in respect of density, Water and Fire are tenuous while Wood and Metal are gross. The Five Agents in combination enter into the composition of all existences. Though they differ in the proportions in which they combine, there is not a single thing in which one of them is lacking. They constitute as it were the atom.

It must be borne in mind that the evolution of the Five Agents in the manner described above is wholly due to the directing and controlling immaterial element, Law, inherent in them ; and the five ethical principles of which Law consists are severally inherent in the Five Agents, each nature-principle having its own Agent as its peculiar vehicle. They

[1] *Matter and some of its Dimensions*, by W. K. Carr, p. 41.

also have each their own special relation to the four seasons. Wood is the reigning (王) Agent in the season of Spring, Fire in Summer, Metal in Autumn, and Water in Winter; while Earth has its own period of eighteen days in which it rules in each of the four seasons, just as Sincerity among the virtues qualifies and gives reality to each of the other four. The Five Agents, therefore, correspond to the five cardinal virtues on the one hand, and to the four seasons on the other, thus:

VIRTUES	AGENTS	SEASONS
Love	Wood	Spring
Righteousness	Fire	Summer
Reverence	Metal	Autumn
Wisdom	Water	Winter
Sincerity	Earth	

From these Five Agents the whole cosmos is evolved, and, although each Agent has its own nature-principle, all five, as has been said above, enter into every individual phenomenon in the universe. The cosmos, therefore, in its infinite vastness and in its infinite minuteness is permeated by these Agents with their nature-principles, so that the processes of creation and transformation are present everywhere in their perfection. From this Chou Tzŭ in his monograph reasons back to the all-comprehensive unity of substance, the mystery of the Infinite, as inherent in every individual thing. For, while the Five Agents differ in their substance, none are without the Two Modes; and while the Two Modes differ spatially in their relation to each other, and in time, the one following the other, the Supreme Ultimate is inherent in both, so that the Supreme Ultimate, which is also the Infinite, is inherent in every single thing.

The Dual Powers Ch'ien and K'un

In the evolution of the cosmos, according to this system, the first to appear out of chaos is Heaven, and the second is Earth. Their evolution is by the union of the Infinite (*Wu Chi*) with, and by the interaction of, the Two Modes and Five Agents. The two forms of existence thus produced are the manifestation of two spiritual powers, the *Ch'ien* and *K'un* of the *Yi Ching*, which may be described as the Two Modes in the sphere of cosmic evolution, and from which all things proceed. They are represented in Chou Tzŭ's Diagram by the circle of Fig. 4. The position which this circle occupies in the Diagram—that is, between Figs. 2 and 3, on the one hand, representing the Two Modes and Five Agents, and Fig. 5, on the other hand, representing the creation and transformation of all things—indicates the place filled by these two principles as the intermediary powers through whose agency all things are produced.

When, therefore, Chu Hsi, as is frequently the case, uses the expression " Heaven and Earth ", in the sense of creative powers, it must not be supposed that he means to imply that the visible and material heaven and earth are the joint creators of all things, for the very obvious reason that they themselves are the " all things ". What Chu Hsi teaches is that the invisible Powers of which Heaven and Earth are the visible manifestation, are the twofold source of all the creative and transforming processes in the universe. " Heaven and Earth are material," he says, " *Ch'ien* and *K'un* are immaterial. Heaven and Earth are the corporeal form of *Ch'ien* and *K'un*, and *Ch'ien* and *K'un* are the operating nature of Heaven and Earth." [1] It must also be understood

---

[1] 全 書, bk. xlix, f. 26.

that when Heaven and Earth, or *Ch'ien* and *K'un*, are spoken of as the twofold source of creative and transforming processes, it is not meant that they are the ultimate source. As we have found repeatedly in our discussion, the ultimate source is one, and one only. The Dual Powers, Heaven and Earth, are but the twofold operations of the one being, Heaven.

The terms "heaven" and "earth" are intimately associated with the terms "spirit" and "matter" both in the Taoist and the Sung philosophy. Both systems agree as to the order of cosmic evolution referred to in this and the following sections, according to which the first to appear in the cosmic cycle is Heaven, then Earth, and then Man the offspring of these Dual Powers. Lao Tzŭ in the *Tao Tê Ching* says, "The *Tao* produced the One (i.e. Heaven). The One produced the Two (i.e. Heaven and Earth) ; and the Two produced the Three (i.e. Heaven, Earth, and Man)." [1] Mr. W. Gorn Old, not without reason, interprets the binomial expression "Heaven and Earth" as spirit-matter. "By Heaven," he says, "we are to understand all that is spiritual in nature, and by Earth all that is material." "By Heaven," he says again, "we may understand the spiritual, causal, or noumenal world, and by Earth the material, physical world of effects," and "man, compounded of heavenly and earthly natures, is at once a spiritual involution and a natural evolution— spiritual as to his soul, and natural as to his body ". [2]

---

[1] Chap. XLII. See the *Tao Teh King*, by C. Spurgeon Medhurst, p. 72. Chu Hsi contradicts Lao Tzŭ with respect to the first of these statements, maintaining that *Tao* and Heaven are identical (see 全 書, xlix, f. 7). But in the other two statements the two systems agree.

[2] *The Simple Way*, by W. Gorn Old, pp. 26, 97.

THE COSMIC CYCLE

In the evolution of the cosmos, according to the Sung School, there is on a vast scale a cycle of four periods analogous to the four seasons of the solar year. Ruling in these four periods are four ultimate principles of the universe, the attributes of the *Ch'ien* and *K'un* referred to in the preceding section. These four ultimates are named *Yüan, Hêng, Li,* and *Chêng,* and are expounded in the *Yi Ching.* Their meaning is fully discussed in the next chapter; here it will be sufficient simply to mention their English equivalents, Origin, Beauty (or Development), Utility, and Potentiality. As illustrated in the accompanying diagram, *Yüan* in the cosmic cycle

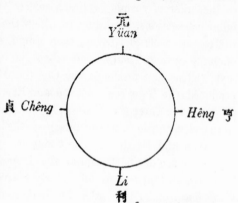

represents the origin of all things. From *Yüan* to *Hêng* is the period, answering to Spring, when all things come into being. The energy thus born continues and develops in the period of *Hêng.* The two periods, Yüan and Hêng are thus the periods of cosmic activity and development: the cosmos is in the Positive or Active Mode. In *Li* is the waning of the cosmos, the Negative or Passive Mode. Energy gives place to inertia, and all nature is on the decline as in Autumn, which decline culminates in the decay and apparent death of the final period, *Chêng*, corresponding to Winter. So all things return to Chaos until *Yüan* again returns and a new cosmos begins. There is therefore an endless succession in the alternation of the Two Modes in the revolutions of the cosmos, of which the *Yi Ching* says, "The efflux which ensues is goodness," and which Chu Hsi compares to the opening and closing of a door. "Were it not for this 'ensuing'," he says—that is the energy following upon the inertia—"and if there were only one opening and closing, then the universe would close and perish." [1] It is owing to the ethical principle inherent in these operations that in *Chêng* there is the root from which Yüan is reborn, and the cosmos proceeds on its way once more.

The idea of a cosmic cycle is elaborated in great detail by Shao Tzŭ in his *Huang Chi Ching Shih Shu*,[2] the study of which would be beyond the scope of the present work. It may be of interest to the reader, however, to reproduce a second diagram, in which the circle is divided into what may be termed the hours of the "Great Year" (太 歲). The complete circle is called *Yüan*, which includes the other three Ultimata.

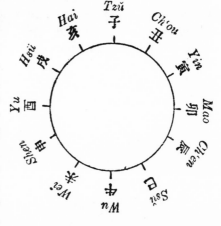

[1] 全 書, bk. xlix, f. 2.   [2] 大 全, bks. vii–xiii.

Each "hour" consists of 10,800 years, and represents a " period " in the development of the universe. Thus, the complete cycle consists of 129,600 years.

The first of these hour-periods, *Tzŭ*, is the opening period in the evolution of the universe ; the last, *Hai*, is the period of Chaos, in which all things come to an end, but which again is but the womb from which all things are born anew. The first to emerge from the darkness is heaven, which " opens " Chaos as if opening the door of a Great Receptacle, and the first period, *Tzŭ*, begins. In the middle of the period the lighter and pure portion of the ether ascends, and the sun, moon, and stars assume visible shape in the heavens. In the second period, *Ch'ou,* the solid earth appears. The heavier and turbid ether consolidates and becomes earth and stone, the humid ether becomes fluid, the caloric ether becomes fire, and thus the four constituents of the earth—water, fire, soil, and rock are formed. In the third period, *Yin*, man appears— the offspring of heaven and earth—and with him the lower animals. In the succeeding periods is traced the course of human history.

CHAPTER VII

THE MORAL ORDER

In a preceding chapter it was shown that the fundamental meaning of the word *Li* is Law; that it is essentially ethical; and that, while it derives its name from the fact that every single thing has its own rule of existence, it also has a universal application. There is another word, *Tao*, which specially expresses both the universal and the ethical aspect of *Li*.

TAO OR MORAL LAW

The term *Tao* (道) fills a large place in Chinese philosophy of all schools. It has given its name to one of the three religions of China, it is a general term for philosophy itself, and it is the word most used as the term for religion. Its primary meaning, which must not be lost sight of in the study of its deeper meanings, is a " road " or " way ".[1] It is called a " road " from the fact that it is a universal law common to all the ages as distinguished from *li*, the law of individual existence; [2] it is a highway " so level that it can be travelled upon for countless myriads of years, and all men find their way to it ".[3] But it is an invisible road; the evidence of its existence is to be found in men's actions. In other words, it is the hidden moral principle from which proceed the common virtues of every day life, the Moral Law followed by all men in all ages.

---

[1] 全 書, bk. xlvi, f. 1. (*P.H.N.*, p. 269).
[2] Ibid.   [3] Ibid.

This is the fundamental meaning of the term *Tao*, and formed the starting-point or line of approach for Chu Hsi in his exposition of its more comprehensive meanings. Shao Tzŭ said : " The Nature is the concrete expression of the Moral Order (*Tao*)." " This," says Chu Hsi, " is what is taught by all the Masters, but by none is it expressed so exactly as by Shao Tzŭ." [1] It is also in accord with the teaching of Mencius. " Love is the distinguishing characteristic of man," said the Sage ; " as embodied in man's conduct it is termed *Tao*." [2] *Tao* is seen in the relations of father and son, sovereign and minister, husband and wife, elder and younger brother, friend and friend. "*Tao* is near," said he, "and men seek it in what is distant. The work of duty lies in what is easy, and men seek for it in what is difficult. If each man would love his parents, and show due respect to his elders, the whole empire would enjoy tranquillity." [3] Chu Hsi's own interpretation of *Tao* was fully in accord with the teaching of the Sage. " Though *Tao* is present everywhere," he said, " how are we to find it ? The answer is : simply by turning and looking within." [4] " We need not talk about empty and far-away things ; if we would know the reality of *Tao* we must seek it within our own nature." [5]

But while this was the line of approach, the Philosopher did not stop there. Looking out from his own heart into the hearts of men in all ages, and beyond the domain of man into

---

[1] Ibid., f. 4 (*P.H.N.*, p. 275).
[2] *Mencius*, p. 361.
[3] Ibid., p. 178 ; cf. Faber's *Mind of Mencius*, p. 76.
[4] 全 書, bk. xlii, f. 13 (*P.H.N.*, p. 32).
[5] Ibid., bk. xlvi, f. 5 (*P.H.N.*, p. 276).

the wider world of phenomena in general, the Philosopher saw the very same principles pervading the universe as those which constituted the law of his own being. They are manifested in the moral excellence of the sages, they are written in the consciences of the most wicked of men. Heaven, earth, and all things follow along the same ethical highway as man himself. The essential meaning, then, of the word *Tao* is that the moral principles which we find engraved upon our own hearts are common to all our fellow-creatures. " From the fact that we ourselves possess the principles of Love, Righteousness, Reverence, and Wisdom, we infer that others possess them also ; that, indeed, of the thousands and tens of thousands of human beings, and of all things in the universe, there are none without these principles. Extend our investigations as far as we will, we still find that there is nothing which does not possess them." [1]

There is thus a co-ordination of the principles underlying all phenomena in what is called " The Moral Order ". Probably no one English word can be found consistently to represent the meaning of the word *Tao*, but of all possible renderings, such as Way, Path, Truth, Reason, or Logos, that perhaps which best expresses its meaning is this term " The Moral Order ". Moral Order, however, is simply Moral Law as pervading the Universe, and it is often more convenient to use the latter form of expression. The essential thing to note is the twofold idea conveyed by either term. It is Law, but it is moral Law ; it is Order, but it is an ethical Order. Dr. Faber speaks of *Tao* as " The Universal Reign of Law ".

---

[1] Ibid., bk. xlii, f. 13 (*P.H.N.*, p. 32).

He says : " According to the Chinese, there is only one
universal law that makes itself known in all the unities
throughout the course of the universe. Physical nature or
spirit life makes no difference. Each follows in its way a
fixed ordered course." [1] That is true, but it is from the ethical
aspect of Law and its co-ordination in a universal moral
standard for man and the universe that *Tao* derives its name.
" According to my view," says Chu Hsi, " *Tao* obtains its
name simply from the principle of inherent right present
in all phenomena." [2] Speaking of the varied species of the
myriad phenomena, he says, " Each one has within it the
principle of right, what we call *Tao*, the road along which we
ought to walk." [3] That is, not only is there a principle of
right in everything, but it is the same " right " for all men and
all things. This is *Tao*. " There must be some reason why,
when the hawk and the fish come into existence they are
hawk and fish. The cause is in the presence of the substance
of *Tao*. The hawk flies and the fish leaps, not by the individual
choice of the hawk and fish, but because of the Divine Law
imparted to them in unceasing flow." [4] " The sun sets and the
moon rises, the cold passes and the heat returns, the four
seasons pursue their course, and all things are continually
being produced." This is the pervading and manifested
operation of *Tao*, while the immovable and abiding element
in all this procession of phenomena is the substance of *Tao*.[5]

---

[1] *Mind of Mencius*, by E. Faber, p. 75
[2] 全 書, bk. xlvi, f. 10 *(P.H.N.*, pp. 285–6).
[3] Ibid.
[4] Ibid., f. 9 *(P.H.N.*, pp. 283–4).
[5] Ibid., f. 1 *(P.H.N.*, p. 270).

It is this wide and comprehensive meaning attached to the term *Tao* which differentiates it from *Li* (Law). It must not be forgotten that both terms refer to the same entity. The unity and universality of *Li* are clearly asserted more than once. The two terms, however, represent different aspects of this unity. The term *Tao* calls attention to the vast and comprehensive ; the term Li calls attention to the minute and infinitesimal,[1] and refers to the innumerable vein-like principles inherent in every individual thing, like the grain in wood, or the lines vertical and horizontal in bamboo, or the strands of a piece of thread, or the bamboo splints of a basket.[2] *Li* derives its name from the fact that everything has each its own rule of existence ; *Tao* expresses the fact that everything conforms to one Moral Law, and is part of one Moral Order. Thus *Li* may be compared to the innumerable trees in a dense forest, whilst *Tao* is compared to a vast, trackless desert with its vision of the illimitable.[3] It is here that we reach the full transcendental meaning of the word *Tao*. Shao K'ang Chieh said : " Moral Law is the Supreme Ultimate," and Chu Hsi confirms his statement as referring to *Tao* as the self-existent law of the universe.[4] *Tao*, as we saw in the preceding chapter, existed before all things, and is the true source of all things.[5]

It was in his doctrine of *Tao* from the transcendental point of view that Chu Hsi came into conflict with Taoism, although

---

[1] Ibid.

[2] Ibid., ff. 1, 12 (*P.H.N.*, pp. 269, 290, 291).

[3] Ibid., f. 16 (*P.H.N.*, p. 298).

[4] Ibid., bk. xlix, f. 14.

[5] 精 義, pt. i, f. 4.

at the same time there were marked affinities between the two systems. Lao Tzŭ, the reputed founder of this sect, in the classic work entitled *Tao Tê Ching* says : " There is an Infinite Being which was before Heaven and Earth. How calm it is, how free ! It lives alone and changes not. It moves everywhere, but is not affected. We may regard it as the universal Mother. I know not its name. I call it *Tao*." [1] Here is the same idea as that which we have found in Chu Hsi's teaching. Moreover, Lao Tzŭ's *Tao* was also the principle of which *Tê* (德), or Virtue, is the manifestation ; which is closely akin to Chu Hsi's doctrine of *Tao* as the comprehensive term for the four cardinal virtues, the principles which become *Tê* (德) when appropriated by man. What, therefore, Mr. Gorn Old says of Lao Tzŭ and Confucius is true : " At most they were not far divided on essential points." [2]

Where, then, was the point of divergence which resulted in the controversy between the two systems ? We must bear in mind that Chu Hsi in his attacks on Taoism and the teachings of Lao Tzŭ was attacking them as interpreted by the representatives of that sect centuries after its founder had uttered his mystical teachings. Chu Hsi's charge against Taoism as interpreted by the scholars of his own day was what he regarded as its ultra-transcendentalism, which, he maintained, tended to destroy all moral distinctions. The chief points of controversy gathered round two passages, or sets of passages, in the *Tao Tê Ching*, which touch on the two aspects of *Tao* referred to above, the ethical and the transcendental. In Chapter XVIII Lao Tzŭ said, " When the

[1] Chap. XXV ; cf. *The Simple Way*, by W. Gorn Old, p. 9.
[2] *The Simple Way*, p. 6.

great *Tao* is lost, men follow after Love and Righteousness," [1]
and in the chapter following he gives utterance to the bold
paradox that " if men would forsake Love and Righteousness they might revert to their natural relationships." [2]
Of the chapter in which the first of these passages occurs,
Mr. W. Gorn Old gives the following explanation : " In this
chapter Laotze (Lao Tzŭ) refers to the doctrines of Confucius
as a system of ' patching up ' that which is already worn out.
The so-called virtue of Charity and Duty to one's neighbour
(translated above as Love and Righteousness), the recognition
of wisdom and learning by marks of merit, filial duty, and
parental indulgence, are all regarded by the Old Philosopher
as so many marks of degeneracy in the people. Against them
he sets the natural virtue of integrity, and to this he would
have us revert." [3] That is, Lao Tzŭ maintained that when
Confucius inculcated Love and Righteousness he in that very
fact confessed that *Tao* was lost, and therefore the only true
remedy is to seek, and revert to, the lost *Tao*. To which Chu
Hsi retorts : " If we separate *Tao* from Love and Righteousness we have no ethical principle at all, in which case how
can *Tao* be *Tao* ? [4] You have nothing left but an empty
abstraction. What is *Tao* but Love and Righteousness ?
If you forsake Love and Righteousness you have forsaken
Tao itself. You cannot destroy them without destroying
virtue, for the simple reason that they *are* virtue. You cannot
weaken the bonds of the Five Relationships without injuring

---

[1] Chap. XVIII.
[2] Chap. XIX.
[3] *The Simple Way*, p. 53.
[4] 全 書, bk. xlvi, f. 3 (*P.H.N.*, pp. 273–4).

the moral sanction itself, because they are the embodiment of it." It may perhaps be questioned whether Chu Hsi did not misconceive the Old Philosopher's meaning. It is hardly likely that when rightly understood the latter would lay himself open to so obvious a retort. The gloss by C. Spurgeon Medhurst suggests what is possibly a truer interpretation : " Virtues and duties are separative, subtle forms of self-assertion, something lower than that Ideal of ideals which identifies itself with the All, and in the joy of service annihilates self. Benevolence, righteousness, filiality, paternalism, loyalty, devotion, is each in its own way a degenerate, when the Tao, the Great Ideal, the One Life, recedes from view. Woe to that captain who, when navigating his vessel into port, allows the various lights and sounds of the harbour to turn his attention from the flashing signals of the lighthouse." [1]

Chu Hsi's point, however, remains. It is just here, indeed, that he joins issue with what he regards as a false mysticism. *Tao* itself *is* Love and Righteousness. It is not some far away, vague, and incomprehensible ideal. It has to do with every-day life and its relationships. This he makes clear in his answer to the other group of classic statements referred to above, in which the great Mystic's love of paradox is still more manifest. " The *Tao* which can be expressed in words," says Lao Tzŭ, " is not the eternal *Tao*. The name which can be named is not its eternal name. Nameless, it is the Beginning of heaven and earth ; with a name it is the Mother

---

[1] *The Tao Teh King*, by C. Spurgeon Medhurst, p. 32.

of all things." [1] " All things in the universe are born of the Existent ; and the Existent is born of the Non-Existent." [2] To quote again from Mr. W. Gorn Old, " The Causal Principle of all effects Laotze calls the Non-Existent. The well-known philosophical gamut of Principles, Causes, Effects, and Ultimates is reduced by the Sage to Non-Existent and the Existent, for seeing only One Cause (*Tao*) he regards all else as a single Effect (Nature)." [3] And in another passage the Sage speaks of *Tao* as the intangible and inscrutable. " Inscrutable, intangible," he says, " yet within are Forms. Intangible, inscrutable, yet within there is substance." [4] Chu Hsi's answer to this doctrine was that *Tao* has a real existence and is not transcendental to such a degree that it has no connexion with men. " The Nature is what men receive substantively ; *Tao* is the natural Law of Right which we find in the phenomena of the universe. The law which we find in phenomena is really inherent in the Nature ; but when we speak of it specifically as *Tao*, our idea is of something which is boundless as a vast desert and diffused in infinite variety so that its substance is invisible, and it is only when we seek it in our own Nature that we see what constitutes

---

[1] See Chap. I; cf. Lionel Giles, *The Sayings of Lao-Tzŭ*, p. 19. Mr. C. Spurgeon Medhurst explains this passage thus : " That aspect of God which is hidden in eternity, without bounds, without limits, without beginning, must be distinguished from that side of God which is expressed in nature and in man. The one, apparently, subjective, certainly unknowable ; the other, a self-manifestation, or a going forth, the commencement of our knowledge, as of our being." *The Tao Teh King*, by C. Spurgeon Medhurst, p. 1.

[2] Chap. XL.

[3] See *The Simple Way*, p. 26.

[4] Chap. XXI; see ibid., pp. 57–8.

its reality—here and nowhere else ! " [1] Chu Hsi therefore did not exclude the transcendental aspect of *Tao*, but he held that the transcendental *Tao* is identical with the *Tao* which we find in our own hearts. " Is it maintained," he says again, " that *Tao* is lofty and distant, inscrutable and mysterious, and beyond the possibility of human study ? Then I answer that *Tao* derives its very name from the fact that it is the principle of right conduct in every day life for all men, that it is like a road which should be travelled upon by the countless myriads of people within the four seas and nine continents ; it is not what the Taoist and Buddhist describe as *Tao* : empty, formless, still, non-existent, and having no connexion with men. Is it maintained that *Tao* is far removed from us, so vast as to be out of touch with our needs, and that we are not called upon to study it ? Then I say that *Tao*, present as it is in all the world in the relation between sovereign and minister, and between father and son, in down-sitting and up-rising, and in activity and rest, has everywhere its unchangeable clear law, which cannot fail for a single instant." [2]

> O world invisible, we view thee ;
> O world intangible, we touch thee ;
> O world unknowable, we know thee ;
> Inapprehensible, we clutch thee.

The antithesis of the Non-Existent and the Existent (有 無) suggests the famous dictum of Chou Tzŭ : " Infinite ! And also the Supreme Ultimate ! " Those who entered into controversy with Chu Hsi frequently referred to this as teaching Lao Tzŭ's doctrine of the Non-Existent, contending

---

[1] 全 書, bk. xlii, f. 22 (*P.H.N.*, p. 48).
[2] Ibid., bk. xlvi, f. 6 (*P.H.N.*, pp. 278).

that it was so implied in the word "not" (無), which enters into the term "Infinite" (無 極). Chu Hsi, however, as was seen in the preceding chapter, was careful to explain that Chou Tzŭ in his doctrine asserted the invisibility and infinity of the Supreme Ultimate, and not that it was a separate entity paradoxically named the Non-Ens.

To sum up : *Tao* is the all-comprehensive Moral Law pervading the universe. It is identical with *Li* the ultimate element in the dualism of the cosmos. It is before all things, in all things, and the source of all things. Illimitable, it nevertheless has a real substantive existence ; and—not least in the emphasis which the Philosopher places upon it—though transcending all things, it is identical with the Moral Law written upon the heart of man. For there is only one Moral Law. Any other hypothesis would conflict with the fundamental thesis of Chu Hsi's philosophy—the unity of the Nature.

THE FOUR ULTIMATA

The opening sentence of the *Yi Ching* contains four words of exceptional interest to the student of the Sung philosophy. They are *Yüan, Hêng, Li, Chêng* (元 亨 利 貞), or the principles of Origin, Beauty, Utility, and Potentiality.

In Section I of the First Appendix of that classic the writer sets forth, somewhat vaguely it must be confessed, the relation of these principles to physical phenomena and to the virtues of the Sage. To quote Dr. Legge's note : "In paragraphs 1, 2, 4 the four attributes in Wên's Text are illustrated by the phenomena taking place in the physical world. In paragraphs 3 and 5, the subject is the sage." [1]

[1] *Yi Ching*, pp. 213–4.

In the Fourth Appendix the relation of these attributes to man's nature, with special reference to the Noble Man, is enlarged upon. The whole passage is as follows :—

1. What is called *Yüan* is in man the first and chief quality of goodness ; what is called *Hêng* is the assemblage of all excellences ; what is called *Li* is the harmony of all that is right ; and what is called *Chêng* is the faculty of action.

2. The Noble Man, embodying love is able to preside over men ; presenting the assemblage of all excellences he is able to show in himself the union of all forms of reverence ; benefiting all creatures he is able to exhibit the harmony of all that is right ; correct and firm, he is able to manage all affairs.

3. The fact that the Noble Man practises these four virtues justifies the application to him, of the words : " *Ch'ien* [1] represents the Principle of Origin (*Yüan*), the Principle of Beauty (*Hêng*), the Principle of Utility (*Li*), and the Principle of Potentiality (*Chêng*)." [2]

In this and the other passage referred to we have two ideas set forth. The first is that pervading the whole cosmos are four principles ; they are ethical in character, they enter into all physical phenomena, and may be termed the Ultimata of the Universe. The second is that these ethical principles which pervade the universe enter into the nature of man ; they are exemplified in the character of the Noble Man, and find their highest expression in the Sage or Saint. These two ideas constitute the germ from which the Sung School doctrine of the Four Ultima was developed.

---

[1] For the meaning of *Ch'ien* see p. 157.
[2] *Yi Ching*, p. 408.

In the preceding pages it has been pointed out that, according to our philosopher, *Li* (Law) consists of the four principles Love, Righteousness, Reverence, and Wisdom, while *Tao* represents the transcendental and universal aspect of *Li*. We have also seen that Chu Hsi, in criticizing what he regarded as the ultra-transcendentalism of Taoist philosophy, maintained that the transcendental *Tao* is identical with the moral principles to be found in our own hearts. What it is now desired to make clear is that just as the term *Tao* represents this transcendental and universal aspect of *Li* (Law), so the four terms *Yüan, Hêng, Li, Chêng*, translated in this work as the principles of Origin, Beauty, Utility, and Potentiality, represent the transcendental and universal aspect of the ethical principles of man's nature—Love, Righteousness, Reverence, and Wisdom. In other words, *Yüan, Hêng, Li, Chêng* are the ethical principles which constitute that Moral Order which was the subject of the preceding section.

Further, in a passage cited in the "Symposium" Ch'ên Ch'un, one of Chu Hsi's most noted pupils, quoting his Master, says : "*Yüan, Hêng, Li, Chêng* are the eternal constants of Heaven's Moral Order ; Love, Righteousness, Reverence, and Wisdom are the governing principles of man's nature. . . . The Decree of Heaven is the diffusion of the Moral Law of Heaven throughout the universe and its impartation to the creature. Regarded as *Yüan, Hêng, Li, Chêng* it is called the Moral Order of Heaven ; regarded as diffused throughout the universe and imparted to the creature it is called the Decree of Heaven." [1] From this passage it will be seen that these Ultimata have both a transcendental and an immanent aspect.

[1] 大 全, bk. xxix, f. 3.

As transcendental, they constitute the *Tao*, or Moral Order ; as immanent they are the Decree of Heaven, which is implanted in the creature and becomes the law of his being.

In their relation to the physical universe, the most conspicuous manifestation of these Four Ultimata is in the Four Seasons. " The first budding forth of things into life is the manifestation of the Principle of Origin, and among the seasons is Spring. The growth and development of things is the manifestation of the Principle of Beauty (or Development), and among the seasons is summer. The attainment to full fruition of things is the manifestation of the Principle of Utility, and among the seasons is Autumn. The storing up of nature's resources is the manifestation of the Principle of Potentiality, and among the seasons is Winter." [1]

The relation of the Four Ultimata, thus manifested in the Four Seasons, to the Four Cardinal Virtues which constitute man's moral nature is also set forth by Ch'ên Ch'un in the passage alluded to above. " Of the principles of which the Decree of Heaven is composed the Principle of Origin when received by me is termed Love ; the Principle of Beauty when received by me is termed Reverence ; the Principle of Utility when received by me is termed Righteousness ; and the Principle of Potentiality when received by me is termed Wisdom." [2]

It will be noted that the Four Ultimata are always named in the same order, namely, Origin, Beauty, Utility, and Potentiality, corresponding to the order of the Seasons. But this order differs from that in which the Cardinal Virtues are almost invariably named, thus :—

[1] Ibid., f. 4.   [2] Ibid., f. 3.

Seasons : Spring Summer   Autumn   Winter
Ultimata : Origin Beauty   ✕ Utility   Potentiality
Virtues : Love   Righteousness ↗↘ Reverence   Wisdom.

The reason is that the order of the Cardinal Virtues arose from the historical development of their doctrine. In the early period Love alone, and later Love and Righteousness, coupled together, were emphasized as comprising all the virtues. Later still, these were further analysed with the result that Reverence and Wisdom were added ; Reverence having a special relation to Love, and Wisdom to Righteousness. In considering, therefore, the anology between the Ultimata and the Cardinal Virtues, it must be borne in mind that there is this difference in the order in which they are named, so that the Principle of Beauty in the universe corresponds to Reverence in man, and the Principle of Utility to Righteousness, while the principles of Origin and Potentiality correspond respectively to Love and Wisdom.

The first of the Four Ultimata is *Yüan*, the Principle of ORIGIN. Chu Hsi thus explains the relation of this principle to Love (仁) : " The Principle of Origin is the beginning of the production of things by Heaven and Earth. The *Yi* says, ' Great is the Principle of Origin indicated by *Ch'ien* ! All things owe to it their beginning.' ' Perfect is the Principle of Origin indicated by *K'un* ! All things owe to it their birth.' From this we learn that the Principle of Origin is the thread running through all stages in the production of things by Heaven and Earth. *Yüan*, the Principle of Origin, is the vital impulse itself ; in *Hêng*, the Principle of Beauty, it becomes the development of the vital impulse ; in *Li*, the

Principle of Utility, it becomes the fruiting, and in *Chêng*, the Principle of Potentiality, the completion of the vital impulse. It is the same with Love. Love in its essence is the vital impulse, the feeling of solicitude. If this vital impulse is wounded, then the feeling of solicitude is called forth. Conscientiousness also is Love manifesting itself in Righteousness ; courtesy is Love manifesting itself in Reverence ; and moral insight is Love manifesting itself in Wisdom." [1] Elsewhere he endorses the statement, " Love is the creative mind of Heaven and Earth, which is received by all men as their mind. . . . It is what is called the Principle of Origin of *Ch'ien* and *K'un*." [2]

The passage here referred to teaches that *Yüan*, the Principle of Origin pervading the physical universe, and Love, the premier virtue in man, are identical ; and that it is to this Principle of Origin, or Love, that all things owe their beginning. But that is not all. Not only do all things physical owe their beginning to this principle, but all four principles are wrapped up in this one. We see it in the case of the Cardinal Virtues in man, and we see it in the material universe as exemplified in the progress of the seasons, which, though they differ one from another, all proceed from the Spring : Spring is the birth of Spring, Summer is its growth, Autumn is its consummation, and Winter is the storing up of Spring. [3]

The second of the Four Ultimata is *Hêng*, the Principle of

---

[1] 全 書, bk. xlvii, f. 14 (*P.H.N.*, p. 336).
[2] Ibid., f. 39 (*P.H.N.*, p. 382).
[3] Ibid., bk. xlviii, f. 12 (*P.H.N.*, p. 407).

BEAUTY. The word *Hêng* is explained by two Chinese words—*t'ung* (通), which has the double significance of "permeating" and "continuing"; and *chia* (佳), which means "beautiful" or "excellent". In the gloss on the original text of the *Yi Ching*, which appears in the passage already quoted from the Fourth Appendix, the meaning of *Hêng* is given as "the assemblage of all excellencies".[1] But the idea of *t'ung* (通), "permeating" or "continuing", is also present to the mind of the Chinese student when considering this word. It is the latter meaning which is most emphasized in explaining the relation of the Ultimata to the seasons. *Hêng* finds its manifestation in the Summer season, which is the "continuance" or "development" of the vital impulse of Spring. "Spring is characterized by the vital impulse; in the Summer we see its persistent and permeating principle."[2] But the meaning "excellence" also in this connexion is obviously appropriate; Summer is the Beauty season just as Spring is the Love season. In fact, the underlying thought in the use of this word seems to be a combination of both ideas—"permeating" or "continuing", and "excellent". Pervading all physical phenomena is a peculiar appropriateness and harmony, a surpassing excellence which produces in us the sense of Beauty. A modern writer on Theistic Philosophy says, "If Beauty be an ultimate element in the Universe—not analysable into anything else, but an essence or characteristic quality which defies the disintegrating effort of the analyst—it may perhaps supply us with one means of escape from that 'slough of despond' into which materialism plunges us. Beauty

---

[1] *Yi Ching*, p. 408.
[2] 全 書, bk. xlviii, f. 13 (*P.H.N.*, p. 410).

is as ultimate as anything that is known in the spheres of the true and the good ; and while the discussion of its ' ultimate ' is as interesting as the problem of metaphysical and ethical philosophy, it may be found to cast much light upon the latter." One of the special characteristics of Beauty, the same writer says, is its prodigality, " and its being diffused in quarters where it is not at first recognized. There is, in truth, ' no speech or language where its voice is not heard.' It is not only in external aspects of form and colour, however, that it is to be seen as an adornment of the world. It exists in the very heart of its laws, as these hold sway over the realm of the organic and the inorganic world. . . . Nature everywhere ornaments herself. There is a process at work which is a real effort of Nature to realize the Beautiful by the production of harmony. That is much the same thing as saying that the inmost spirit of Nature is itself beautiful, and that it strives to disclose itself through this channel. It is not the world of matter, or dull inert substance, however, that is beautiful, or that ornaments itself. It is the spirit of the cosmos that shines through, and irradiates, or trans- figures material substance. It thus becomes a genuine apocalypse. . . . So far as, and so long as, it is discerned, our apprehension of it is a knowledge of the very essence of things, and therefore of that which transcends Nature." [1] In this passage Professor Knight admirably expresses in modern phrase the underlying thought which this word *Hêng* repre- sents to the Chinese philosopher. The " assemblage of all excellencies " manifest in physical phenomena, or the prodigality of beauty diffused throughout the cosmos, is

[1] *Aspects of Theism*, by William Knight, pp. 191-3.

due to an ethical principle behind and beneath it all which ranks among the ultimata of the universe, and this principle is termed *Hêng*, or the principle of Beauty.

This meaning of the term best explains its relation to its corresponding virtue Reverence. " The Principle of Beauty (*Hêng*) inherent in the Decree of Heaven when received by me is termed Reverence." [1] The connexion is sufficiently apparent. Poet and artist alike will tell us how near akin are Beauty in the universe and Reverence in man, and there is no need to enlarge upon it here. But this is not the only connexion between the two terms. Reverence is itself beautiful, it is " Love in graceful expression ".[2] It is the spirit of worship, the essence of ceremony. Worship and ceremony are perhaps the most common meanings of *Li* (禮), the word which in this work is translated Reverence ; and worship and ceremony, though they include much more, are, or are intended to be, forms of Beauty. While " Beauty " (隹) best explains the relation of *Hêng* to Reverence, the other meaning of the word *Hêng*, namely " continuance " or " development " (通), is not excluded. Reverence is the development of Love just as Summer is the development of Spring. Love seeks expression. It cannot stop at the subjective, it must find its continuance in objective manifestation. Love seeks to express itself in *deferring* to the object of its solicitude, and deference or courtesy is Reverence in operation.

The third of the Ultimata is *Li* (利), the Principle of UTILITY. The use of the word " utility " to express that

[1] 大 全, bk. i, f. 2.
[2] 全 書, bk. xlviii, f. 17 (*P.H.N.*, p. 417).

ultimate principle in the Moral Order which answers to Righteousness in man is at least arresting, if not startling. A little reflection, however, will show its peculiar appropriateness. At the very root of the idea of Righteousness is that of order; and order in the philosophical sense implies not only regularity but, what is another name for the same thing, adaptation or useful collocation also. These two ideas are coupled together in one of the " Proofs " so familiar to the student of Theism. The late Professor Flint in his Baird Lecture said, " In what may be called general order, that which strikes us chiefly is regularity; in what may be called special order, that which chiefly strikes us is adaptation or adjustment. . . . While we may readily admit the distinction to be so far valid, it is certainly not absolute. Regularity and adjustment are rather different aspects of order than different kinds of order, and so far from excluding each other, they will be found implying each other. . . . Wherever regularity can be found adjustment will also be found, if the search be carried far enough." [1] It is the aspect of adaptation or useful collocation which is most suggested by the term *Li* (利). A phrase which has been much used in connexion with the doctrine of Evolution is " the survival of the fittest ". Chinese philosophy sees something deeper, namely, mutual service. All things are made to serve. Everything has stamped upon it as the law of its being the creative purpose that it should be of service to its neighbour.

> Oh, we live ! Oh, we live !
> And this life which we conceive
> Is a great thing, and a grave,
> Which for others' use we have.

[1] *Theism*, by Robert Flint, pp. 132–4.

This principle of Utility is manifested in the Autumn season. The vitality which is born in the Spring and of which the Summer is the growth and development, finds its consummation and full fruition in Autumn, the harvest or fruit season. Western science teaches us that fruit in contrast to the leaf is self-giving.

In fruiting, the tree expends its life for the enrichment of others, so that Autumn may be characterized as the service season. The fulfilment of such service for all, says the Chinese philosopher, is what constitutes Order in the universe and Righteousness in the individual. Righteousness, then, is the fulfilment by each individual of the purpose of his existence in serving and benefiting his fellow creatures. " Benefiting all creatures he is able to exhibit the harmony of all that is right." [1] This principle pervading the universe is termed *Li* (利), the Principle of Utility.

The last of the Four Ultimata is *Chêng* (貞), the Principle of POTENTIALITY. Its physical manifestation is in the Winter season. In man it becomes Wisdom. Like the word for the Principle of Beauty, *Chêng* has a double interpretation, *chêng* (正) and *ku* (固). Legge translates it " correct and firm ". Its meaning is : " strong to do, and to do rightly." In the gloss given in the Fourth Appendix this principle is defined as the " faculty of action " and is said to confer on the noble man ability to " manage all affairs ".[2] It is, however, a reserve faculty ; and this is the special characteristic of

[1] *Yi Ching*, p. 408.
[2] Ibid.

Wisdom : a reserve of knowledge and ability adequate to all emergencies.

But this sense of reserve is not the characteristic of man alone ; it is everywhere, in all the phenomena of the universe. Its typical manifestation is in the season of Winter. Life's powers to all outward seeming have died down. The fruit has passed, the leaves have fallen, the tree itself is dry and hard. But we are not deceived. We know that there are hidden resources reserved within it ; the forces of its vitality are stored up for future need, and when the need emerges they will be called forth to the new task, strong and unerring in their efficiency. " Of the Four Attributes of *Ch'ien*, Origin is the chief and next to it is Potentiality as revealing the meaning of the end and beginning. Apart from the Principle of Origin there could be no birth ; apart from the Principle of Potentiality there could be no end ; apart from an ending there would be no means of making a beginning ; and without a beginning the end could never be consummated ; and so on in endless rotation." [1] In other words, Spring is the Mother of the Seasons, but Winter is the Mother of Spring. The hidden reserves of Winter are the guarantee of the permanence of the cosmos. This is *Chêng*, the Principle of Potentiality. And what Winter is among the seasons, that is Wisdom among the virtues. Love as Love is creative ; as Reverence it finds its development and expression in humility and self-repression, as Righteousness it finds its consummation in sacrifice and service, and as Wisdom it is fathering up its energies for new creations of love and humility, of service and sacrifice.

[1] 全 書, bk. xlviii, f. 14 (*P.H.N.*, p. 411).

These then are the Four Ultimata, the Attributes of Heaven. We see the creative principle at work throughout the universe ; we see its development in all-pervading beauty and harmony ; we see its consummation in a universal perfection of adjustment the secret of which is mutual service ; and we see everywhere, not less in the tiniest insect than in the mightiest physical forces, a reserve of efficiency which ensures the permanence of all things. These principles find their expression in the typical characteristics of the Four Seasons—in the Love season of Spring, in the Beauty season of Summer, in the Service season of Autumn, and in the Reserve season of Winter ; their highest manifestation is in Man—in his Love, in his Righteousness, in his Reverence, and in his Wisdom ; and among these Love is pre-eminent as the source and sum of all the rest.

Part III

CHU HSI'S DOCTRINE OF HUMAN NATURE

CHAPTER VIII

THE ESSENTIAL NATURE

The term Nature (性) as applied to man has a double significance, which, though implied in the Classics, was not clearly expounded until the emergence of the Sung School. In certain contexts the term refers to the " Original and Essential Nature " (極 本 窮 源 之 性),[1] while in others it refers to the " Physical Nature " (氣 質 之 性);[2] that is to the Essential Nature as conditioned by the physical element. This twofold interpretation of the term is the chief contribution by this School to the Chinese doctrine of human nature, just as Chou Lien Hsi's doctrine of the Supreme Ultimate is its chief contribution to the Chinese theory of the Universe. Notwithstanding the fact that these two conceptions of the Nature are almost inextricably intertwined, it is necessary for the sake of clearness that they be treated more or less separately. The consideration of the doctrine implied in the term " Physical Nature ", therefore, will be reserved for the next chapter. In the present chapter we shall confine ourselves as far as possible to the subject of the " Essential Nature ".

In the voluminous discussions on the Nature characteristic of the Sung period two questions stand out prominently as the most crucial. The first is : " What is it ? " And the second : " Is it good ? " It is evident that the answer to the one very

[1] 全 書, bk. xliii, f. 5 (*P.H.N.*, p. 87).   [2] Ibid.

much determines what the answer to the other will be. Indeed, it may be said that much of the controversy which raged round this term from the time of Mencius to that of Chu Hsi would have been avoided if at the outset its meaning had been free from ambiguity. Chu Hsi admits that the differences which appeared even in schools which may be regarded as comparatively orthodox are to be attributed to the fact that the term itself was not clearly defined ; but this, he maintains, is not the fault of the sages, while he refers in words of scorn to the heretic's blind gropings after a consistent theory. " The sages," he says, " understood the meaning of the term Nature ; the divisions in the later schools were simply because the word itself was not understood. The philosopher Yang flounders, while the philosopher Hsün is like the proverbial man who tries to scratch his leg through his boot." [1] The fact, however, that by the sages themselves the term was used in two senses contributed not a little to the confusion. For example, when Mencius says, " The Nature is good," [2] and when Tzŭ Ssŭ in the *Doctrine of the Mean* says, " The Decree of Heaven is what is termed our Nature," [3] both are speaking of the Essential Nature with which man is originally endowed. Confucius, on the other hand, when he says, " Men in their Nature are nearly alike, but by practice they grow wide apart," [4] is speaking of the physical nature ; and

[1] Ibid., bk. xlii, f. 6 (*P.H.N.*, p. 17).

[2] *Mencius*, p. 110.

[3] *D.M.*, p. 247.

[4] *Analects*, xvii, ii (p. 182). " The moral nature," says Legge, in his explanatory note on this passage, " is the same in all, and though the material organism and disposition do differ in different individuals, they at first are more nearly alike than they subsequently become."

Mencius also obviously uses the term in the latter sense when he speaks of the appetites of the senses as the Nature.[1] But such divergence in the use of the term was not unnatural in an age when as yet exact philosophical statement was hardly to be expected ; nor should it have been difficult for subsequent writers to discern the different senses in which the term was used in its different connexions. Chu Hsi enunciates the obvious canon of interpretation that in all such passages the word in question must be interpreted according to its context.[2] If this canon had been observed many a treatise of the Sung period would have remained unwritten.

WHAT IS IT ?

The paramount question, then, in the Sung philosophy is : " What is the Nature ? " The answer to it is given in the dictum just quoted from the *Doctrine of the Mean*, and is one of the chief battle grounds of the schools. " The Decree of Heaven," says the author, " is what is termed the Nature." As translated by Legge, it reads : " What Heaven has conferred is called the Nature." [3] But this rather misses the point. Legge, in his notes, supports his rendering by quoting a gloss on a passage from the *Yi Ching*, which says : " *Ming* is what men are endowed with " (命 者 人 所 稟 受). The gloss, however, is simply descriptive and must not be taken as a definition. Mr. Ku Hung Ming has interpreted the passage correctly in his rendering : " The ordinance of God

---

[1] *Mencius*, p. 365.

[2] 全 書, bk. xlii, f. 2 (*P.H.N.*, p. 7).

[3] *D.M.*, p. 247.

is what we call the law of our being " [1]; and Legge himself quotes Chu Hsi's definition of *Ming* (命) as *ling* (令) " to command ", " to order ". *Ming*, in fact, is the immanent and all-pervading creative will of God, which, imparted to man, becomes his Nature.

There are three respects in which these two terms *hsing* and *ming* are distinguished from each other. In the first place they represent respectively the Divine and human aspects of the one entity. " As imparted by Heaven to the universe it is called the Decree, as received by the creature from Heaven it is called the Nature. It is the point of view from which the terms are used that differs." [2] In the second place, " The word Nature," says Chu Hsi, " refers to what is individualized, the word Decree to that which is all-pervading. The Decree is like water flowing as in this stream ; the Nature is as if you took a bowl and filled it from the stream." [3] In the third place, " The Decree of Heaven," says Chu Hsi, " is like the command of a sovereign, and the Nature is the receiving of office from the sovereign." [4] " Heaven may be likened to the Emperor. The Decree is like his handing to me letters patent. The Nature is the duty attached to the office which I thus receive, just as the duty attached to the office

---

[1] *The Conduct of Life*, by Ku Hung Ming. Mr. Ku's translation is some-what free, a very desirable feature in a work of that kind, but hardly admissible, in argumentative works like those of Chu Hsi, where appeal is repeatedly made to the literal and exact meaning of a word or phrase, so that the one rendering must be made to fit many and varied contexts. We have therefore to content ourselves with the more rigid word " decree ".

[2] 全 書, bk. xlii, f. 2 (*P.H.N.*, p. 7).

[3] Ibid., f. 3 (*P.H.N.*, pp. 10–11).

[4] Ibid., f. 1 (*P.H.N.*, p. 5).

of district police is to arrest robbers, and the duty of the Comptroller of the Archives is the custody of documents." [1] In these similes there is clearly indicated not only the idea of what Mr. Ku calls " the law of our being ", but also the Divine authority by which this " law " is implanted within us, and which gives it its moral sanction. Divine Law (天 理) stands in opposition to human desire (人 欲), and because it is Divine Law it is man's " duty " to obey it, however contrary to his own flesh-born desires it may be, just as the paramount duty of the magistrate is to obey his sovereign in the discharge of the duties of his office.

What, then, is the " law of our being ", the " duty attached to the office ", which is conferred by the sovereign will of Heaven ? Here, on the very threshold of our subject, we find how necessary was our preliminary survey of Chu Hsi's theory of the universe. For it is in terms of *Li* (理) Law and *T'ao* (道) Moral Law, which we were considering in Part II, that the content of the term Nature is to be explained. We saw there that Law, which as the ultimate element in the universe enters into every individual thing that exists, consists of the four ethical principles Love, Righteousness, Reverence, and Wisdom ; and it was shown that, according to our philosopher, this universal Law is what constitutes our Nature. But there is an important difference between the two terms, parallel to the distinction we just now saw to exist between the Decree and the Nature. " The Nature is Law," says Chu Hsi ; " subjectively it is the Nature, objectively it is Law." [2] Regarded as informing all phenomena, the rule of existence

---

[1] Ibid., f. 2 (*P.H.N.*, p. 6).

[2] Ibid., f. 6 (*P.H.N.*, p. 16).

for everything that is, it is Law. Regarded as within us, the centre of our life, the ethical sanction which we cannot deny without denying our very existence, it is the Nature. Ch'ên Pei Hsi, a pupil of Chu Hsi, gives a similar explanation : " The Nature is Law," he says, " why then is it called ' the Nature ' and not ' Law ' ? Because ' Law ' is the comprehensive expression for law as common to men and things throughout the universe. The Nature is Law as it is in myself. It is simply that this Law received from Heaven becomes my own, and therefore is called my Nature. The word ' Nature ' (性) is composed of the two words ' birth ' (生) and ' heart ' (忄), and indicates that man from his ' birth ' has this Law complete in his ' heart '." [1]

The relation of the term Nature to *Tao* is equally apparent, and is repeatedly emphasized by our philosopher. The classic statement which he endorses as an exact expression of this relation is that of Shao Tzŭ : " The Nature is the concrete expression of Moral Order (道 *Tao*)." [2] Here, again, as might be expected, there is the same difference between the two terms : " The term Moral Order is used in a universal sense, the term Nature is used in the individual sense." [3] " The Moral Order is Law as we find it in the external world ; the Nature is Law as we find it in ourselves." [4] And if we ask what is the content of the term *Tao*, or Moral Order, again the answer is the same as in the case of *Li*, or Law. It consists of the four ethical principles Love, Righteousness, Reverence, and Wisdom.

---

[1] 大 全, bk. xxix, f. 4. [2] 全 書, bk. xlii, f. 6 (*P.H.N.*, p. 18).
[3] Ibid., f. 9 (*P.H.N.*, p. 23). [4] Ibid.

We see, then, that the Nature is nothing less than the individuation in the creature of that immaterial principle which as *Li* is regarded as the fundamental element in the universe, as *Tao* is recognized as constituting its Moral Order, and as *Ming* is the immanent creative will of God. It is " the seat of the assemblage of principles " [1] on which all moral distinctions are based. It is not necessary here to repeat what has been said in previous chapters, nor to anticipate what in a later chapter has still to be said, with reference to these four principles in detail. The point to note now is that at least we may say as the result of our discussion that for Chu Hsi the Nature is nothing less than the Divine Law written upon the heart. The philosopher of the far distant and isolated East confirms by his independent testimony the earnest contention of the Apostle Paul that in man as man, apart from any special revelation, there is a law written in the heart which conscience tells him it is his duty to obey.[2] And, further, as shown elsewhere, this law is the law of Love, comprehending all virtues in all relationships.

The aspect of the Nature thus presented to us is undoubtedly its most important aspect in the view of our philosopher, as it certainly is that around which there was most controversy. It does not, however, represent the whole content of the term. Indeed, it would be strange if " The Nature " resolved itself into nothing more than " Law ", lofty though that Law be in its ethical ideals. There is one other important element in the meaning of the word, which,

---

[1] Ibid., f. 14 (*P.H.N.*, p. 34).
[2] The very phrase " Divine Law " is of frequent occurrence in his writings, as representing the heaven-born nature.

though less prominent in the writings of the school—for the simple reason that it was less the subject of controversy—is nevertheless an essential part of it. A famous dictum by Ch'êng Ming Tao, couched in the language of Kao Tzŭ the opponent of Mencius, was : " Life is what is termed the Nature." [1] This statement is frequently endorsed by Chu Hsi, and is of the first importance in our analysis of his doctrine of Human Nature. Chu Hsi himself says : " The principle of life is termed the Nature." [2] He also endorses the statement that " in the term Nature the reference is to that complete substance by which all things have their life ".[3] Chang Tsai, too, says : " The Nature is that by reason of which we cannot but be acted upon by the external world " ; [4] in other words, it is the seat of sensibility, or consciousness. It must not be forgotten that the word " life " here includes the material element, and to that extent goes beyond the " Essential Nature ", which is the proper subject of this chapter.[5] But this does not affect the present argument. The point to be emphasized is : The Nature is that principle which, when it is imparted to, and becomes inherent in, the physical element results in a living being. It is the seat of that relation between man and his environment which constitutes his life. It is the principle or law of that life by which he not only receives his

[1] 遺 書, pt. i, f. 10.

[2] 全 書, bk. xlii, f. 6 (*P.H.N.*, p. 16).

[3] Ibid., bk. xlii, f. 1 (*P.H.N.*, p. 3).

[4] Ibid., f. 13 (*P.H.N.*, p. 31). The immediate application of this statement as cited by Chu Hsi is in an ethical sense ; the statement itself, however, covers all phenomena.

[5] Cf. I Ch'uan's gloss in the 遺 書, pt. xxiv, f. 2.

life but continues to live—" to breathe and eat." [1] Chinese
philosophy teaches us in effect that God formed man of matter
(shall we say " of the dust of the ground " ?) and imparted to
the material element this immaterial principle, and so " man
became a living soul ". A passage which in an earlier chapter
was cited from Sir Oliver Lodge's *Man and the Universe* may
be repeated here, as illustrating this aspect of the term *hsing*.
" Life is not matter," he says, " nor is it energy, it is a guiding
and directing principle, and when considered as incorporated
in a certain organism, it, and all that appertains to it, may well
be called the soul, or constructive and controlling element, in
that organism. The soul in this sense is related to the
organism in somewhat the same way as the Logos is related
to the universe, it is that without which it does not exist—
that which vivifies and constructs or composes and informs
the whole." [2] It is not suggested that the Chinese word *hsing*
means " soul ", which Sir Oliver appears to regard as
a synonym for " life ". There are other words which the
Chinese use to express the idea of " soul ". The reason for
quoting this passage in this connexion is that if the Chinese
word *hsing*, or Nature, be substituted for the word " soul "
in each place where the latter occurs in the above passage, we
shall have an almost perfect statement of what Chu Hsi
appears to mean by the term. It would not be a complete
statement, because it does not include that essential element
in the content of the term which we have already dwelt upon,
and which must be combined with it. The " constructive

---

[1] 全 書, bk. xlii, f. 24 (*P.H.N.*, p. 53).
[2] *Man and the Universe*, p. 166.

and controlling element in the organism", "that without which it does not exist", is the moral element in man's constitution, consisting of the four ethical principles which constitute the Moral Order of the universe. Such is what is meant by the term Nature, according to Chu Hsi—an ethical principle imparted by the creative will of God to the material organism and constituting the life of that organism. It is interesting to note, in passing, that in modern Chinese colloquial the common word for "life" is *hsing ming* (性 命), a combination of the two words "nature" and "decree". That is, life, in ordinary parlance to-day, is the Nature imparted to man by the Divine Decree; and to lose one's life is to *tiu ming* (丟 命),[1] to lose the Decree which was imparted by Heaven.

The bearing of all this on the ethical questions "Is the Nature good?" and "Whence comes moral evil?" will be considered in the section following, and in the third section of the next chapter. It will be convenient also to reserve till then the consideration of those erroneous views on the constitution of the Nature which had their roots more especially in the ethical side of the problem, and which for that reason Chu Hsi found it necessary vigorously to combat. There were other views, however, which, though of less moment in the ethical controversies of the period, nevertheless called for question and criticism in the lecture-room, or by letter. These may be briefly indicated here. The first is the theory that confounded the Nature with Mind. This view originated in Buddhism and the answer to it is for the most part covered by

---

[1] *Tiu* (丟) = to lose.

Chu Hsi's answer to the Buddhist view of Mind. What Chu Hsi insists upon is that the Nature must be clearly distinguished from Mind, which is but the envelope of the Nature —its organ of consciousness, as the Nature itself is the seat of consciousness.[1] " We of the Confucian Cult," he says, " regard the Nature as real. Buddhists regard it as unreal. To define the Nature as the Mind, as is done so frequently in these days, is incorrect." [2] " If we point to that which possesses Consciousness as the Nature, we are speaking of what is really the Mind." [3] He contends that " the words Nature and Mind have each a different connotation ",[4] and endorses Shao Yung's statement of the relation between the two that " the Mind is the *enceinte* of the Nature ", [5] and " contains the principles of the Nature as a city wall does its inhabitants ". [6]

An error in the opposite direction was that which made the Nature, and the ethical principles of which it consists, to be separate entities, and the four principles themselves to be separated from each other as if by partition walls. According to Chu Hsi's own philosophy " The Nature is the seat of the assemblage of principles ".[7] It was but going one step further to contend that it was a receptacle separate from, though containing, these principles ; and, under the

---

[1] See p. 194. Similarly, the Nature is the seat of life, and the physical frame the organ of the vital functions.

[2] 全 書, bk. xlii, f. 7 (*P.H.N.*, p. 18).

[3] Ibid., f. 7 (*P.H.N.*, p. 18).

[4] Ibid., f. 20 (*P.H.N.*, p. 45).

[5] Ibid., f. 2 (*P.H.N.*, p. 6).

[6] Ibid., bk. xliv, f. 10 (*P.H.N.*, p. 175).

[7] Ibid., bk. xlii, f. 10 (*P.H.N.*, p. 34).

Buddhist and Taoist influences of the time, to maintain that the Nature itself is pre-existent[1] and eternal,[2] an empty shell,[3] as it were, to be received by man as the receptacle for those four ethical principles which become his own by a voluntary acceptance.[4] This was substantially the view held by the Su School,[5] who maintained further that the term Decree, in the dictum of Tzŭ Ssŭ, on which Chu Hsi's philosophy is largely based, was merely a name borrowed by the sages to represent a certain phase in the evolution of the Nature which had no substantive existence in itself.[6]

This whole position Chu Hsi pulverizes with a *reductio ad absurdum* argument. Granted that the Nature is the seat of the assemblage of principles, it does not follow that there is " a pre-existent Nature without such principles, and waiting for them to assemble within it ".[7] " Since it is called the Nature," he says with merciless sarcasm, " it is manifest that it is so-called because man has received it. Here, however, it is said that at a certain stage it has not yet become man's own ! So then Heaven in creating a man does not at once confer the Nature upon him, but deposits it in a place apart and the man must rise and take it for himself ; only then does he possess it as his own ! The exponents of this view do not realize that before man has received this Nature, according to their theory, he is already a man ! What is it that enables

[1] Ibid., ff. 6, 23 (*P.H.N.*, pp. 15, 51).
[2] Ibid., f. 5 (*P.H.N.*, p. 13).
[3] Ibid., f. 23 (*P.H.N.*, p. 51).
[4] Ibid., f. 24 (*P.H.N.*, p. 53).
[5] Ibid., f. 5 (*P.H.N.*, pp. 14–15).
[6] Ibid.
[7] Ibid., f. 14 (*P.H.N.*, p. 34).

him to breathe and eat in the world, and so to receive this Nature ? And further, how comes this Nature as a separate entity to be placed in some particular spot, so that it may be laid hold of and deposited in the body ? Love, Righteousness, Reverence, and Wisdom, inherent in the Nature, are the substance of the Nature ; but here it is said that man embodies the Nature as his own, and afterwards it clothes itself with these principles ! This means that these four principles are placed on one side, and subsequently the Nature comes in on the other side and clothes itself with them : but where the four principles are to come from before the Nature does so clothe itself with them we are not informed ! " [1] Chu Hsi's own position is perfectly clear. It is true, there is a sense in which the Nature as the individuation of the universal *Li* is said by the Philosopher himself to be pre-existent and even eternal. " Before the etherial element exists," he says, " the Nature is already in existence. The former is transitory, the latter is eternal." [2] But the subject he is discussing in this connexion is the relation between Matter and Law, the latter being fundamental and ultimate, and still continuing to be so after it becomes the Nature. As Law it is pre-existent and eternal. Our philosopher, however, is very clear that Law is not the Nature in its true meaning until it is individualized in man and combined with the physical element. There is no pre-existent Nature *qua* Nature. Before birth the very word Nature is inapplicable.[3] He is equally clear that the four ethical principles ARE the Nature, and not " contained

[1] Ibid., f. 24 (*P.H.N.*, p. 53).
[2] Ibid., f. 16 (*P.H.N.*, p. 43).
[3] Ibid., bk. xliii, ff. 15, 16 (*P.H.N.*, pp. 108, 109, 110).

in " the Nature ; they constitute its substance. Moreover, though there are clear distinctions between them, these principles are not " separate " one from the other as if in water-tight compartments, any more than, in the view of the modern psychologist, Intellect, Feeling, and Will are separate faculties, though they may be distinguished as three " phases " of mind. " Within this one all-embracing Law, while not regarding them as separated one from another as if by a wall or fence, we nevertheless recognize them as having distinctive qualities." [1]

Is it Good ?

In the discussions of the Sung School on human nature the question, " Is it good ? " is hardly second in importance to the question, " What is it ? " It may even claim to be the *fons et origo* of all the controversies that the term Nature has evoked—beginning with the statement of Mencius that " The Nature is good ". It will be expected from the discussion of the preceding section that the Sage's doctrine was defended, developed, and more clearly expounded by the philosophers of the Sung School. Chu Hsi teaches that the Nature is the Law of God written upon the heart ; and it is in the light of this doctrine that Mencius is interpreted by him. When Mencius says, " The Nature is good," he is not speaking of the Nature as actually seen in the adult man, nor even as in the infant, who is already caught in the meshes of the physical element of his being. For the Nature of which the assertion is made is not the Nature as conditioned by the physical element, or as modified by external environment, or as warped and tainted by fleshly entanglement, and

[1] Ibid., bk. xlii, f. 23 (*P.H.N.*, p. 51).

least of all as perverted and ruined by evil conduct, but as ordained by the Divine purpose when imparted to man. And who shall say that this is not " good " ? Or who shall say that it is not designed for good ?

There is another statement by the Sage which otherwise would be still more difficult to explain, but which becomes clear in the light of this same doctrine. " The tendency of man's nature to good," he says, " is like the tendency of water to flow downwards." [1] On the face of it, this would appear contrary to the experience of most. Not so easy, one would say, is the quest after goodness. The saintliest among men have chosen language very different to express their experience. Mencius was a sage of rare virtue ; he was nevertheless delightfully human, a man manifestly of like passions with ourselves. Did he escape the temptations common to man ? If not, how came he to speak in such a different vein from, say, that of the Apostle Paul ? Chu Hsi seems rarely if ever to have made reference in his philosophical discussions to this classical saying of Mencius, nor did any of his numerous questioners propound a question concerning it, which fact seems to show that the accepted interpretation was not discordant with their experience. That interpretation in the light of Chu Hsi's doctrine of the Nature becomes perfectly plain. Just as St. John says of the new nature, " Whosoever is begotten of God doeth no sin, because his seed abideth in him, and he cannot sin, because he is begotten of God," [2] and so teaches the inherent impossibility of that Divine element in the child of God committing sin, so the

[1] *Mencius*, pp. 271–2.
[2] Ibid., *Prolegomena*, p. 68.

Sage of the Far East declares of that original nature Divinely implanted in man its " tendency to good is like the tendency of water to flow downwards ". In neither case does the statement deny the obvious facts of life. The Christian Apostle recognizes the possibility of even the regenerate falling into sin, and the Chinese Sage was ready enough to admit that, with the rare exception of such saintly men as Yao and Shun, men in general do evil and violate the law of their Nature. But, he would maintain, the Nature itself is never other than perfectly good.

The most famous opponent of Mencius was the philosopher Kao who maintained in opposition to the theory of the Sage that originally there was no distinct moral element in man's nature. What is termed the Nature is simply the life of the organism, wholly material in its essence. Man's nature, he said, is like whirling water in the corner of a rocky cliff ; [1] it will flow in any direction in which an outlet is given to it, a position which was met by the Sage with derisive scorn. Now the remarkable thing is that Ch'êng Tzŭ, a follower of Mencius and the one of all others whose teachings had most influence with Chu Hsi, expressed his own doctrine of the Nature in exactly the same words as those used by Kao Tzŭ : " Life is what is termed the Nature." [2] It is not surprising that this fact gave rise to questions among the followers of Chu Hsi, and that the Philosopher's explanation was sought. The answer given [3] was at first somewhat

---

[1] Ibid., p. 271. The heresy was called the " Whirling Water " heresy ; see 全 書, bk. xlii, f. 12 (*P.H.N.*, p. 27).

[2] *Mencius*, p. 272.

[3] 全 書, bk. xliii, f. 11 (*P.H.N.*, pp. 100–1).

enigmatic, designed to lead the students to elucidate the matter for themselves. The explanation, however, is simple. The Philosopher admits the verbal correspondence between the two statements and that the one seems to confirm the doctrine of the other; but he argues from the vehement opposition of Mencius that Kao Tzǔ must have meant by his statement something altogether different from what Ch'êng Tzǔ meant, and finds the solution of the difficulty in the different value attached to the word "life" in each case. As we have shown in the preceding paragraphs of this chapter, Ch'êng Tzǔ's use of the word "life" included both the immaterial ethical principle and the physical element. With Kao Tzǔ the word carried a wholly material significance. Trammelled by the idea of uniformity and failing to recognize diversity, he took account of the material element, but lost sight of the ethical principle.[1] "The phenomena of benevolence and righteousness were akin to those of walking and sleeping, eating and seeing."[2] Such a philosophy in the eyes of Mencius and the Sung philosophers alike, "went to deny any essential distinction between good and evil, virtue and vice."[3]

Mencius and Kao Tzǔ were followed by Hsün Tzǔ who, not content with what might be called the middle position assumed by Kao Tzǔ, went to the other extreme and maintained that the Nature is positively evil. This latter doctrine had no representative in Chu Hsi's day. The heresies he had to combat, in so far as they were not forms

---

[1] Ibid., bk. xlii, f. 8 (*P.H.N.*, p. 63).

[2] *Mencius, Prolegomena*, p. 61.

[3] Ibid., p. 60.

of Buddhism and Taoism, were more or less modifications of the position maintained by Kao Tzŭ. The most important of these were the teachings of the Hu School,[1] the tenets of which are to be found in the treatise entitled *Chih Yen* (知 言) or *Words of Wisdom*.[2] It is difficult to understand how Chu Hsi with his keen intellect found the patience to reply in detail to anything so palpably illogical and self-contradictory as the mixed medley of quasi-philosophical utterances to be found in this and the other writings of that School. The reason no doubt is that the system, if such it may be called, had many adherents, who were more or less within the circle of the Sung School. It was necessary, therefore, for Chu Hsi to combat the errors of the Hu-s in order to preserve his own disciples from their injurious influence, and his teachings from heretical admixture in their transmission to posterity. The tenets to which he gave most attention were three :—

First.—It was maintained that it is impossible to predicate good of the Nature without thereby predicating evil of it also, because " good " is a relative term implying the existence of evil as its opposite. Therefore, what Mencius meant by the statement " The Nature is good " was not good in the moral sense at all. The statement was simply an exclamation of admiration at its mysterious excellence.

Second.—To the Nature in its original mystery and excellence the word " good " in the relative sense is inapplicable. It is " good " in an absolute and transcendental sense only, a good which transcends all contraries. When

---

[1] See p. 76.   [2] Ibid.

you have what is generally called the Nature you have both good and evil, but this is not the real Nature.

Third.—To support these positions it was maintained concerning the Nature itself as it exists in men that it is simply the faculty of liking and disliking. "The noble man in his liking and disliking is actuated by Moral Law and the ignoble man by selfishness." [1]

It is obvious that the first and second of these statements were self-contradictory. It is maintained that good cannot be predicated of the Nature because it implies evil, and at the same time, that a transcendental good, which does not imply evil, is predicated of the original Nature! Chu Hsi's answer to all this shows the usual keenness of his analytical powers. That the term "good" is relative, he admits, but maintains that it does not necessarily imply contemporaneous evil nor even eventual evil, but potential evil. It is absurd, he maintains, to say that you cannot predicate good of the Nature without implying the presence in it of evil also. Apply this reasoning generally, and there is nothing of which you could affirm either goodness, or activity, or even real existence! "Good and evil, truth and error, activity and repose, the antecedent and the sequent, the former and the latter, all receive their names from their mutual opposition. Apart from its contrast with evil, good cannot be predicated of anything. Apart from its opposition to activity repose cannot be predicated of anything. If a thing cannot be false then neither can it be true, and there is nothing of which these things can be predicated at all." [2]

---

[1] 全 書, bk. xlii, f. 12 (*P.H.N.*, p. 29).

[2] Ibid., f. 17 (*P.H.N.*, p. 41).

To the contention that when Mencius said, " The Nature is good," he was using the language of admiration the reply is that admiration itself implies goodness. " Just as Buddha," says the Philosopher, " when in admiration he exclaims ' Excellent ! Excellent ! ' implies that the Path is good, and so calls forth his admiration." [1] The very idea of a distinction between a transcendental, absolute good and a relative good involves a doctrine of two Natures which Chu Hsi emphatically rejects.[2] Though endorsing Ch'êng Tzǔ's doctrine of the Physical Nature he maintains that this is not a second nature, but the same Essential Nature conditioned by the physical element.[3] Similarly, the good mingled with evil, which we find in man as he is actually, is not a different good but the same good as existed before any evil had emerged.[4]

The heresy we are told originated in the orthodox school, in a conversation between Yang Kuei Shan and Ch'ang Tsung, a man deeply versed in Buddhist literature. Ch'ang endorsed Mencius's doctrine that the Nature is good, and when Yang asked whether both good and evil could be predicated of it, said, " The Original Nature is not contrasted with evil." This statement was learned from Yang Kuei Shan by Hu Wên Ting, the founder of the Hu School, and became the dictum on which its heresy was based, but divorced altogether from its original meaning.[5] Although the heresy originated in the orthodox school, however, Chu Hsi regarded it very seriously. His severest charge was that it was but another

---

[1] Ibid., f. 11 (*P.H.N.*, p. 27).　　　[2] Ibid., f. 10 (*P.H.N.*, p. 25).
[3] Ibid.　　　[4] Ibid.
[5] Ibid., f. 10 (*P.H.N.*, p. 26).

form of Kao Tzŭ's " Whirling Water Heresy ".[1] The statement that the Nature is simply " the faculty of liking and
disliking ", though not in the same language, carries the same
import as the statement " The life is the Nature ". Moral
Law on this theory has no place within the Nature, moral
distinctions themselves are obliterated, and the Nature
comes to be no more than the seat of physical or psychical
functions.[2] It is this materialistic trend that to him appeared
so grave.

Such was Chu Hsi's answer to the prevailing heresy of
his time. The positive argument by which he established
his main proposition that the Nature is good was essentially
the same as that of Mencius. " If we look at the feelings
which flow from the Nature, we may know that they are
constituted for the practice of what is good." [3] We see men
exercised by solicitude, by conscientiousness, by the feeling
of respect, and by moral insight. Notwithstanding that
these feelings exist in varying degrees, and that they are
responded to with more or less of imperfection, they are
nevertheless present in every man. From them you may
trace the existence of their corresponding nature-principles,
Love, Righteousness, Reverence, and Wisdom, with the same
certitude as you infer the nature of the source from that
of the stream which flows from it. Even in the wicked man
the fact that he knows that his actions are evil, is the evidence
of the existence in him of a nature that would lead him in
a contrary direction.

[1] Ibid., f. 12 (P.H.N., p. 29).
[2] Ibid.
[3] *Mencius*, p. 278.

CHAPTER IX

THE PHYSICAL NATURE

The Chinese philosopher's acceptance of the doctrine of the perfection of man's Essential Nature raises the question : How does he account for the differences between men in respect of good and evil ? Why are they not all saints and sages ? And whence come such men as the notorious Chieh and Chou ? [1] How, too, are we to account for the differences in the physical lot of men ? Why are good men poor and short-lived, while evil men are rich and live to old age ? Such questions have troubled serious thinkers in all ages. Allied to the problems of moral evil and destiny is that of the relation between man and the brute. Chu Hsi asserts that the nature in man and the universe is one. How then does he account for the manifest gulf existing between man and the lower animals, not to speak of the differences between different species, between animal and plant life and between the animate and inanimate ? Yet another question— arising out of the first of these two problems—cannot but suggest itself to the Christian student. What light, if any, does Chu Hsi offer on the problem of Redemption ? Is there any way by which men caught in the toils of sin may shake off those toils and regain the perfect goodness of their Essential Nature ? The answer of Chu Hsi and his Masters to these questions is found in their doctrine of the Physical Nature.

[1] 全 書, bk. xlii, f. 9 (*P.H.N.*, p. 23).

This doctrine is claimed by Chu Hsi as the distinctive merit of the Sung School. He asserts that it was first developed by Chang Tsai and the two Ch'êngs, to whom he not only acknowledges his own debt of personal gratitude, but declares that they have placed the sages under obligation to them as their interpreters, and have done great service to posterity. For " no one previously ", he says, " had ever given utterance to this doctrine. Han T'ui Chih, for example, in his essay on ' The Original Nature ' (原 性), propounded his theory of the ' Three Grades ', and what he says is true, but he does not state clearly that he is speaking of the physical nature. Where can you get ' three grades ' in the original nature ? Mencius in his assertion that the Nature is good speaks of it only in respect of its origin, making no reference to the physical nature, so that in his case, too, there must be careful discrimination ; while of the rest of the philosophers, some assert that the Nature is evil, others that it is both evil and good, whereas if the doctrine of Chang and the two Ch'êngs had been propounded earlier there would have been no need for all this discussion and controversy. If, then, the doctrine of Chang and the two Ch'êngs stands, that of the rest is shown to be confusion." [1] Chu Hsi thus makes no small claim for this particular doctrine ; and it must be conceded that with Chu Hsi himself the controversy ended, and, in the issue, his own prediction was verified, that though he failed to convince his contemporaries of the truth of his theories posterity would accept them.[2]

What, then, was this doctrine which achieved so much ?

----

[1] Ibid., bk. xliii, f. 6 (*P.H.N.*, p. 88).
[2] Ibid., f. 9 (*P.H.N.*, p. 95).

In brief it was the enunciation of a clear distinction between the essential nature as it is in itself, and as it is conditioned by the physical element. While the real nature is what I Ch'uan calls the " Original and Essential Nature ", with which man is endowed by Heaven, it is never found except in conjunction with its material vehicle, and therefore any account of the Nature which treats of the one apart from the other must be inadequate, if not positively erroneous.[1] " Take light as an illustration," says the Philosopher ; " there must be some reflecting body, whether a mirror or a sheet of water, in order to have light. The light is the Nature ; the mirror or water is the physical element ; without the mirror or water the light is dispersed and lost." [2] This combination of the essential nature with its physical medium is termed the Physical Nature. It is to the inequalities in the physical element that the inequalities of virtue and vice, as well as the differences of species, are due ; as in an old mirror which is marred by the blotches on its surface and so reflects the light unequally.[3]

It must not be supposed, however, that there are two natures, the Essential and the Physical. There is only one nature ; that is, the Essential Nature. The Physical Nature is still the Essential Nature, but conditioned by the physical element. The physical element in and by itself can never be termed the Nature.[4] It is the necessary medium for the individuation of the immaterial element by which the essential

---

[1] Ibid., bk. xlii, f. 35 (*P.H.N.*, p. 72).
[2] Ibid., bk. xliii, f. 1 (*P.H.N.*, p. 80).
[3] Ibid., bk. xlii, f. 25 (*P.H.N.*, p. 59).
[4] Ibid., f. 4 (*P.H.N.*, p. 13).

nature comes to be; and as that medium it conditions, impedes, and even distorts, the manifestation of the Essential Nature. It is the Essential Nature as it is thus affected that is called the Physical Nature.

MAN AND THE BRUTE

"The Uniformity of Nature" is a phrase with which nineteenth century philosophy has made us familiar. By it is meant a uniformity underlying all phenomena, and expressed in the physical laws of the universe. The Chinese philosopher also saw uniformity underlying the infinite diversity of phenomena, but the uniformity which he saw was an ethical uniformity. In other words, he attributed the uniformity to an all-pervading ethical principle, and the diversity to the infinite variety and intricate complexity of the manifesting medium. By the interaction in different degrees of the two modes of matter, the *Yin* and the *Yang*, the Five Agents are evolved. These Five Agents, again, in varying proportions, all enter into every individual thing, and thus are produced the infinitely diversified forms of existence. The diversity and inequality in the manifesting vehicle caused by the innumerable transformations of the Two Modes and Five Agents are what is to be regarded as the source of the differences between species, and between man and other creatures.[1]

This theory the Philosopher illustrates in considerable detail, showing how, for example, the differences between fish and land animals, beasts and bird, grasses and trees, are due to the predominance of the negative or positive

[1] Ibid., bk. xliii, f. 21 (*P.H.N.*, p. 119).

ether as the case may be.[1]   Referring specially to the difference
between man and other creatures we are told : " When Heaven
and Earth stored up the subtle essences, it was man who
received the choicest excellence of the Five Agents." [2]   And
again : " The Two Ethers and the Five Agents mutually
interact and pass through a myriad transformations, so
that in the production of men and things there are differences
in the degree of their etherial fineness.   From the point of
view of the Ether as one, men and other creatures all come
into being by receiving this one ether.   From the point
of view of the varying degrees of fineness the Ether as received
by man is perfect and free from impediment ; as received by
other creatures it is imperfect and impedes.   Man receiving
it in its perfection, the ethical principle permeates it completely
and without impediment ; while in the case of other creatures,
in which it is imperfect, the ethical principle is impeded
and unintelligent." [3]

There is a striking similarity between the idea thus presented
to us and Bergson's theory of the *élan vital*.   To quote one
of his expositors : " We have the creative life-force and the
dying matter upon which it acts.   The law of the dissipation
of energy tells us that matter is ever sliding down the slope
of life towards inertia, decay and death.   The life-force
is pushing up the slope, interrupting its downward impetus,
moulding it into increasing adaptation to environment.
Thus matter is at once a hindrance and a stimulus.   The
forward push of the *élan vital* is beset with resistance, failure,

[1] Ibid., bk. xlii, f. 30 (*P.H.N.*, p. 66).
[2] Ibid., f. 16 (*P.H.N.*, p. 37).
[3] Ibid., f. 31 (*P.H.N.*, p. 67).

deviations, reversions. It drives its way through many a mass of resistance and is checked, now sooner, now later. Here it can go no further, and the end of the line is called vegetism. There it bores deeper and the terminus is instinct. In one instance only it has tunnelled its way through matter and come out at the other end as consciousness." [1] In Chu Hsi's doctrine the important thing to note is that from the point of view of Law the variation is a variation in manifestation only, or rather in the degree in which the Ether is permeated, the difference in the degree of the latter's permeation being due to the difference in the degree of its own density. Law, the Supreme Ultimate, is present, and wholly present, in every individual thing.[2] " Seeing that the physical element differs in the degree of its opacity and grossness," it is asked, " does the Nature as conferred by the Decree of Heaven differ in the degree of its completeness ? " " No," is the answer, " there is no difference in the degree of its completeness. It is like the light of the sun or moon. In open spaces it is seen in its entirety, but under a mat-shed it is hidden and obstructed so that some of it is visible and some not. The opacity and grossness belong to the Ether and result in the Nature being hidden and obstructed as if by a mat-shed. In man, however, this obstruction is capable of being completely penetrated by the ethical principle ; whereas in birds and animals, though they still possess this Nature, it is nevertheless restricted by the corporeal element, which creates an impenetrable barrier." [3]

[1] *Eucken and Bergson*, by E. Hermann, pp. 159–60.

[2] 全 書, bk. xlii, f. 27 (*P.H.N.*, p. 60).

[3] Ibid., f. 27 (*P.H.N.*, pp. 60–1).

That the ethical principles which exist in man are to be found in the differing ranks of creation's hierarchy is shown by various illustrations from the realm of Nature. Before referring to these it will be well to recall the attention of the reader to the theory of the Five Agents as explained in Chapter VI. It was there shown that the Five Agents are the physical embodiment of those five ethical principles which constitute the moral order of the universe and man's essential nature. Each Agent corresponds to, and is the embodiment of, one particular principle. Thus Wood corresponds to Love, Metal to Righteousness, and so on. A very pertinent question, in the light of this theory, was asked with reference to man and the universe. "Does man," said the questioner, "embody the Five Agents while other beings receive only one? Does man, for example, receive all these Agents, and therefore all the five ethical principles, while certain species receive Wood only, and therefore exhibit only the virtue of Love?" The whole discussion shows that this was a problem which, as much perhaps as any other, perplexed the student of that time. The answer, however, is clear and categorical. All beings possess all the Five Agents, the difference being that the lower animals receive them more or less partially.[1] This being the case with the Five Agents it follows that the ethical principles, of which they are the physical embodiment, are all possessed by all beings, though differing in the degree of their manifestation.

It is the partial and imperfect character of the manifestation of these nature-principles in the lower animals which appears to have been most apparent to Chu Hsi's questioners. But

[1] Ibid., f. 25 (*P.H.N.*, p. 54).

Chu Hsi insists that they are there, and adduces many instances to establish his point. For example, the affection between parent and offspring in tigers and wolves, and the relation between sovereign and subject in ants and bees, he maintains, show that the same Law is present though partial and warped.[1] Even plant life shows by its sensitiveness to injury that it is akin to ourselves, as Chou Tzŭ felt when he refrained from clearing the grass from the front of his window because it manifested the same shrinking from death as he himself possessed.[2]

Asked whether inanimate things possess the Nature, Chu Hsi's answer was that in the universe there is not a single thing without the Nature. As he walked up some steps he said : " The bricks of these steps have the law of bricks." Sitting down he said : " A bamboo chair has the law of the bamboo chair." [3] This may not appear to us very conclusive as showing the presence of ethical principles in these things. Neither did it to some of the Philosopher's hearers ; for when, using the illustration of a pen, he said : " As soon as the pen exists Law is inherent in it," he was asked, " How can a pen possess Love and Righteousness ? " Nor does the answer to the conundrum thus propounded seem altogether satisfactory. " In small things like this," he said, " there is no need for such distinctions as that between Love and Righteousness." [4] We must not miss Chu Hsi's point, however, which is that there is not a single thing in existence

---

[1] Ibid., f. 8 (*P.H.N.*, p. 20).
[2] Ibid., f. 31 (*P.H.N.*, p. 68).
[3] Ibid., f. 29 (*P.H.N.*, pp. 64–5).
[4] Ibid., f. 30 (*P.H.N.*, p. 65).

without Law, and that this Law is ethical, the degree in which its ethical nature is apparent varying according to the nature of the thing in which it is embodied. Some, indeed, put forward the contention that withered things have only the physical nature and do not possess the original nature. But Chu Hsi would have none of it. " If it were really so," he says, " other creatures would have only one nature, while men would have two ! " [1] So tenaciously does he hold to the doctrine that the nature in man and the universe is one.

> Many a thrill
> Of kinship, I confess to, with the powers
> Called Nature : animate, inanimate,
> In parts or in the whole, there's something there
> Man-like that somehow meets the man in me.

But that is not all. Though Chu Hsi holds thus tenaciously to the doctrine of the unity of the Nature, he recognizes not less clearly the great gulf between man and his fellow-creatures. " Occasionally, indeed," he says, " affection between parent and offspring and the bond between sovereign and minister exist in some degree, and are not eclipsed ; but in the Love that masters self and returns to right principle, in the Righteousness that loves good and hates evil, there are heights which to them (the lower animals) are impossible of attainment." [2] To account for this great gap not only does he tell us, as we have seen, that man receives Law in its perfection and unimpeded, while other creatures receive it partially and with impediment ; [3] he goes further, and says

[1] Ibid., f. 33 (*P.H.N.*, p. 71).
[2] Ibid., f. 32 (*P.H.N.*, p. 70).
[3] Ibid., f. 28 (*P.H.N.*, p. 62).

that man, in receiving Law thus perfectly and unimpeded, possesses its four component ethical principles each in their perfection and all in harmony and mutual poise. In other words, that which differentiates man from the brute is his possession of the MEAN or EQUILIBRIUM, that perfect balance of the elements in the constitution of his Nature of which Tzŭ Ssŭ teaches in his famous classic the *Doctrine of the Mean*.

To sum up in Chu Hsi's own words : " It is not the case," he says, " that Man, as the being possessed of the highest intellect, stands alone in the universe. His mind is also the mind of birds and beasts, of grass and trees. MAN, HOWEVER, IS BORN ENDOWED WITH THE MEAN, the attribute of Heaven and Earth." [1]

DESTINY

Somewhat related to the problem of the differences between species is that of the differences in men's physical lot. Some are rich and powerful, others are poor and of lowly birth ; some are long-lived while others are prematurely cut off. There is, moreover, the problem of the prosperity of wicked men while the virtuous are poor and despised. These differences are also accounted for by the differences in the Ether with which men are endowed, and this endowment differing in different individuals is termed " Ming ", or " Decree ".

The word " Ming " has two meanings which must be carefully distinguished the one from the other. In the one case the word refers to the Divine Immanence, the all-pervading creative will of Heaven ; and in the other case it

[1] Ibid., f. 27 (*P.H.N.*, p. 61).

refers to what we may term Destiny, the physical lot of men as decreed for them by the Divine will. The distinction is not simply in the application of the word, however, but in its content also. It corresponds to the distinction between the two senses in which the word Nature is used—the Essential Nature and the Physical Nature; as Divine Immanence " Ming " is purely Law; as determining human destiny it includes Ether as well as Law. Of this important distinction a partially inaccurate statement was submitted by one of Chu Hsi's questioners and corrected by the Philosopher. " The Decree is that which Heaven imparts to the creature," says the questioner, " and the Nature is that which is received by the creature from Heaven, but the Nature and the Decree have each two applications. From the point of view of Law, Heaven decrees it to inhere in the creature, and therefore it is called the Decree; while the creature receives it from Heaven, and so it is called the Nature. From the point of view of the Ether, Heaven decrees it to inhere in the creature, and therefore this, too, is called the Decree; and, as the creature receives the Ether from Heaven, it is also called the Nature." To this the answer given is that the Ether cannot be called the Nature or the Decree, all that you can say is that the Nature and Decree exist by reason of it. Therefore, when the Nature of heaven and earth is spoken of, it is Law only that is referred to; when the Physical Nature is spoken of, Law and Ether are referred to in combination. But the Ether alone can never be regarded either as the Nature or the Decree.[1]

---

[1] Ibid., f. 4 (*P.H.N.*, pp. 12–13).

As we have seen, the Ether thus " decreed " and imparted differs in its quality in different individuals ; and to this the differences in destiny as well as character are due. " Those in whom the endowment is clear and translucent," we are told, " are eminent and refined ; those in whom it is simple and generous are gentle and genial ; those in whom it is clear and elevated are honourable ; those in whom it is abundant and generous are rich ; those in whom it is enduring and extended are long-lived ; those in whom it is feeble and deteriorating, attenuated and turbid, are the foolish and degenerate, the poor, the mean, and the short-lived." [1]

It is obvious that, according to this theory, a man may be rich in his ethical endowment, and poor in his physical lot, as in the case of Confucius, who, on the one hand, " was endowed with the clear and translucent ether, and was therefore a sage ; while, on the other hand, his endowment was low and attenuated, and therefore his lot was one of poverty and lowliness ; " [2] whereas, in the case of Yao and Shun, the Ether was received in its perfection in both respects ; with the result that not only were they morally perfect, but they also filled the high position of Emperor.[3]

A fatalistic application of such a doctrine was not only possible but inevitable. By some it was developed to such a degree that Chu Hsi's protest was called forth. Coupled with Shao Yung's theory of Numbers it became a system of fortune telling. But Chu Hsi maintained that the doctrine has its legitimate use, and that the Decree with regard to

[1] Ibid., bk. xliii, ff. 27–8 (*P.H.N.*, p. 133).

[2] Ibid., f. 29 (*P.H.N.*, p. 136).

[3] Ibid., f. 32 (*P.H.N.*, pp. 140–1).

man's Destiny rightly regarded is a stimulus in the path of virtue. From it men will learn that "wealth, honour, and fame are not to be obtained by coveting them ; nor poverty, lowliness, and calamity to be avoided by man's skill. They will therefore take the straight path and follow destiny and their own virtuous resolves ".[1]   Quoting Mencius, he says : " When neither premature death nor long life causes a man to hesitate, but cultivating his personal character he awaits them whatever the issue may be—this is the way in which he established his Destiny." [2]   On the other hand, as Mencius again teaches, a man who rightly interprets Destiny will not with impious presumption invite calamity. He will receive the Decree submissively in its true meaning and not stand beneath a precipitous wall.[3]

The Problem of Evil

" The Nature of all men is good, and yet there are those who are good from their birth and those who are evil from their birth." [4]   Here is the great problem which the philosophers of the Sung School set themselves to solve. Given the perfection of man's nature, how are we to explain the existence of evil ?   Again, the solution of the problem is found in the inequality of the material endowment.[5]

From the very moment of birth, with the rare exception of the sages, the nature of Man is tainted by the admixture of the physical. As Ch'êng Hao expresses it in paradoxical form,

[1] Ibid., ff. 35–6 (*P.H.N.*, p. 149).
[2] Ibid., f. 36 (*P.H.N.*, p. 150).
[3] Ibid., f. 33 (*P.H.N.*, p. 144).
[4] Ibid., f. 4 (*P.H.N.*, p. 85).
[5] Ibid.

" The moment you use the term Nature, you are speaking of what is no longer the Nature." Like the mountain stream which, from the moment it leaves the spring to which it owes its rise, becomes muddied by the channel through which it flows, so the Nature of man, from the moment it has come to be the Nature—that is, from the moment that Law has become individualized in the new-born man—has become tainted by the very medium of its individuation, and so ceased to be that absolutely pure Nature of which Mencius said : " It is good." This, indeed, requires qualification, for it is a tenet of the School that the essential Nature is still what constitutes man's Nature. Ch'êng Hao loved paradox and for that reason was apt to be unguarded in his statements ; and, though perhaps by his very boldness he contributed most to the solution of the problems which perplexed his contemporaries, Chu Hsi was called upon to solve more difficulties raised by his sayings than by those of anyone else. But the meaning of the statement quoted is made sufficiently clear by Ch'êng Hao's own explanation in the same context. The Nature, of which it is said " It is good ", he says, is like water flowing downwards, and it is all water. Though in some streams it flows even to the sea itself without pollution, while in others it becomes defiled within but a short distance from its source, and in others again it is not till far on in its course that it becomes muddied in its flow ; still, whether clear or turbid, the water is one ; it is the channel which makes the difference in the different streams. Even when the stream is muddy the water IN ITSELF IS CLEAR. That is, the Nature, though conditioned by the physical element, remains in itself pure. In the simile of the flow to the sea without defilement the reference is to the saints who from their youth up are perfectly good ; the stream which before it has proceeded far on its way has already become turbid is like one who is evil from his youth ; whilst the stream which becomes turbid after it has proceeded some distance in its course is like a man fully grown who " has lost his child-heart ". [1]

Moral differences in men, therefore, are accounted for in part by inequalities in their physical endowment. Some of those inequalities are due to the unequal proportions in which the Five Agents are imparted to the subject. " There are those," for instance, " in whose endowment the ligneous ether predominates, and in them the feeling of solicitude is constantly uppermost, while the manifestation of conscientious-ness, the courteous spirit, and moral insight is impeded . . . It is only when the Two Modes unite all the virtues and the five nature-principles are all complete that you have the due MEAN and the perfect uprightness of the sage." [2] " If my nature be good, what is there to prevent my being one of the holy and wise men ? Nothing but the etherial endowment. For example, when a man's etherial endowment has excess of strength he is tyrannical, when it is gentle to excess he is weak." [3] But there are inequalities also in the character of the Ether itself. It may be clear or turbid, translucent or opaque, pure or mixed, true or distorted, perfect or defective, all of which affect its permeability by Law. When the Ether is received, " if in respect of its clearness and translucence there is neither

[1] Ibid., f. 25 (*P.H.N.*, pp. 128–9).
[2] Ibid., f. 8 (*P.H.N.*, p. 92).
[3] Ibid., f. 5 (*P.H.N.*, p. 86).

obscurity nor obstruction, Law flows forth freely ; if there be obscurity and obstruction but in lesser degree, then in its outflow Divine Law is victor ; if there be obscurity and obstruction in greater degree selfish desire obtains the victory. Thus we see that the original nature is invariably good . . . but it is obstructed by the opacity and grossness of the physical element." [1] It is like the rays of the sun or moon which are obstructed by the opacity and density of the clouds and mist. [2] " When the ether with which the individual is endowed is clear and translucent there is freedom from the entanglement of creaturely desire, and we have the saint. When the ether with which the individual is endowed is clear and translucent, but neither pure nor perfect, some entanglement of creaturely desire is unavoidable, but it can be overcome and got rid of, and then we have the wise man. When the ether with which the individual is endowed is blurred and turbid, there is the beclouding by creaturely desire to such an extent that it cannot be shaken off, and we have the foolish and degenerate. All this is the action of the etherial endowment and creaturely desire, but the goodness of the Nature itself does not vary. The Nature received by Yao and Shun at their birth was the same as that of others, but because of the clearness and translucence of their etherial endowment there was no beclouding by creaturely desire." [3]

To charge moral evil upon the physical endowment, however, is obviously not the whole account of the matter. If this explanation stood alone it would manifestly involve a

[1] Ibid., f. 3 (*P.H.N.*, p. 82).

[2] Ibid., f. 9 (*P.H.N.*, p. 94).

[3] Ibid., f. 20 (*P.H.N.*, p. 117).

negation of moral responsibility which was the very thing against which Chu Hsi was contending. Two principles are maintained by Chu Hsi and his school which are complementary to, and, indeed, must be regarded as an essential part of, their doctrine of the Physical Nature. The first is that it is man's duty to overcome the impurity of his physical endowment. And the second is that the original impurity of the physical endowment is accentuated by man's own self-indulgence. "The means by which we all may day by day banish human desire and return to Divine Law lie within our reach and to use them is our duty."[1] "Men who excuse themselves by saying that their etherial endowment is bad, and so do not persevere, will fail; while those who pay no regard to the injury possible from it, but go blindly on in their heedless course, will also fail. The one thing we must realize is that we must use our earnest effort and master it, out of its excesses, and restore the MEAN."[2]

The failure, therefore, to overcome the physical nature, and the positive indulgence in the selfish desires which spring from it, are the two factors which, in conjunction with the original impurity, are held to account for moral evil. There are various ways in which this failure is accounted for in detail. To begin with, Chu Hsi fully endorses and expands the saying of Confucius, "Men in their nature are nearly alike, by practice they grow to be wide apart"; on which the Philosopher comments: "What is here termed the Nature includes the physical element, in which, indeed, men do differ in respect of good and evil, but at the very outset

[1] Ibid., f. 20 (*P.H.N.*, p. 118).
[2] Ibid., f. 5 (*P.H.N.*, p. 86).

none differ greatly from another : those who are trained in goodness become good, and in evil, evil ; hence it is in the training that the differentiation begins." [1]

Another cause of evil is the lapse into desire through lack of watchfulness, by which it is possible even for the saint to fall. " Are those in whom the ether is pure," asked one, " therefore free from creaturely desire ? " " That cannot be asserted," was the reply, " the desire of taste and the desire for musical sounds are common to all. Even though the ether with which he is endowed be clear the man will drift into desire at the least relaxation of watchfulness and self-control." [2]

And, finally, evil proceeds from excess or shortcoming. Evil is a disturbance of the MEAN or the perfect equilibrium of the principles of our nature. If there be an inequality of these principles in the original endowment, evil results ; and, similarly, if through man's own act there is excessive or insufficient development of them, evil follows. " We do not know whence comes this human desire," said one of Chu Hsi's disciples. " It is in the deviation in the flow of Divine Law that human desire originates," was the reply. " When Ch'êng Tzŭ says ' Good and evil are both Divine Law ', what he calls evil is not evil originally, but it comes to be such by excess or by shortcoming." [3] But when all is said that can be said as to man's duty to overcome the flesh, and without retracting one word as to human responsibility, so true to the facts of experience is our philosopher that, joining hands

---

[1] See *Analects of Confucius*, by W. E. Soothill, p. 812.

[2] 全 書, bk. xliii, f. 14 (*P.H.N.*, pp. 106–7).

[3] Ibid., bk. xlii, f. 14 (*P.H.N.*, p. 35).

with the great Apostle himself, he confesses, " Though my nature is good, when I would act in accordance with it I fail, and find that it has been made captive by human desire." [1]

From what has been said it will be apparent that for the Sung philosophers, though Law is the ultimate element in the universe, and Matter is subject to its direction and control, Law itself in its conjunction with Matter is nevertheless subject to a certain measure of limitation. " Although Ether is produced by Law, nevertheless, having been produced, Law cannot control it." [2] Matter is strong while Law is weak, much as a faithless magistrate because of his proximity to the people may defeat the gracious intentions of his sovereign. Or as, when a graceless son refuses to follow the footsteps of his father, the father is unable to compel him.[3] And yet this limitation of Law must not be interpreted as meaning that Law and Matter are two opposing principles. In the ultimate, Law is the controlling factor to which is to be attributed the distinction between good and evil ; while the actual good or evil varies according to the degree of purity, and therefore of the permeability, of the Ether.[4]

CONVERSION

The Chinese philosopher, then, confesses with the Christian apostle that the law of God written upon the heart we fail to fulfil ; and the fact that we do so fail is accounted for in part by the flesh in which we are entrammelled, but also by our own self-indulgence for which we ourselves are responsible. If that be the case, surely the supreme question is : How is the

---

[1] Ibid., f. 9 (*P.H.N.*, p. 23).
[3] Ibid.
[2] Ibid., bk. xliii, f. 7 (*P.H.N.*, p. 89).
[4] Ibid., f. 25 (*P.H.N.*, p. 127).

Nature to be restored to its original purity ? What, then, is the Sung School contribution to the solution of this problem ?

" Those whose etherial endowment is clear," says Chu Hsi, " are the saints and sages in whom the Nature is like a pearl lying in clear cold water. Those whose etherial endowment is turbid are the foolish and degenerate, in whose case the Nature is like a pearl lying in muddy water. ' To make manifest illustrious virtue ' is to cleanse the pearl from the muddy water." [1] Two things are indicated in this passage. The Nature, though obscured and in a sense defiled by the contamination of moral evil, still remains incorrupt and incorruptible ; and, though hidden beneath the filthiness of sinful flesh, it is recoverable in all its original purity. Lying at the bottom of the slimy pool the lost pearl is still a pearl unsullied in its beauty, and may yet be cleansed from its surrounding filth, when its " illustrious virtue " will shine forth once again with undimmed lustre. The illustration is not intended to suggest that the processes of recovery and cleansing are in any sense easy ; the contrary, indeed, is the manifest teaching of our philosopher. The point of the simile lies in the incorruptible purity of the pearl, and in the fact that it can be recovered and cleansed. Herein, according to Chu Hsi, is man's hope ; the possibility of purifying the beclouded and turbid stream is due to the fact of its original purity.[2] Or, to refer again to the figure of the mirror which was originally bright and clear, but because of the dust has become blurred ; " if you wipe away the dust you will find the

---

[1] Ibid., f. 7 (*P.H.N.*, p. 91).
[2] Ibid., f. 13 (*P.H.N.*, p. 104).

brightness and clearness still there." [1] But so far from the process being easy, it is only when " a man will courageously and fiercely press forward " that he will find the inequality of the etherial endowment disappear, and his task be accomplished.[2] So imperative is this work of transforming and converting the physical element that the earnest seeker will strain every nerve to achieve success. " If another succeeds by one effort the noble man will use a hundred efforts. If another succeeds by ten efforts he will use a thousand." [3] The laboriousness and almost hopelessness of the task in the case of the lowest and most degenerate is suggested by another illustration given by the Philosopher. " In earlier times," he tells us, " it was the custom for people to fill their vessels with water at the Hui Hill Well and carry them into the city. If, after a while, the water became foul the city people had a way of cleansing it. They filled a bamboo pipe with sand and stones, and poured water on them, letting it run through. By doing this several times, the water would gradually be restored to its original purity." [4]

Leaving the language of metaphor and coming to the nature of the process, we find that it is twofold. There is first the preservation of the essential nature as imparted to us, and next there is the conversion of the physical element. In expounding the difference between man and the brute the Philosopher said, " The passage, ' The great God has conferred on the people below a moral sense,' and, in the Odes, ' The

[1] Ibid., bk. xlvii, f. 12 (*P.H.N.*, p. 332).
[2] Ibid., bk. xliii, f. 5 (*P.H.N.*, p. 86).
[3] Ibid.,f. 2 (*P.H.N.*, p. 82).
[4] Ibid., f. 13 (*P.H.N.*, p. 104).

people possess this normal principle of good,' both represent
the difference. The saying, ' The masses of the people cast
it away, while the noble man preserves it,' means that we
must preserve this difference." [1] But, says our philosopher,
the preservation of this " normal principle of good " must be
supplemented—and indeed only thus can it be securely
preserved—by that which is complementary to it, the conversion of the physical nature. This physical nature must
be reversed : then only will the Divinely given nature abide.[2]
" Form implies the psychical Nature," said Hêng Ch'ü ; he
who succeeds in reversing his physical nature will preserve
the nature of heaven and earth.[3]

If it be asked by what method this conversion is to be
achieved, the answer is : by self-culture. " The object of
self-culture is to transform the etherial endowment," a task
" exceedingly difficult to accomplish ".[4] But such self-
culture, it is held, is fully adequate to the task ; for, in
comparison with the operations of the physical element,
which are limited, the achievements of this ethical culture are
vast.[5] Self-culture again is twofold. On the one hand, the
noble man will not recognize the physical nature to be his
Nature.[6] To all its enticements he is deaf ; and he does not
allow himself to be deceived into regarding it as his master,
or himself as its slave. And, on the other hand, he will
persistently strive towards the MEAN. The source of evil is in

[1] Ibid., f. 10 (*P.H.N.*, p. 97).
[2] Ibid., f. 3 (*P.H.N.*, p. 79).
[3] Ibid., f. 6 (*P.H.N.*, p. 88).
[4] Ibid., f. 5 (*P.H.N.*, p. 86).
[5] Ibid. (*P.H.N.*, p. 87).
[6] Ibid., ff. 3, 6 (*P.H.N.*, pp. 83, 88).

the disturbance of the equilibrium in the principles of his nature ; the objective, therefore, in the self-culture of the earnest man is to restore the equilibrium. Every virtue must be balanced and so corrected by its opposite, affability must be balanced by dignity, mildness by firmness, and so on with all the nine virtues enumerated by Kao Yao.[1] In this way the physical element will be transformed.[2] Therefore " men should not fail to apply themselves to the work of purification. It is only when by self-culture a man overcomes the etherial element that he knows that this Nature is all-comprehensive and has not perished ! " [3]

The Sung doctrine of the Physical Nature has not inaptly been compared with St. Paul's doctrine of the Flesh. The similarity between the two is striking, mainly in the struggle between the higher and lower natures which both set forth. But the contrast is equally striking. The note struck by the Sung philosophers is very different, on the one hand, from that of the Apostle's cry, " Who shall deliver me from this body of death ? " or, on the other hand, from that of his pæan of triumph : " Thanks be to God which giveth us the victory through our Lord Jesus Christ ! " It is true that the inadequacy of man's own unaided wisdom is recognized : that the means whereby victory is to be achieved is the Divine principle within reinforced by the example of the sages.[4] But apart from this there is no suggestion in Chu Hsi's philosophy of redemption from without, or, indeed, of the need

---

[1] *Shu Ching*, p. 71.
[2] 全 書, bk. xliii, f. 2 (*P.H.N.*, p. 77).
[3] Ibid., f. 26 (*P.H.N.*, p. 129).
[4] Ibid., f. 26 (*P.H.N.*, p. 130).

of it. The helping hand of that Divine Being who implanted in man His own Nature is not called upon to assist in the recovery of the lost pearl. "When men have sought the conversion of the physical element in their constitution," he says, "their success in that conversion and their return to their original nature are not imparted from without." [1] Conversion is wholly from within. Man holds within himself all that is needed for his own redemption. Such is the teaching of Chu Hsi and his Masters.

[1] Ibid., ff. 14-16 (*P.H.N.*, p. 107).

CHAPTER X

MIND

Chu Hsi's doctrine of mind, it must be confessed, is not easy to follow. It is perhaps the least clear of all the doctrines which make up his philosophical system. The difficulty, no doubt, is partly due to the fact that here, as in his theory of the universe, his standpoint throughout is solely that of the ethical. He is not concerned with the question "What is mind?" as a problem which in itself invites discussion, but only in so far as it enables the student of ethics to discover how the mind may be maintained in its original purity, or how, if its purity has been lost, it may be restored. There is therefore no separate and direct discussion of what constitutes mind. What definition we have is incidental and fragmentary. It is necessary for our purpose, however, that we arrive at some clear idea of Chu Hsi's conception both of what mind is in itself, and of its relation subjectively to the ego, and objectively to the external world.

One clue at least we have, of a negative sort, in the fact referred to above. Not only is the Philosopher's treatment of mind from the standpoint of practical ethics, but, in his theory of the universe, the ultimate element—the foundation of all things—is also regarded from the moral point of view rather than from that of intelligence. We must rid ourselves, therefore, of any expectation of a discussion of the antithesis between mind and matter so familiar to the Western student.

We must remember, too, that, while to the Indian philosopher Intelligence is what fastens itself upon the imagination as the great source from which all things spring, to the purely Chinese philosopher—as distinct from those who have been affected by Buddhist and therefore foreign influences—it is Goodness and not Intelligence which first and last presents itself to his mind as the Great Source. " God is Law," he says ; that is, God is moral perfection. But so far is he from regarding Intelligence as fundamental that he does not seem to lay stress even on the consideration that Goodness necessarily includes Intelligence.

The fundamental element in human nature, as in the universe, is Law. What then is Mind ? What is its relation to the Nature ? To man's own body ? And to the external world ? Chu Hsi's answers to these questions, in addition to certain allied ethical questions of a practical nature, are the main subjects of our inquiry in this chapter.

WHAT IS MIND ?

The first question then which presents itself for consideration is : What is Mind ? In answer, we are told incidentally that mind is consciousness,[1] and also that mind is that which has consciousness.[2] But neither of these statements carries us very far. What is consciousness ? Is it identical with the mind-substance or is it a function of mind ? What is the mind-substance, if indeed it is substance and not simply a function or relation ? There are two isolated statements which though they stand alone, nevertheless furnish the key to

---

[1] 全 書, bk. xliv, f. 2 (*P.H.N.*, p. 159).
[2] Ibid., f. 11 (*P.H.N.*, p. 177).

Chu Hsi's answer to such questions. The first is: "Its substance is termed Flux"; [1] and the second is: "Mind is the Ether in its purity and brightness." [2] The first explains more particularly the relation of mind to the nature and the feelings, and the second its relation to the body.

In the first of these statements the word translated "Flux" is *Yi* (易). It is the word which gives its title to the *Yi Ching*, or *Canon of Changes*, and literally means "change" or "transformation". As Legge points out in the Introduction to his translation of that word, the character *Yi* (易) is composed of 日 "the sun", placed over 勿, a form of the old 𝕯 (= 月) "the moon". [3] "As the sun gives place to the moon, and the moon to the sun, so," Dr. Legge explains, "is change always proceeding in the phenomena of nature and the experiences of society." [4] In the classic itself a clear and explicit definition of the word is given: "Production and reproduction are what is called 'change'." [5] Legge's explanation of this is: "In nature there is no vacuum. When anything is displaced, what displaces it takes the empty room." [6] On this interpretation of the original text, which no doubt is the correct one, the word *yi*, as applied to mind, would refer to that characteristic phenomenon of consciousness which is emphasized by all psychologists,

[1] Ibid., f. 1 (*P.H.N.*, p. 157).

[2] Ibid., f. 2 (*P.H.N.*, p. 159).

[3] Suzuki gives an alternative explanation of this ideograph as having "primarily represented the form of a chameleon", from whom we get the meaning "change". *Early Chinese Philosophy*, p. 159.

[4] *Yi Ching*, p. 38.

[5] 生 生 之 謂 易; see ibid., p. 356.

[6] Ibid., p. 39.

namely CHANGE. " Consciousness is a continuum," but the " continuum " consists of a succession of states of consciousness. As Confucius, standing by a stream, said of the nature—of which mind is the manifesting vehicle—" It passes on just like this, not ceasing day or night," [1] so of the mind itself, we may say, states of consciousness follow one upon the other in an unbroken flux. A Chinese gloss on the definition just cited from the *Yi* gives another interpretation of *yi* : the phrase " production and reproduction " is referred, not to the transformations of the visible cosmos, but to the mutual production of the two modes of the Ether, the *yin* and the *yang* ; the *yin* produces the *yang*, and again the *yang* produces the *yin* in endless succession.[2] In the *Li Ch'i* a statement by Chu Hsi suggests a combination of both these interpretations. " In the universe," he says, " there are only two modes of being, movement and rest, which succeed each other in an unending circle. This is what is called *yi* (易)." [3] Again, in his commentary on the *T'ung Shu* he explains *yi* as " alternation and succession ", referring to the alternation of the *yin* and the *yang*.[4] Mind, therefore, is Flux, not only

---

[1] *Analects*, ix, xvi (p. 86). N.B.—Legge's note cites Chu Hsi as applying this saying to the course of nature (i.e. the phenomena of the universe) ; but in the *Philosophy of Human Nature* Chu Hsi specifically applies it to the nature of man (全 書, bk. xlii, f. 13 ; *P.H.N.*, p. 30). The two statements, of course, are not inconsistent.

[2] This interpretation has a still closer connexion with the composition of the character, because the sun and moon are the most realistic representations of the *yang* and the *yin*, so that the former is often termed the *T'ai Yang* (太 陽), or Great Light, and the latter the *T'ai Yin* (太 陰), or Great Shadow.

[3] 全 書, bk. xlix, f. 16.

[4] 精 義, pt. i, f. 19.

in the sense intimated above, but also as the alternation of the two modes of the Ether, the *yin* and the *yang*.[1]

The above definition, thus understood, gives us the clue to the relation of Mind to the Nature and the Feelings, and explains why the whole of the first section of Book IV in the *Philosophy of Human Nature* is devoted to this aspect of the subject. On the one hand we have the Nature, which is purely Law, and on the other hand we have the four feelings which are Law and Ether combined. Between them is mind as the connecting link. Just as Law, the Supreme Ultimate, is inherent in the Two Modes as its manifesting vehicle, so the Nature is inherent in mind; and mind, which also, as we have just seen, is the Ether in its two modes, is its manifesting vehicle.[2] But though Law is inherent in the Two Modes as its organ of manifestation, the manifestation itself is in the Five Agents pervading all phenomena; that is, the Two Modes are the intermediate stage between Law and the Five Agents. Similarly the manifestations of the Nature are in the feelings, but by way of Mind. As expressed by Chang Tsai in a statement frequently quoted by Chu Hsi, " The Mind unites the Nature and the Feelings." [3]

---

[1] 全 書, bk. xlix, f. 16.

[2] This explains the question raised by Chih Tao, recorded on the first page of Book III of the *Philosophy of Human Nature*, as to whether mind is the Supreme Ultimate or indwelt by the Supreme. Ultimate. The Philosopher did not give a direct answer to the question. What he does say means in effect that it is both, but that the one must not be confounded with the other ; just as, in the cosmical relation between the Supreme Ultimate and the Two Modes as its manifesting vehicle, the Supreme Ultimate is the Two Modes and is in the Two Modes, but must not be confounded with them. See p. 137.

[3] 學 案, bk. xviii, f. 14.

The *modus operandi* of this relation may be explained thus : The Mind contains within it the component principles of the Nature. As Shao Tzŭ expresses it : " The Mind is the *enceinte* of the Nature," [1] containing within it the nature-principles, as a city wall contains within it the inhabitants of the city.[2] The Mind is thus a receptacle for the principles which constitute the Nature.[3] It is also the agent by which those principles are set in operation and objectively manifested in the Feelings. To take a concrete case : the principle from which the knowledge of the difference between right and wrong springs is Wisdom—a principle of the Nature. The operation by which we actually regard a particular act as right or wrong is Feeling. The agent which possesses the principle and is conscious of the distinction made is Mind.[4] Thus the Mind is said to be the Nature plus Consciousness.[5] It is the nexus between the immaterial principle and its manifestation in consciousness. A favourite illustration is taken from Ch'êng Tzŭ's writings. " The Mind," he said, " is like the seed-corn : the principle of life contained in it is the Nature ; the putting forth of life on the part of the positive ether is Feeling." [6] In relation to the Nature, then, the Mind is the receptacle of its four component principles, and in relation to the Feelings it is the organ of their manifestation. In other words, the Nature is the seat of consciousness, and the Mind is the organ of consciousness.

---

[1] In the Preface to the *Chi Jang Chi* ; see p. 37.
[2] 全 書, bk. xliv, f. 10 (*P.H.N.*, p. 175).
[3] Ibid., bk. xlv, f. 2 (*P.H.N.*, p. 231).
[4] Ibid., f. 7 (*P.H.N.*, p. 240).
[5] Ibid., f. 4 (*P.H.N.*, p. 235).
[6] Ibid.

This close relation of the Mind to the Nature is expressed in
the statement that " to the Mind the Nature stands in the
relation of substance ",[1] for the mind in itself is without
substance ; the Nature is its substance.[2]   In view of such
intimate relation to the Nature, it is not surprising that the
Mind is spoken of also as life, and the principle of life.[3]
Expounding the word mind the Philosopher said : " One
word will cover it, namely life." [4]   What has been said of the
Mind and the Nature, therefore, in relation to consciousness
may also be said of them in relation to life.   The Nature is
the seat of life and the Mind is the organ of its manifestation,
while the manifestation itself is in the Feelings.

That this relation between the Mind, on the one hand, and
the Nature and the Feelings, on the other, is no novel interpretation, but simply the historical development of the
teachings of the past, is shown by our philosopher both from
the writings of Mencius and from the derivation of the words
themselves.   To take the philological argument first, it is
pointed out that the " mind " radical (忄) [5] enters into the
composition of both hsing (性), the Nature, and ch'ing (情),
feeling.   The word hsing (性), the Nature, suggests the idea
that the nature-principles are inherent in the mind (忄)
from the moment of birth (生).[6]   With regard to the writings
of Mencius, this connexion is illustrated by the Sage's use of

---

[1] Ibid., f. 2 (P.H.N., p. 231).

[2] Ibid., f. 5 (P.H.N., p. 236).

[3] Cf. Chap. VIII, pp. 194 ff.

[4] 全 書, bk. xliv, f. 2 (P.H.N., p. 159).

[5] 忄 is the shortened form of 心 (hsin), the mind.

[6] 全 書, bk. xlv, f. 3 (P.H.N., p. 233).

terms. The four nature-principles, Love, Righteousness, Reverence, and Wisdom, are spoken of by the Sage as having their root in the mind, while among the feelings solicitude and conscientiousness are spoken of as the solicitous mind and the conscientious mind. Chu Hsi, therefore, claims that his doctrine of the relation between the Mind and the Nature, and between Mind and Feeling, while not explicitly stated by Mencius, was, nevertheless, implied in his use of these and related terms.

This inquiry has an important bearing on the question of personality. We have seen that the mind is the nexus between the Nature and the Feelings, or between the immaterial principles of the Nature and their manifestation in consciousness. Expressed differently, this means that mind is the seat of unity in the complex being, man. In the statement of Chang Tsai, which was cited as expressing this nexus : " The mind unites the Nature and the Feelings," the word " unites " (統) also means " rules ". The union is union under one head. In Book xlix of Chu Hsi's works it is also definitely stated that "mind means ruler ", [1] and that "the mind is the agent by which man rules his body ". [2] We have then these two ideas combined : mind is the seat of unity, and mind is the ruler in man's complex being ; and to these must be added a third, mentioned at the beginning of this section : " Mind is consciousness." [3] Man is a conscious being and free, and the organ of his consciousness and freedom is in mind as the seat of unity. What is this but in effect to

[1] Ibid., bk. xlix, f. 23 ; cf. bk. xlii, f. 20 (*P.H.N.*, p. 43).

[2] Ibid., bk. xliv, f. 28 ; cf. f. 21 (*P.H.N.*, p. 209 ; cf. ibid., p. 196).

[3] Ibid., f. 2 (*P.H.N.*, p. 159).

say that mind in man is the seat of personality ? It must be remembered that the Chinese language does not love abstract terms, and there is no word answering precisely to our word personality. But here, surely, is the idea. When Chang Tsai says : " The Mind unites under its headship the Nature and the Feelings," and when Chu Hsi says : " Mind means ruler," both are conveying to us the idea of personality, and of mind as the seat of that personality. This interpretation is supported by the illustration, repeatedly used by the Philosopher, of the relation between the Decree, the Nature, the Feelings, and Mind, in which it is stated that the Decree is like letters patent appointing a man to office, the Nature is the duty pertaining to that office, the Feelings are the performance of that duty, and " mind is the man himself ". [1]

BODY, SOUL, AND SPIRIT

In the second definition referred to above Chu Hsi states that Mind is the Ether in its purity and brightness.[2] As a definition this would more properly have been treated in the preceding section, but its exposition inevitably leads to a consideration of spirit in its relation to the body, and of the mutual relation between the soul, or sentient mind, and spirit, or intellectual mind. It is more convenient, therefore, to consider it in connexion with this part of our subject.

As was shown in Chapter VI, the Primordial Ether, according to this school, divides into the Two Modes ; and of these two modes one pertains to the world of spirit and the other to the

[1] Ibid., bk. xlii, f. 1 (P.H.N., p. 4).
[2] Ibid., bk. xliv, f. 2 (P.H.N., p. 159).

world of matter. Attention was also drawn to the resemblance between this view and that of Spinoza and other Western philosophers, who hold that mind and matter are but two different aspects of an underlying unity. " Given the one supreme principle, Existence," according to Spinoza, "we see its necessary duplicate manifestation, as Mind, under one aspect, and under the other as Matter." [1] Leibnitz, though his system is essentially different from that of Chu Hsi, nevertheless comes near to the Chinese conception of the individual soul when he maintains that " every monad is at once both body and soul, a besouled body, a living machine, a complex of active and passive Forces, and that the active Force is living, spontaneous, planning; while the passive is movable, mechanical, efficient ". [2]

Ether, therefore, is both spiritual and material ; and, conversely, mind and matter are both forms of the Ether— the one the positive and the other the negative mode. According to the definition which was before us in the preceding section, however, Mind is Flux, or the Ether in the alternation of its *two* modes. The explanation of what at first sight might be deemed a discrepancy is that there are two aspects from which Mind is treated by Chu Hsi, each of which is complementary to the other. The Ether which in its purity and brightness is contrasted with the gross and material Ether is itself the Primordial Ether alternating in the Two Modes. Hence, the statement is made that " Mind alone is absolute ", or, more literally, " Mind alone is

[1] Lewes' *History of Philosophy*, ii, 198.
[2] Ibid., p. 280.

without a contradictory." [1] It is in itself the higher synthesis of the two contrasted modes of existence, mind and matter.

It will be recalled that, according to this school, the principle of dualism obtains in each of the Two Modes in infinitely varying gradations; so that we have the positive and negative modes of spirit, and the positive and negative modes of solid matter also. Thus Mind in its two modes is the ruler of the entire personality, and as such enters into both of the two ethers, which become respectively spirit and body: "It is the home of the spirit and the ruler of the body." [2]

Spirit, *shên* (神), is defined in terms similar to those used in the above definition of Mind. "The Ether in its purity and brilliance," says Chu Hsi, "is Spirit," and the Philosopher goes on to say: "Metal, Wood, Water, Fire, and Earth are not Spirit, though that by reason of which they are what they are is Spirit." [3] According to this statement, while Spirit is said to be Ether, it is not Ether as developed in the Five Agents. And yet we found in Chapter VI that there are both Celestial and Terrestrial Agents, corresponding to the spirit portion of the Ether and to solid matter respectively. The truth is that, just as in the case of Mind, so in the case of Spirit, the word is used in two senses. In the one case it is *shên*, spirit, as distinguished from *p'o*, the body: both of which are the outcome of the Five Agents. In this sense *shên* is

[1] 全書, bk. xliv, f. 1 (*P.H.N.*, p. 158).
[2] Ibid., f. 21 (*P.H.N.*, p. 196).
[3] 全書, bk. xlix, f. 4.

the positive ether, and *p'o* the negative. In the other case *shên* is the primordial ether, the organ of the operations of the Divine Being, of which more will be said later.

The terms mind and spirit, then, are both used in two senses. In the one case they are contrasted with matter, as the positive ether in contrast to the negative, and so we have Spinoza's twofold distinction of mind and matter, or spirit and matter. In the other case they are the Ether in its primordial form, the higher synthesis which, for Chu Hsi, is pure spirit or mind.

The word spirit (*shên* 神) occurs in several pairs of terms in which its meaning varies according to the meaning of the term associated with it. Two of these pairs of terms, *shên p'o* (神 魄) and *kuei shên* (鬼 神), are closely related to our subject. In the expression *shên p'o*, *shên* is spirit, or the rational part of man, as contrasted with *p'o*, the body, or physical part of man, and is interchangeable with *hsin* (心), mind.[1] In the expression *kuei shên*, *shên* is spirit, or the intellectual mind, as contrasted with *kuei*, soul, or the sentient mind. This pair of terms has been variously translated: by McClatchie as " gods (神) and demons (鬼) ", by Le Gall as " *âmes* (鬼) *et esprits* (神) ", and by Legge as " *the anima* (鬼) and *animus* (神) ". A further explanation of the terms will make the reason for this difference of rendering apparent.

It was just now stated that the principle of dualism enters

---

[1] Two other expressions synonymous with *shên p'o* (神 魄) are *ch'i p'o* (氣 魄) and *hun p'o* (魂 魄). Of the three expressions, the last named is the one most generally used.

into the different elements of man's being in infinitely varying gradations. Hence, mind not only belongs to the positive ether in contrast to the body, but is itself the ether in its two modes. These two modes are exhibited in *shên* and *kuei*. *Shên* is the positive mode, and, as such, is the expanding principle of mind. It represents the intellectual and spiritual element in man, and is akin to the New Testament concept πνεῦμα. *Kuei* is the negative mode, the contracting principle of mind. It represents the animal or sentient soul, the ψυχή. It is the animating principle of the body, and is also called *p'o* (魄).[1]

On the dissolution of the body at death the expanding *shên*, or spirit, is said to ascend on high, while the contracting *kuei* or soul descends to earth.[2] Thus, in their disembodied condition, *shên* and *kuei* are superior and inferior spiritual beings, and as such are referred to several times in the Classics, notably in the *Doctrine of the Mean*.[3] By an easy transition the terms came to mean, respectively, beneficent spirits whose seat is in heaven, and malevolent demons or ghosts haunting the abodes of men. The superstitious possibilities of such a conception, needless to say, are endless; and the Sung School, resisting its mischievous tendency, gave a more rationalistic interpretation to the terms explaining them as representing the

---

[1] This is the primary meaning of *p'o* (魄). The word *ching* (精) in the expression *ching shên* (精 神) also means the principle of sensation as contrasted with *shên* (神), the intellectual principle. *Ching* emphasizes the functional, *p'o* the physical aspect, while *kuei* (鬼) is more allied to the psychic.

[2] See *Yi Ching*, Introd., p. 45.

[3] Chap. XVI.

operations of creation and transformation in nature, or as the activity of the two modes, which in mind are manifested in intellectual and sentient consciousness respectively. Ch'êng Tzŭ, in consequence of his teaching in this direction, was charged with denying the existence of spiritual beings ; but Chu Hsi defended him from the charge as untrue. These various interpretations explain the different renderings that have been adopted for these terms. McClatchie's " gods and demons " represents the superstitious interpretation, while Legge's " *animus* and *anima* " represents the more rationalistic interpretation. Le Gall's " *âmes et esprits* " is probably more strictly accurate as a translation, and, for that very reason, admits of the double interpretation.

To sum up the results of our inquiry : Mind is a form of the primordial ether, which is the original substance underlying both mind and matter. In contrast to the body it is the pure and refined portion of the ether, the positive mode, active, expanding, independent of gravitation or resistance. But mind itself has its negative and positive modes and thus has a double manifestation in soul and spirit, or as sentient mind and intellectual mind.

BUDDHISM AND THE EXTERNAL WORLD

A problem that can hardly fail to emerge in the development of a doctrine of mind is the mind's relation to the external world. In the case of Chu Hsi this phase of the subject has special prominence in his controversy with Buddhism.

A concise statement of the attitude of Buddhism towards

the problem occurs in Part II of the *Surangama Sutra*. Ananda
and all the great congregation, it is said, after listening to the
abstruse argument unfolded by Buddha Tathagata, " perceived
that each one's Heart [1] was co-extensive with the universe,
seeing clearly the empty character of the universe as plainly
as a leaf or trifling thing in the hand, and that all things in
the universe are all alike merely the excellently bright and
primeval Heart of Bodhi, and that this heart is universally
diffused, and comprehends all things within itself." [2] Thus the
ego and the non-ego alike are manifestations of the universal
mind—" the excellently bright and primeval heart of Bodhi."
There is therefore no objective external world in the ordinary
acceptation of the term ; subject and object are identical,
their individuality being submerged in the universal mind ;
and what we call mind is merely " the false connexions of
external things, and the distinctions of mere shadowy
appearances ". [3]

Of this monistic view of the universe the method of Buddhism was the natural corollary. " The whole world of
sentient creatures," said Buddha, " from the first till now,
have been involved in the nexus of (endless) births and deaths,
from the fact of their ignorance of the ever fixed and true
state of Being (heart), essentially pure, and substantially
glorious." [4] And the only remedy for this evil is knowledge,
a true understanding of what the true mind is. Only when we
know and realize that our true mind is not what is commonly

---

[1] *Hsin* (心), the word which in this work is translated mind.

[2] *A Catena of Buddhist Scriptures from the Chinese*, by S. Beal, p. 343.

[3] Ibid., p. 309.

[4] Ibid., p. 290.

and mistakenly called mind or heart, but the one universal mind, the only real existence—then only shall we regain our true mind and be freed from the " nexus of births and deaths " in which our ignorance has involved us. In the *Surangama Sutra*, again, it is said : " Ananda and all the great congregation, listening to the explanations of Buddha, with rapt attention, began to recognize the fact that from the earliest moment till now they had utterly *overlooked and lost the true Heart* (mind), and mistaken for it the false connexions of external things, and the distinctions of mere shadowy appearances. But now they began to understand, just as a lost child does who suddenly meets with its tender mother ; and so with closed hands they adored Buddha, desiring above all things to hear Tathagata open out and explain the differences between that which is body and that which is mind, the true and false, the empty and the real, and contrasting that which is visible and perishing with that which is invisible and eternal, to cause them to attain to a *clear comprehension* of the true nature (which is the basis of all which is called Mind)." [1]

The Method, therefore, was meditation [2] and mind contemplation,[3] by which we are to illumine the mind and understand our true nature [4]; and its practical application was the meditation trance in which the subject sought oblivion of all phenomena, and even of the *ego* itself. Thus only could the true universal mind be realized. In his admonitions to the Bikshus recorded in the Sutra of *Forty-two*

---

[1] Ibid., p. 309.

[2] *Ch'an* (禪).

[3] 觀 心.

[4] 明 心 見 性.

Sections, Buddha said : " Never tire of self-reflection ; the four constituents (elements) in your body are merely names, and therefore without any personal reality. That which one calls ' Self ' is but a passing guest, and its concerns all like the mirage of the desert." [1]

Chu Hsi, as well as the Buddhists, teaches that the human mind is one with the universal mind ; but the oneness of which he speaks is of a different kind. In a treatise on Mind approved by Chu Hsi, his pupil Ch'ên Ch'un says : " ' The decree of Heaven how profound it is and undying ! ' That by means of which it rules over the production of things is the Mind of Heaven. Man receives the Decree of Heaven and so is born ; and because this, by which Heaven gives me birth, is received by me in its entirety, to be lord of my complete personality, and in its entirety to reside in me, spiritual and intelligent, continuously illuminating and unclouded, living and imperishable—this we call the Mind of Man. Its substance, answering to what are termed the principles of Origin, Beauty, Utility, and Potentiality, is inherent in me as the nature principles—Love, Righteousness, Reverence, and Wisdom. Its operation, answering to what are termed the ethers of Spring, Summer, Autumn, and Winter, is manifested in me as the four feelings, Solicitude, Conscientiousness, Courtesy, and Moral Insight. Therefore, although the substance of the Mind resides in a very minute spot, that which constitutes it the substance is really as great as heaven and earth ; the countless laws of the universe are present in their completeness, and there is not a single thing outside

---

[1] *A Catena of Buddhist Scriptures from the Chinese,* by S. Beal, p. 197.

their scope. Although its operation proceeds from a very minute spot, that which constitutes its operation is really in union with the all-pervading activity of Heaven and Earth ; the countless phenomena of the universe are united by it, and there is not one of its principles which does not operate in them." [1] Later on in the same treatise the writer shows that this unity is because " permeating the whole universe there is but one Law as the ultimate reality, the pivot of creation and transformation, received in all ages alike by men and all other creatures. The Moral Law of Heaven is all-comprehensive, and the law of my mind is all-comprehensive ; the Moral Law of Heaven is limitless, and the law of my mind is limitless ; the Moral Law of Heaven enters into every single thing without exception, and there is not one thing in the universe which is not Divine ; and the Law of my mind also enters into everything without exception, and there is not one thing in the universe which is not my mind . . . To whatever point Law reaches the thought of my mind follows it. If in its greatness it reaches to infinitude, or if it be so fine as to pierce things indescribably minute, the mind penetrates and permeates all. If it reaches back to the most ancient times, or forward ten thousand generations, the mind comprehends all. Whether it be near or distant, a foot or ten thousand miles, it is all alike. Even though it extend to ' establishing order in heaven and earth, and nourishing all things ' it still does not go beyond the fullness of the original mind-substance : it is not something accomplished outside its sphere ".[2]

[1] 全 書, bk. xliv, f. 32 (*P.H.N.*, pp. 217-18).
[2] Ibid., ff. 33-4 (*P.H.N.*, pp. 220-1).

This oneness of mind with the universal mind carries with it a true oneness of the ego with the non-ego, an identity of subject and object, of the internal and external. It is true that Chu Hsi asserts a real difference between them. " You have to divide them and say that this is substance and that is operation before you can say that they have one source. You have to say that this is the phenomenon and that is its principle before you can say that they are inseparable. If they were merely one entity there would be no need to speak of one source and of their being inseparable." [1] But he is not less emphatic in the assertion of unity, the secret of which lies in the Mind. In the Treatise on Mind by Ch'ên Ch'un, and following immediately after the first of the passages just quoted, the writer says : " Herein lies the mystery of the Mind : it unifies activity and repose, the manifest and the hidden, the external and the internal, the end and the beginning, in an unbroken unity." [2] The unity asserted, however, is ethical ; the oneness is the oneness of sympathy. " Let men's desires be pure, and their feelings far-reaching, with no barrier in their all-pervading operations, then they will be continuously in union with the all-pervading operations of Heaven and Earth." [3] " If in all the innumerable threads of life we follow the simplicity of the laws of Heaven, and there is on the part of the Mind an all-round carrying of them into effect, then in its operation it will be one with the principles of Origin, Beauty, Utility, and

---

[1] Ibid., xlvi, f. 11 (*P.H.N.*, pp. 288–9).
[2] Ibid., bk. xliv, f. 32 (*P.H.N.*, p. 218).
[3] Ibid., ff. 34–5 (*P.H.N.*, p. 222).

Potentiality in their pervading activity throughout the universe." [1]

In Western philosophy the theory of Being is intimately related to the theory of knowledge, if, indeed, they are not inseparable; and with Chu Hsi the discussion of the one imperceptibly merges into the discussion of the other. Hence oneness with the external world is explained as " entering into " things in an intellectual and ethical sense. Bergson postulates " as a necessary presupposition of metaphysical knowledge a species of ' intellectual sympathy ' between the knowing mind and the object known; a kind of ' intellectual suscultation ' in which the heart of reality is felt to palpitate; a process of intellectual *dilatation* by which one *places oneself in the object one is studying*". [2] Using almost identically the same terms, Chang Tsai says : " When the mind is enlarged it can enter into everything in the universe. When there is anything into which the mind does not enter it is egoistic. The mind of the man of the world rests within the narrow limits of the senses, and therefore cannot enter into everything in the universe. It is only the sage—who develops his nature to its utmost, and does not allow his mind to be fettered by what he sees and hears—whose mind is large enough to embrace all things, so that under the whole heaven there is not a single thing which he does not look upon as he looks upon himself." [3] When asked the meaning of " entering into things " Chu Hsi

---

[1] Ibid., ff. 35–6 (*P.H.N.*, p. 223).

[2] *A Critical Exposition of Bergson's Philosophy*, by J. Mckellar Stewart, p. 92.

[3] *Chêng Mêng* (大 心 篇).

explained : " It means to import the mind into the phenomenon and to investigate that phenomenon in such a way as to grasp its principle. It is the same meaning as that of the expressions ' investigation of things ' and ' perfection of knowledge '." [1] But the " entering into things " is not a merely intellectual process. " The expression ' enter into ' is like what is spoken of as ' the universal embodiment of love in actions ' and means that the principle of the mind permeates everything just as the blood circulates in the body. If there is a single thing into which it does not enter its permeation is incomplete, and it fails perfectly to embrace all things ; and this is egoism. For selfishness produces separation between the ego and the non-ego, so that they stand opposed the one to the other." [2] And explaining " egoism " in answer to a further question, he said : " When there is selfish thought, obstruction arises between the subject and object. We see only ourselves, and everything external is regarded as having no relation to the self. Such is egoism." [3] As expressed by one of Bergson's exponents, " To understand in the fashion in which one loves—if there be a Soul of the world, a supra-materialistic, psychical element in life, that must be the only fashion of understanding." [4]

Such in brief is Chu Hsi's teaching on the oneness of the individual mind with the universal mind, and of the ego with the external world. At times the language he employs is

---

[1] 全 書, bk. xliv, f. 12 (*P.H.N.*, pp. 180–1).

[2] Ibid. (*P.H.N.*, p. 180).

[3] Ibid., f. 13 (*P.H.N.*, p. 181).

[4] *Eucken and Bergson*, by E. Hermann, p. 152.

similar to that of Buddhism, possibly due to its early influence upon his own thought. He speaks of the mind being so enlarged as to take in the whole universe, so that nothing is but what is regarded as oneself, and the distinction between the Ego and the Non-Ego is submerged. He speaks of the oneness of the individual mind with the universal mind in terms which suggest that there is but the one ALL. Chu Hsi's position, however, differs from that of the Buddhists in two fundamental particulars. In the first place Chu Hsi's philosophy does not obliterate the individual. If the mind enters into everything in the universe, it does not lose itself in the process. If it embraces all things, its own individuality is only intensified thereby. In the second place, this embracing all things, this incarnation of the individual mind in everything that exists is ethical. In fact, for Chu Hsi the second is really a corollary of the first, for if the unity of mind throughout the universe is coexistent with a real individuality, the ground of unity must be ethical rather than metaphysical.

These then are the essential features of the two systems. Buddhism says : There is one mind in the universe, the Buddha mind. We receive it, and it is ours. Our mind, therefore, is a part of the universal mind. But our individuality consists in our entanglement in the mesh of connexions with external things, and what we call our mind, that is, our individual mind, is not our real mind. So, then, our real mind is outside what we call our mind, and the Law of the Universe is to be found outside our hearts. Our business, therefore, is not to develop, but to sink our individuality, to lose our individual mind that we may find our true mind, the universal mind of Buddha. The result is the destruction of the social relations and the cardinal virtues. Chu Hsi, on the other hand, says : There is one mind of the universe, the manifestation of Divine Law. We receive it and it is ours. And because the mind of the universe is ours, the Law of the universe is also ours inherent in our hearts. Our business is to develop our mind to the utmost and bring it into harmony with its source. To do this means that our individuality will be not obliterated, but intensified, and the cardinal virtues perfected.

In all that has preceded we have endeavoured to state as briefly and fairly as possible the teaching of Chu Hsi in contrast to that of the Buddhists, but nothing has been said as to methods of controversy. It is necessary, in a few words, to indicate some of the lines of attack which Chu Hsi adopted. It may be said at once that here, as in the case of the controversy on *Tao*, his appeal is in the main an appeal to common sense. The Buddhist method, he says, is both ineffective in itself, and based on a false philosophy. The position of the Buddhist is that we need only to understand our true mind. " But," Chu Hsi contends, " they them-selves do not know what the mind-substance really is. Although they assert that all laws have their origin in the Mind, they really hold that there is yet another law external to it. Hence there is no room in their philosophy for the Great Source of the universe." [1] That is, they in effect set up two laws of the universe, but how can there be two laws in the ultimate sense ? In the endeavour to understand the true mind the Buddhist method is that of contemplation

----

[1] 全 書, bk. xliv, f. 18 (*P.H.N.*, p. 191).

with " rigid posture and hard discipline ". In this way "they indeed observe and contemplate the mind", he says, "and yet, with it all, we cannot in their company attain to the moral ideal of Yao and Shun, simply because they fail to perceive the Divine Law, and regard the mind alone as Ruler." [1] Not only is the method ethically ineffective, it even destroys the end it seeks. The meditation trance is based upon the idea that " when thought reaches the point at which its stream is cut off, Divine Law is perfectly manifested ". But " true thought is Divine Law ; its continuous flow and operation are nothing else than the manifestation of Divine Law. How can it be that we are to wait till the stream of thought is cut off before Divine Law is manifested ? " [2] Moreover, what is Divine Law ? What but the virtues ? What but the sacred relationships ? " If the Buddhist really apprehends Divine Law, why must he," by his asceticism, " act contrary to and confuse, cut off and destroy all these, beclouding his own mind and losing his true knowledge of himself ? " [3]

Thus Chu Hsi's chief complaint of the Buddhists is that their negation of Mind resulted in the destruction of the essential principles of man's nature. " The presence of the Four Terminals and the Five Cardinal Virtues in man's nature they regard as masking the Nature," and therefore to be cleared out of the way. " The indispensable relationships between father and son, sovereign and minister, husband

[1] Ibid., f. 17 (*P.H.N.*, p. 189).
[2] Ibid., bk. xlvi, f. 18 (*P.H.N.*, p. 301).
[3] Ibid., f. 18 (*P.H.N.*, p. 302).

and wife, senior and junior, they regard as accidental." [1]
The Buddhist negation of mind, therefore, was the chief
point of attack. Chu Hsi asserts that "what is termed
self—so termed in opposition to external things—is a selfish
recognition of self", from which spring selfish desires.[2] The
remedy is the mastery of this self, not the destruction of the
ego. "The Mind has a real existence. It is pure, undivided,
penetrating, and all-pervading in its influence. The perfect
development of the nature and the practice of Moral Law
both proceed from it. You, however," he says to a correspondent, "regard it as vain and would get rid of it," and so
you would destroy the very thing of which you are in search.[3]

In an ironical passage comparing this method with that of
the sages, he says : " The teaching of the sages is, that with
the mind we exhaustively investigate principles, and by
following these principles we determine our attitude to
external things, just as the body uses the arm, and the arm
the hand. Their doctrine is even and clear, their attitude
broad and calm, their principles real, and the practice of
them spontaneous. The teaching of Buddhism, on the other
hand, is that with the mind we are to seek the mind, with
the mind to control the mind, like the mouth gnawing the
mouth, or the eye gazing at itself. Its methods are uncertain
and feverish, its course is dangerous and clogged, its principles are hollow, and its tendency antagonistic to what is
right." [4]

[1] Ibid., f. 7 (*P.H.N.*, p. 280).
[2] Ibid., bk. xliv, f. 23 (*P.H.N.*, p. 201).
[3] Ibid., f. 24 (*P.H.N.*, p. 201).
[4] Ibid., f. 29 (*P.H.N.*, pp. 212–13).

Such is Chu Hsi's answer to Buddhism. To quote a summary of his position in his own words : " The mind is the agent by which man rules his body. It is one and not divided. It is subject and not object. It controls the external world and is not its slave. Therefore, with the mind we contemplate external objects, and so discover the principles of the universe. According to this (the Buddhist) theory, however, and contrariwise, we examine the mind by means of an external object ; that is, in addition to this my mind, I have another mind external to it, by which it is controlled. But is this thing that we call mind one entity or two ? Is it subject, or is it object ? Is it free, or is it the slave of the external ? We do not need to be told in order to see the fallacy of it all." [1]

MIND CULTURE

As was pointed out at the beginning of this chapter, Chu Hsi's standpoint is wholly ethical. He never leaves it. Mind culture therefore fills a large place in his teaching.

In the admonition addressed by the emperor Shun to his successor Yü, the following passage occurs : " The natural mind [2] is unstable, the spiritual mind [3] is but a spark. Be discriminating, be undivided, that you may sincerely hold fast to the Mean." [4] In explanation of the term " natural mind " and " spiritual mind ", Chu Hsi says : " The intellectual powers of the mind when they manifest themselves on the plane of ethical principle, constitute the

---

[1] Ibid., f. 28 (*P.H.N.*, pp. 209–10).
[2] Lit. " mind of man ".
[3] Lit. " mind of *Tao* ".
[4] *Shu Ching*, pp. 61–2.

'spiritual mind'; when they manifest themselves in the region of desire, they constitute the 'natural mind'." [1] The definition does not mean that the natural mind is evil in its origin, it represents the psychic powers which manifest themselves in desire, but the desire may be good or evil or colourless. [2] It is that part of the personality through which man becomes involved in evil, but in the beginning is neither good nor evil. It is unstable. The spiritual mind is the ethical element in mind which cannot be anything but good. Thus, mind, like the nature inherent in it, is originally good, and in regard to one element in its constitution can never be other than good, while in regard to the etherial element it is capable of both good and evil.

Mind culture consists in the effort to preserve this originally good mind, or if it has been lost, to regain it. Mencius quotes Confucius as saying : " Hold it fast, and it is preserved. Let it go, and you lose it. Its outgoing and incoming cannot be defined as to time or place." Chu Hsi applied this exhortation to holding fast the spiritual mind. If in his quest of the good the seeker will exert his strength to this end he will find that his higher nature will be preserved, and its manifestations will be those of Love and Righteousness. [3] If the spiritual mind is thus allowed to rule as the predominant element in the personality, the natural mind, or the element of desire, will be transformed into the spiritual mind. [4] But while there is the great man who " does not lose his child

---

[1] 全 書, bk. xliv, f. 20 (P.H.N., p. 194).

[2] Cf. 遺 書, pt. xviii, f. 24.

[3] Mencius, p. 285 and note.

[4] 全 書, bk. xliv, ff. 27–8 (P.H.N., p. 209).

heart ", [1] the mass of men lose it early in their career. For these the urgent necessity is to regain it. Lamentable indeed is the case of the man who loses this mind and does not seek it again.[2]

The processes of mind culture by which the " lost mind " is regained are given in the treatise on the Buddhist method of mind contemplation. [3] They are :   (1) To be discriminating and single, and thus " to fasten upon what is right and discern all that diverges from it ", to " discard everything that is opposed to it and restore all that is in accord with it ". (2) To " hold fast " the true mind, not by sitting in rigid posture and preserving what is thus a useless intelligence, but by " not allowing the doings of the day to fetter and destroy the natural goodness of the virtuous mind ".   (3) To " develop the mind to the utmost " by the investigation of phenomena, by the exhaustive study of the laws of the universe, and by a wide and far-reaching penetration ; " and so to have that by means of which we may develop to their utmost extent the principles inherent in the mind."

Such mind culture as is here described results in what Ch'êng Tzǔ called the " Steadfast Nature ".   " The expression ' Steadfast Nature '," Chu Hsi tells us, " means the attainment of the original quality of the nature through the completed work of preservation and nurture." [4] The term originated with Chang Tsai,[5] and became the text of a treatise by

---

[1] *Mencius,* p. 198.

[2] Ibid., p. 290.

[3] 全 書, bk. xliv, f. 28 ff. (*P.H.N.,* p. 209 ff.).

[4] Ibid., f. 15 (*P.H.N.,* p. 256).

[5] Ibid., p. 245, n. 1; cf. 明 道 文 集, pt. iii, ff. 1-3.

Ch'êng Ming Tao. The treatise itself is very short, extending over hardly more than two pages, but in its turn becomes the text for discussions occupying a whole section in Book IV of Chu Hsi's work on Human Nature. Its most important teaching is in substance expressed in the assertion that in the studies of the noble-minded there is no higher attainment than with broadness of mind to be actuated by a high altruism, and to respond naturally and fittingly to external things as they present themselves. This is the true characteristic of the Steadfast Nature, the real objective of that mind culture which fills so large a place in the Sung system of philosophy.

CHAPTER XI

VIRTUE AND THE VIRTUES

VIRTUE

The ethical content of the word *Tao* (道), or Moral Law, as shown in Chapter VII, brings it into close relation to the word *Tê* (德), or Virtue. So close is this relation that the two words are often coupled together, as in the title of the Taoist classic, the *Tao Tê Ching*. *Tê* is the embodiment of *Tao* in the individual : for it is when *Tao*, or Moral Law, is so appropriated by the individual that it becomes his own disposition and inevitably manifests itself in conduct, that it is called *Tê*, Virtue.

The above statement of the meaning of Virtue as defined by Chu Hsi includes three ideas, all of which are emphasized by the Philosopher. The first is obvious : Virtue has to do with conduct. " Virtue," says Chu Hsi, " is the practice of Moral Law." [1] The second is hardly less obvious. Virtue is in the heart before it is manifested in conduct. " Virtue is what is received into the heart. Before serving one's parents and following one's elder brother, already to possess a perfectly filial and fraternal mind : this is what is termed Virtue." [2] But it is assimilated in such a way that spontaneously and inevitably it manifests itself in conduct. It is not enough, therefore, to say that Virtue is Moral Law in the concrete. " You must be continually watchful, and make

[1] 全 書, bk. xlvi, f. 19 (*P.H.N.*, p. 304).
[2] Ibid., f. 20 (*P.H.N.*, p. 305).

the principle which is in you such that action is certain to be in accordance with it. For example, when sitting in meditation alone, before serving my parents and my sovereign, and before holding intercourse with my friends, there must already be in me the perfectly filial and fraternal, loyal and faithful disposition, which so inspires my conduct that in serving my parents I cannot be other than filial, in serving my sovereign I cannot be other than loyal, in intercourse with friends I cannot be other than faithful, and this spontaneously without waiting for special preparation." [1] Chu Hsi, therefore, draws a distinction between Virtue, or the virtuous disposition, and conduct. " As cherished in the heart it is called Virtue, as seen in action it is called conduct." [2] None the less its definite relation to conduct must not be lost sight of : it is the disposition that leads to virtuous action.

The third idea emphasized by Chu Hsi is that virtue is the appropriation of Moral Law by the individual. Moral Law is all-comprehensive and universal, Virtue is that which is received by the individual for himself alone.[3] " When Virtue is perfected in me, it is as though there were a man in me, who, if necessity is filial and fraternal, loyal and faithful, and would not in any wise do anything that is not filial and fraternal, loyal and faithful." [4]

Virtue then is *Tao*, or Moral Law, appropriated by the individual in such a way that it manifests itself in the spontaneous practice of good.

[1] Ibid., f. 20 (*P.H.N.*, pp. 305–6).
[2] Ibid., f. 21 (*P.H.N.*, p. 306).
[3] Ibid., f. 20, cf. f. 3 (*P.H.N.*, p. 304 ; cf. pp. 272–3).
[4] Ibid., f. 21 (*P.H.N.*, p. 306).

Love the Premier Virtue

The Virtues are Love, Righteousness, Reverence, and Wisdom. The first of these is by far the most important. The analytical study of this one virtue and the discussions resulting from it occupy the whole of Book VI in Chu Hsi's work on Human Nature. It has a twofold significance, a wider and a narrower meaning. In its wider meaning it includes all four virtues. Even in its narrower meaning as one of the four, it is the premier virtue and demands separate consideration from the rest.

The word translated Love throughout the present work is *Jên* (仁). It is defined by Soothill as " composed of 亻 or 人 "man" and 二 "two", indicating the right relationship of one man to his fellows ; in other words, a man of 仁 considers others as well as himself ". [1] Suzuki gives the same derivation of the ideograph, and says, " It is very difficult to find a proper English equivalent for the Chinese *jên*. Broadly speaking, it is sympathy or loving-kindness or friendly feeling or, better, feeling of fellowship. Its signification is that there is an inborn feeling in every man's heart which is awakened to its full actuality when he comes in contact with another fellow being, forming the permanent bond of association between them." [2] The word has been variously translated by different sinologues. Giles renders it "Charity in the theological sense ", and explains it as "the natural goodness of the heart ". Faber renders it " Benevolence " and also "humanity ". [3] Legge translates it " benevolence " and

[1] *Analects of Confucius*, p. 104.
[2] *Early Chinese Philosophy*, p. 51.
[3] *Mind of Mencius*, pp. 99 ff. ; also *Digest of Confucius*, pp. 46 ff.

" virtue ". Soothill, in his work on the *Analects*, with a flexibility which adds much to the value of his translation, uses many renderings. " In general," he says, " it may be translated by virtue, the root of each being 人 *vir*, and both words representing man at his best. Its synonyms are humanity, humaneness, generosity, altruism, charity, kindness, etc." [1]

In estimating the use of this word and its suitable translation, two considerations must be noted. First, more than a thousand years intervened between the sages—with whose writings the scholars above quoted are chiefly concerned—and the philosophers of the Sung School. Second, it must be remembered that in quoting from philosophical works such as those of Chu Hsi and his Masters, in which the exact meanings of the terms employed are exhaustively discussed, we cannot permit ourselves that variety of rendering which would otherwise be desirable. We have to discover the nearest English equivalent and use it as consistently as the word itself will allow, otherwise the point of much that is written will be lost.

The fundamental meaning of the word, Chu Hsi insists, is to be found in its relation to *ai* (愛), the word for the emotion of love, or affection. He says : " The saints and sages repeatedly expounded the word *jên* (仁), one in one way and another in another. Their use of words and the meanings attached to them differ ; but when we have definitely ascertained what the meaning is in each case, and when we have carefully examined their statements—scattered as they

---

[1] *Analects of Confucius*, p. 104.

are like the stars—we shall find that this is the invariable interpretation, and that it is everywhere consistent : namely, that, as defined in the *Collected Comments*, *jên* is ' the principle of *ai* (the emotion love), and the virtue of the mind '. *Ai* is solicitude, and solicitude is feeling ; its principle is *jên*. In the phrase ' the virtue of the mind ', virtue, again, is simply *ai*—because the reason why *jên* is called 'the virtue of the mind' is that it is the source of *ai*." [1] Again, " the expression ' the principle of *ai* ' is exactly what is meant when we say that *jên* is *ai* (the emotion love) before it is put forth, and that *ai* is *jên* (the love principle) after it is put forth." [2] The same idea is repeated again and again. *Jên* is the principle from which the feeling of love, or affection, proceeds. The love-principle is the substance, the love-feeling is its operation. Whatever else it connotes this is the basic meaning of the word which must be the starting-point in any adequate consideration of its content. The fact is that in the Chinese language there are two words to express two different ideas, both of which are expressed by the one word " love " in English. There is the pure altruistic disposition of love, and there is the emotion love which may be selfish or unselfish. These two ideas are represented by *jên* (仁) and *ai* (愛) respectively. The latter as an emotion may be misdirected or vitiated ; the former is never other than purely altruistic.[3]

---

[1] 全 書, bk. xlvii, f. 1 (*P.H.N.*, pp. 311–12).

[2] Ibid., f. 34 (*P.H.N.*, pp. 373–4).

[3] For the sake of clearness the word *ai* (愛) in this discussion is, with few exceptions, translated " affection ", and the word " love " is reserved for the rendering of *jên* (仁).

Chu Hsi did not mean to imply that the feeling of love was the only meaning of *jên* (仁). He says that while in earlier times the word was construed in terms of affection, from the time of the two Ch'êngs scholars began to realize that the content of the word *jên* (仁) was not exhausted by this meaning. This, however, itself resulted in some scholars going to the other extreme and expounding the term in such a way that there was a complete divorce from the idea of affection, or the love feeling. This, Chu Hsi says, resulted in wild theories which were worse than the initial error of a too poor conception of the word.[1] In other words, the emotion love is the root idea of the word *jên* (仁). If you eliminate it you will have eliminated its essential element ; but true love is the emotion love based upon an ethical foundation. " If we desire to understand the content of the term *jên*, we cannot do better than follow up the word *ai* (affection). If we understand how *jên* comes to be *ai*, and how the latter still cannot fill out the idea of *jên*, then the meaning and content of the term *jên* will stand out clearly before our eyes." [2]

The typical illustration of *ai*, or the emotion love, which is frequently quoted as explaining *jên*, is the classic case, instanced by Mencius, of a child about to fall into a well, with the result that all who see it, without exception, experience a feeling of alarm and distress.[3] The emotion thus evoked is the outflow of *jên*. " The saints and sages," says Chu Hsi, " in expounding *jên* all start from this passage." [4]

---

[1] 全 書, bk. xlvii, f. 27 (*P.H.N.*, p. 362).
[2] Ibid., f. 28 (*P.H.N.*, p. 363).
[3] Ibid., f. 8 (*P.H.N.*, p. 325), cited from *Mencius*, p. 78.
[4] Ibid., f. 8 (*P.H.N.*, p. 325).

But they do not end there. At the beginning of the present section it was said that Love has a twofold significance, a narrower and a wider meaning. This dual aspect of Love was specially emphasized by Ch'êng Tzŭ in his statement : " In the narrow sense it is but one, in the comprehensive sense it includes the four." On which Chu Hsi's comment is : " The statement preceding this, ' The Principle of Origin, of the four Attributes, corresponds to Love among the Five Cardinal Virtues,' seems to imply that there is a small love and a great love. In the sentence, ' In the narrow sense it is but one,' the small love is referred to, which is simply the one thing, Love. In the sentence, ' In the comprehensive sense it includes the four,' the great love is referred to, and includes Reverence, Righteousness, and Wisdom, in addition to Love." [1] And, again, " Love itself is the original substance of Love, Reverence is love in graceful expression, Righteousness is Love in judgment, and Wisdom is Love in discriminating." [2] It should be added, however, that although there is this twofold significance, Love is but one. The Love which is the parent of, and includes, all four virtues, is the same as that which in its narrow sense ranks as simply one of the four.

Love, then, is the parent virtue and includes all virtues. In this sense it comes to be equivalent to virtue itself. " Love is the fulfilling of the Law." It is therefore not incorrect to translate it in many places as " virtue ", as Legge, Soothill, and others have done. Moreover, as Chu Hsi points out more than once, Confucius in the *Analects* discourses chiefly upon

---

[1] Ibid., f. 2 (*P.H.N.*, p. 313).
[2] Ibid., bk. xlviii, f. 8 (*P.H.N.*, p. 401).

the " practice of love " in various forms of virtuous conduct,
and in such connexions " virtue " is a not inappropriate
rendering.   But it must not be forgotten that it is virtue
because it is Love ; and, indeed, to lose the " love " idea from
the content of this noble word would be disastrous to a true
understanding of the Sung philosophy, and an injustice
to the rich vein of humanity in its exponents.

In explaining what Love is, the Philosopher is careful to
make clear what it is not.   Of the explanations current in
his time one was that it was to be interpreted as " one-ness
with the universe", and a second was that it was to be
interpreted as " consciousness "—that is consciousness of
moral principle.[1]   These explanations grew out of statements
by Ch'êng Tzǔ which were appealed to as their source and
justification.   Chu Hsi was questioned with respect to both
these theories.   " The disciples of Ch'êng Tzǔ," said the
questioner, " give various explanations of Love.   Some say
that affection is not Love, and regard the unity of all things
with myself as the substance of Love.   Others say that
affection is not Love, and explain the term as the mind's
possession of consciousness.   Do you, explaining it as you now
do, mean to imply that these are all wrong ? "   To which Chu
Hsi replied : " From the statement, ' The universe is one with
myself,' we may learn how Love includes all things within the
sphere of its affection ; it does not tell us what Love is in its
real essence.   From the statement, ' The mind possesses

---

[1] *P.H.N.*, p. 323, n. 1 ; cf. 遺 書, pt. ii, 上, f. 2. " Consciousness "
is consciousness of moral principle whereby solicitude is evoked ; as, for
example, when a man sees a child about to fall into a well.

consciousness,' we may learn how Love includes Wisdom ; it does not tell us from what it really derives its name." [1]

But if Love is not " oneness with the universe " nor " consciousness ", neither can it be defined as altruism, or as the absence of selfishness. Love is an innate principle of man's Nature. " If there is no selfishness with its separative barriers the entire substance of man's personality is Love." [2] " If altruism, then there is Love ; if egoism, then there is not Love. But you must not, therefore, regard altruism as Love." [3] Altruism clears the way for Love. " It is like the water in a dyke which, obstructed and clogged by sand and earth, ceases to flow ; if you can remove the obstructions the water will flow freely." [4] Similarly, if we can remove the egoism and be altruistic, Love will have free course.

Love, too, must be distinguished from sympathy (恕). " The outflow of Love (*jên*) is simply affection (*ai*). Sympathy is that which conveys the affection, and affection is that which is conveyed by sympathy ; but for the sympathy conveying the affection, the affection could not reach to the object loved—there could be no ' attachment to parents, love of the people, or kindness to other creatures ', but simply a feeling of affection. If there were no affection there originally what would there be to be conveyed ? It is like the clearing of a dyke. The water is there originally, and, therefore, when the

---

[1] 全 書, bk. xlvii, f. 23 (*P.H.N.*, p. 354 ; cf. pp. 321, 374).
[2] Ibid., f. 19 (*P.H.N.*, p. 346).
[3] Ibid., f. 19 (*P.H.N.*, p. 347).
[4] Ibid., f. 18 (*P.H.N.*, p. 343).

dyke is cleared the water flows. If there were no water in the dyke originally, how could there be a flow of water when the dyke is cleared ? On the other hand, although there is water there, how can it flow out if the dyke is not cleared ? The water is the feeling of affection, that which clears the dyke is sympathy." [1]

The relation of Love to altruism, affection, and sympathy is expressed in a sentence : " Altruism is antecedent to Love, sympathy and affection are subsequent, because where there is altruism there can be Love, and where there is Love there can be affection and sympathy." [2] In a word altruism prepares the way for love, affection is its outflow, and sympathy is its application to the object loved.

Having laid down what is the fundamental meaning of the word Love as a principle of the Nature, Chu Hsi gives a clear exposition of what it is in practical conduct. " If," he says, " we can truly embody and preserve it, we have within us the spring of all goodness, the root of every virtue. This is what is taught by the school of Confucius ; and for this reason we are bound to induce the student to be eager in his pursuit of Love." He then proceeds to a summary of its practical manifestation in everyday virtues, as taught by the great sage, Confucius himself. The chief of these, and the one most frequently referred to as the most comprehensive, is " the mastery of self and the return to right principle ". The full statement will be found in Book VI of the *Philosophy of Human Nature*,[3] to which the reader is referred.

---

[1] Ibid., ff. 18, 19 (*P.H.N.*, pp. 344–5).

[2] Ibid., ff. 19–20 (*P.H.N.*, p. 347).

[3] See ibid., ff. 22–3 (*P.H.N.*, pp. 352–3).

The Five Cardinal Virtues

The history of the development of the doctrine of the Five Cardinal Virtues is both interesting and important. It is pointed out by one of Chu Hsi's questioners that in the *Analects* Love alone is for the most part the subject of discourse, whereas when we come to the works of Mencius we find that he combines Love and Righteousness.[1] Moreover, Mencius speaks sometimes of two Virtues, Love and Righteousness, and sometimes of four, Love, Righteousness, Reverence, and Wisdom. Later still we have the fifth, Sincerity, added.

The explanation given of this development is that in the time of Confucius there was no controversy as to the goodness of the Nature, and that it was the defence of this doctrine in Mencius' day that brought out the detailed analysis of the Nature into the four principles.[2] It was not that there was any essential difference in the teaching of the two sages, for Confucius when he spoke of Love spoke of it in the comprehensive sense as including the other three.[3] In the time of Mencius, " if the all-comprehensive entire substance alone had been stated, the fear was that it would be like a steel-yard with no marks to indicate the different weights, or a foot-rule without inches." " He therefore found other language to express the truth, marking off its fourfold distinctions. This was the beginning of the doctrine of the Four Terminals." [4] Thus Mencius did not import an additional concept, Righteousness, into the teaching of

[1] Ibid., bk. xlviii, f. 16 (*P.H.N.*, p. 414).
[2] Ibid., f. 10 (*P.H.N.*, p. 404).
[3] Ibid., ff. 17, 18 (*P.H.N.*, p. 417).
[4] Ibid., f. 10 (*P.H.N.*, p. 404).

Confucius; still less three additional concepts; he simply made distinctions within the one concept, Love.[1]

And, similarly, the reason why Mencius himself sometimes spoke only of two virtues, Love and Righteousness, and at other times of four, was that the two included the four. "Love is Love, but Reverence is the manifestation of Love; Righteousness is Righteousness, but Wisdom is hidden Righteousness." [2] " Reverence is the going forth of Love (in expression), Wisdom is the storing up of Righteousness." [3]

" How was it that a fifth virtue came to be added ? " was a question put to the Philosopher by an unnamed inquirer. To which the reply was : " Sincerity gives reality to the four." "It is like Earth, one of the Five Agents, if there were no Earth, there would be nothing to contain the other four." [4] " Sincerity is reality, and reality means that a thing IS." [5] " Sincerity, therefore, is the expression of the fact that the virtues and the feelings alike have a real existence." [6]

The respective virtues are analysed in considerable detail. Love, the most important of them, has already been considered. Closely akin to Love is Reverence. Like Love it is contrifugal; its operation is outward, away from itself. The Chinese word is Li (禮), translated by Legge as " Propriety ". It is the word in common use for " rites " and " ceremonies ". Rites and ceremonies, however, are the external manifestation; and neither these words nor the word " propriety " can be considered a suitable rendering of li as one of the principles of the Nature. Li is the nature-principle from which courtesy

[1] Ibid., f. 18 (P.H.N., p. 417).   [2] Ibid., f. 11 (P.H.N., p. 406).
[3] Ibid., f. 9 (P.H.N., p. 402).   [4] Ibid., f. 13 (P.H.N., p. 409).
[5] Ibid., f. 14 (P.H.N., p. 411).   [6] Ibid.

springs, and is fittingly rendered "reverence", as by Professor Soothill in his work on the Analects.[1]

Righteousness is the complement of Love, and is next to it in importance. It is the principle of obligation,[2] the *oughtness* of actions.[3] Using water as an illustration, its flowing movement is said to be a picture of Love; while its flow as rivers, or its collection in pools and ponds, corresponds to Righteousness.[4] "Subjective righteousness," we are told, "is the determinate decision (in favour of what is objectively right); "[5] whilst objective righteousness, or the "rightness of an act", is that rightness which is inherent in all phenomena : "Whatever it is that presents itself to us, there is some duty embedded in it, and the performance of that duty is Righteousness."[6] The quality of "decision" which is thus characteristic of Righteousness is compared to a "sword held horizontally, by which everything as it presents itself is cut in two".[7] Choice must be made between right and wrong action with regard to every matter that comes before us, and the choice of the right is the outcome of Righteousness. Righteousness, therefore, stands in contrast to Love. "Righteousness is self-conserving. Love is self-imparting."[8] And yet, while standing in contrast to Love, it is still a form

---

[1] *Analects of Confucius*, p. 104.

[2] 全 書, bk. xlviii, f. 6 (*P.H.N.*, p. 396).

[3] Ibid., f. 4 (*P.H.N.*, p. 393).

[4] Ibid.

[5] Ibid., f. 2 (*P.H.N.*, p. 390).

[6] Ibid., f. 3 (*P.H.N.*, p. 391).

[7] Ibid., f. 2 (*P.H.N.*, p. 390 ; cf. pp. 389, 391).

[8] Ibid., f. 3, cf. f. 9 (*P.H.N.*, p. 392, cf. p. 403).

of Love. It is Love in judgment. "The awful majesty of Righteousness is the conserving aspect of Love." [1]

Wisdom is still more divisive than Righteousness, and its self-conserving quality more prominent. "You know a thing to be true, or you know it to be false. You know it, and that ends it." "Wisdom knows, and then hands on the matter to the other three, . . . so that its gathering-in quality is more keen even than that of Righteousness." [2] That is, Wisdom is self-assertive; it is clear-cut, decisive, and uncompromising in its manifestation, in contrast to the gentleness and deference of Love and Reverence.

The four virtues thus divide into two pairs. "Love and Reverence represent the idea of giving out life. Righteousness and Wisdom represent the idea of gathering in." [3] In this they are compared to the Seasons; Spring and Summer are the progression; Autumn and Winter are the retrocession. All, however, are forms of the one all-comprehensive virtue, Love.

The Four Feelings

In Chapter VII the relation of the Virtues to the Four Ultimata—the principles of Origin, Beauty, Utility, and Potentiality—which constitute the Moral Order was somewhat fully discussed. Their relation also to the Four Seasons was shown in the same chapter, and in Chapter VI their relation to the Five Agents. We have now to add another set of terms to which they are parallel—the Feelings or Terminals.

---

[1] Ibid., f. 1 (*P.H.N.*, p. 387).
[2] Ibid., f. 7 (*P.H.N.*, p. 399).
[3] Ibid., f. 9 (*P.H.N.*, p. 402).

As we saw at an early stage in our study, Love, Righteousness, Reverence, and Wisdom are principles of the Nature; and from these the Four Ultimata, the ethical principles pervading the universe, are inferred. But principles are invisible; and if Love, Righteousness, Reverence, and Wisdom are themselves principles, how are they to be known? The answer is: " It is from affection, the sense of obligation, respectfulness, and moral insight, that we know that there are the principles Love, Righteousness, Reverence, and Wisdom in the mind." [1] These four feelings—more often named solicitude, conscientiousness, courtesy, and moral insight—are the " clues " to. the hidden principles of the Nature, from which again the existence of the Four Ultimata in the Universe is deduced.

The word " clues " is used designedly, because in a classic passage in Mencius, on which is based the doctrine we are discussing, this is undoubtedly one of the meanings of the term *tuan* (端). The passage reads: " Hence we may see that were it not that he possesses a solicitous mind man would not be man; were it not that he possesses a conscientious mind man would not be man; were it not that he possesses a courteous mind man would not be man; were it not that he possesses a morally discriminating mind man would not be man. Solicitude is the terminal of Love; conscientiousness is the terminal of Righteousness; courtesy is the terminal of Reverence; moral insight is the terminal of Wisdom." [2] The word *tuan*, here translated " terminal ", literally means " end " or " term ". In this connexion it has the meaning of

[1] Ibid., bk. xlvii, f. 9 (*P.H.N.*, p. 326).
[2] *Mencius*, pp. 78–9.

" thread " or " clue ". " When they are called *tuan*, it is as though there were things within, which are invisible, and it is only by means of threads (端 緒) put forth and manifested externally, that we are able to trace their existence." [1] The word *tuan* in itself may be used of either extremity of the thread, although as applied to the Four Terminals it is to be interpreted as the outer extremity. The English word " terminal " has the advantage of being the literal meaning of the word, and also of suggesting the idea of " clue ".

In the original text the names of the Four Terminals, or Feelings, are in each case double terms. Chu Hsi in his exposition of the subject gives a detailed analysis of them. " In each one of the expressions," he says, " solicitude, conscientiousness, courtesy, and moral insight, there is a combination of the meanings of two words. ' Solicitude ' combines the word ' grief ', which is the initial word, with ' distress ' which means ' pain ' ; the word ' conscientiousness ' combines the word ' shame ', meaning shame at my own wickedness, with ' hatred ', meaning hatred of wickedness in others ; ' courtesy ' combines the word ' humility ', having reference to myself, with ' complaisance ', having reference to others ; the expression ' moral insight ' explains itself." [2]

From the feelings, then, we infer the principles of the Nature, " just as from the purity of the stream we know the purity of its source," or as we know " the presence of an object from the shadow it casts ".[3] From the feeling of

---

[1] 全 書, bk. xlviii, f. 17 (*P.H.N.*, p. 416).
[2] Ibid., bk. xlvii, ff. 5, 6 (*P.H.N.*, p. 319).
[3] Ibid., bk. xlv, f. 2 (*P.H.N.*, p. 231).

solitude at the sufferings of others the principle of Love is inferred ; from the hatred of evil in oneself or others the principle of Righteousness is inferred ; from humility and complaisance towards men the principle of Reverence is inferred ; and from the discrimination between right and wrong the principle of Wisdom is inferred. It is to be noted that in the case of the first two the inference of the principles from the feelings is by their opposites. " It is when we see something calculated to wound that the feeling of solicitude is stirred ; it is when we do something hateful that the feeling of conscientiousness is stirred." [1]

In an earlier section it was said that Love is the parent virtue and includes all virtues. What is said of Love among the virtues is also said of solicitude among the Feelings or Terminals. In answer to the question : " How does the solicitous mind include the Four Terminals ? " Chu Hsi said : " Solicitude is manifested in the first movement of the mind. Conscientiousness, moral insight, and respectfulness are possible only when solicitude has become active ; they are seen only in its movement." [2] And again, " The feeling of solicitude is solicitude from beginning to end ; the other three are solicitude in their beginning, but in their issue are conscientiousness, courtesy, and moral insight respectively. Without solicitude these three are dead, because solicitude is the fountain head from which the other three proceed." [3]

[1] Ibid., f. 5 (*P.H.N.*, p. 236).
[2] Ibid., bk. xlvii, f. 14 (*P.H.N.*, p. 335).
[3] Ibid., bk. xlviii, f. 9 (*P.H.N.*, p. 402).

We are now able to complete the table of parallels which was given in part in Chapters VI and VII.

FEELINGS	VIRTUES	ULTIMATA	AGENTS	SEASONS
Solicitude	Love	Origin	Wood	Spring
Conscientiousness	Righteousness	Beauty	Fire	Summer
Courtesy	Reverence	Utility	Metal	Autumn
Moral Insight	Wisdom	Potentiality	Water	Winter
	Sincerity		Earth	

PART IV

THE THEISTIC IMPORT OF
CHU HSI'S PHILOSOPHY

CHAPTER XII

HEAVEN

In Part II, under different names and from different points of view, the subject of our inquiry was the fundamental element in the constitution of the universe. It was first presented to us as omnipresent Law, a guiding and directing principle inherent in every individual thing. We then found, from the point of view of causality, that Chu Hsi, following his predecessor Chou Tzŭ, traces the evolution of the cosmos back to the Primordial Ether, in which this same principle, Law, as the Supreme Ultimate or First Cause, is inherent. Pursuing our inquiry further, we found that this Law is an all-comprehensive and ethical principle pervading the universe ; that it is the basis of that Moral Order which we see everywhere, the component principles of which are, in the physical universe, the principles of Origin, Beauty, Utility, and Potentiality, and, in moral beings, Love, Righteousness, Reverence, and Wisdom.

One other aspect of this monistic principle remained to be considered in order to complete our survey of the subject. The question was asked : What is Chu Hsi's conception of the Final Cause from the theistic point of view ? Immaterial and ethical as it is, does it possess the attributes of deity ? In other words, is Chu Hsi's monism a form of theism ? This question, however, involved not only a careful study of the term " Heaven ", but also of the expression " The Mind of the Universe ", with its implications for this school, and could be adequately considered only after our examination of Chu Hsi's doctrine of human nature, and of man's mind as the seat of personality. The question, therefore, was reserved until this stage of our inquiry. It will be convenient if in this chapter and the following we investigate the problem from these two points of view—the import of the term " Heaven " and the meaning of the phrase " The Mind of the Universe "—keeping in view in each case the relation of the conception under consideration to the problem of personality.

THE DIVINE IMMANENCE

T'ien (天), the Chinese word for Heaven, is of frequent occurrence in the Classics. According to Chu Hsi it is there used in three senses, which, he says, should be carefully distinguished by the reader. " In some passages the word refers to the Empyrean, in others to the Ruling Power, and in others to Law only." [1] It will help us to clearness in our discussion if we consider each of these in turn. The last named, however, needs to be considered from two standpoints : from the standpoint of Divine immanence, in which case *Li* or Law is termed *T'ien Ming*, the Decree of Heaven ; and from the standpoint of the relation of *Li* to the question of personality in the Divine Being. The former is the subject of the present section.

In the opening paragraph of his work on Human Nature, Chu Hsi endorses the statement that Heaven, Law, the Decree, and the Nature are synonyms for the same entity regarded from different points of view ; and, in the paragraph

[1] 全 書, bk. xlix, f. 25.

immediately following, he himself says : " Law is Heaven's substance." [1]   From which it appears that Heaven is identified with the ultimate element in the dualism of Law and Matter.   There are other great words with which the term Heaven is also thus identified.   As might be expected, it is recognized as identical with the Supreme Ultimate or First Cause.   In his comment on the first sentence in the *T'ai Chi T'u Shuo*, Chu Hsi says : " Among the attributes of High Heaven there is nothing that can be perceived by the senses and yet (He) is the true Pivot on which all creation turns, the ground of all distinctions in the world of beings.   Hence the statement is : ' Infinite ! and also the Supreme Ultimate ! ' It is not said that beyond the Supreme Ultimate there is also an Infinite." [2]   In other words, High Heaven is the Supreme Ultimate, the infinite First Cause.

As First Cause it follows that Heaven is self-existent.   In the paragraph already cited Chu Hsi's questioner gives the attribute of self-existence as the content of the term Heaven, which differentiates it from the other terms with which it is compared.   This meaning brings the term into close connexion with *Tao*, or Moral Law.   Referring to a correspondent's statement that Moral Law is Heaven as the self-existent, our Philosopher says : " He is passing on the teaching inherited from the earlier Confucianists," [3]   and thus endorses the identity of *Tao* and Heaven as one and the same being.   The Four Ultimata, also, are regarded as the attributes of Heaven. [4]

---

[1] Ibid., bk. xlii, f. 1 (*P.H.N.*, p. 3).

[2] 精 義, pt. i, f. 4.

[3] 全 書, bk. xlii, f. 19 (*P.H.N.*, p. 44).

[4] Ibid., bk. xliv, f. 34 (*P.H.N.*, p. 220).

As transcendental they are the Moral Law of Heaven, as immanent in the universe they are the Decree of Heaven.[1] *Li*, then, is Law as individualized, *Tao* is Law as ethical, *T'ai Chi* is Law as the Final Cause, *T'ien* is Law as the self-existent, and *Ming* is Law as immanent in the universe; and all are synonyms of *T'ien*, Heaven.

It will be observed that in the last of the statements to which reference has just been made Heaven is represented as both transcendent and immanent, and that the term used to express the latter idea is *T'ien Ming*, the Decree of Heaven. As previously noted, this term has two meanings, Divine Immanence and Destiny; but the former is its most distinctive meaning. *T'ien Ming* is the "Moral Law of Heaven as diffused throughout the universe and imparted to the creature". [2] "The theistic interpretation of force, or cosmic energy," says Professor Knight, "is this. The universe is pervaded from centre to circumference—although in truth in the happy allegoric phrase of Pascal, 'the centre is everywhere, and the circumference nowhere'—by a vast transcendent Power, known yet unknown, its action being mirrored to us in our own moods of conscious energy, but surpassing these immeasurably. The energy of which we are conscious, in the forth-putting of volition, gives us the root idea of force; and, in the light of this idea, we are warranted in interpreting the myriad minor forces of the universe, not as in themselves divine, but as the outcome or manifestation of a Power which underlies and yet pervades them, which animates and at the

---

[1] 大全, bk. xxix, f. 5.
[2] Ibid., f. 4.

same time transcends them." [1] Remembering that in the thought of Chu Hsi it is the ethical idea rather than that of force that is uppermost, this passage expresses the twofold conception conveyed by the terms *Tao* and *Ming*. " Regarded as the principles of Origin, Beauty, Utility, and Potentiality, it is called the Moral Order of Heaven, regarded as diffused throughout the universe and imparted to the creature, it is called the Decree of Heaven." [2] Thus, in every creature that exists there are principles which are the " manifestation of a Power which underlies and yet pervades them." " The Decree of Heaven is diffused throughout the whole universe, and is thus the Heaven of each individual creature." [3]

The term *Ming*, then, connotes the Divine Power as immanent, in contrast to the transcendent *Tao*. But that is not all; added to the idea of immanence is that of authority. The word *Ming* means the command of a sovereign; and the word " decree ", in the old theological sense of the " Divine Decrees ", is the nearest equivalent to it in the English language. As imparted to man, it becomes his conscience, his sense of obligation to act in accordance with its component principles, Love, Righteousness, Reverence, and Wisdom, just as a magistrate is under obligation to fulfil the duties attached to his office. " Heaven may be likened to the Emperor," [4] we are told, " the Decree is like letters patent appointing a man to office, the Nature is the duty pertaining

---

[1] *Aspects of Theism*, by William Knight, p. 85.

[2] 大 全, bk. xxix, f. 4.

[3] 全 書, bk. xlii, f. 4 (*P.H.N.*, p. 12).

[4] Ibid., f. 2 (*P.H.N.*, p. 6).

to such office." [1] From this point of view, the word *Ming* is closely related to the term Nature on the one hand, and to human destiny on the other. Both of these, however, were considered in Chapters VIII and IX. That to which it is desired to draw attention here is, from the theistic point of view, the idea of authority in the content of the term *Ming* as the all-pervading creative will of God.

T'ien Ming, then, in its fundamental sense is the immanent creative will of Heaven, pervading the whole universe, and constituting the essential nature of man. It consists of the Four Ultimata of the universe, the principles of Origin, Beauty, Utility, and Potentiality, which in their transcendental sense are termed *Tao*, or the Moral Order, and in man are Love, Righteousness, Reverence, and Wisdom.

THE EMPYREAN

The first of the three senses in which, according to Chu Hsi, the word Heaven is used in the Classics is that of the Empyrean. In the paragraph already referred to, in which Chu Hsi endorses the statement that Heaven is Law, he goes on to say : "In the present day it is maintained that the term Heaven has no reference to the Empyrean, whereas, in my view, this cannot be left out of account." [2] What, then, is the meaning which Chu Hsi attaches to this expression, which he deems necessary to a true understanding of the term Heaven ?

The word "Empyrean" (蒼蒼) is literally "Azure Azure", and is interpreted by both McClatchie and Le Gall as referring to the Azure Vault or visible sky. Does Chu

---

[1] Ibid., f. 1 (*P.H.N.*, p. 4).　　　　[2] Ibid., f. 1 (*P.H.N.*, p. 3).

Hsi, then, take back his endorsement of the statement that Heaven is Law, with the statement which he himself makes that Law is Heaven's substance, and look upon the material sky as the being termed Heaven by whose creative decree all things exist ? Did he, who as a child, when his father pointed to the Azure Vault with the words " That is Heaven ", asked " What is there beyond Heaven ? " [1]—did he in his maturer years find intellectual rest in the thought that this material dome of sky is in a fundamental sense the Heaven which is to be regarded as the source of all things ? On the contrary, according to Chu Hsi, the whole cosmos, including the heavens and the earth, owe their origin to the Supreme Ultimate or First Cause, which, as already stated, is the same Being as that which is termed Heaven ; and, further, Chu Hsi distinctly asserts, in the passage alluded to above, that the attributes of High Heaven cannot be perceived by the senses.

What, then, is meant by this reference to the Empyrean ? In the Philosopher's work on *Law and Matter* we are told : " The Empyrean is what is termed Heaven. It is that which revolves in endless revolution." [2] This refers not to the revolution of the seasons, but to the rotation of the Primordial Ether, by means of which the Two Modes come into existence. The *Li Chi* refers to the same thing in a passage which says : " The Supreme Unity divided and became heaven and earth. It revolved and became the Two Modes." [3] The Supreme Unity here is identified by Medhurst and McClatchie with Heaven. Legge criticizes this interpretation ; but, though his

[1] See p. 55.
[2] 全 書, bk. xlix, f. 25.
[3] *Li Chi*, Book VII, p. 378.

main conclusion is correct, he is mistaken in this particular, for the *T'ai I*, or Supreme Unity, is another name for the *T'ai Chi*, or Supreme Ultimate, with which, as we have already seen, Heaven is identified. Both these terms, *T'ai I* and *T'ai Chi*, are sometimes applied to the manifesting vehicle ; but the real Ultimate, the real Unity, it is again and again emphasized, is not the manifesting vehicle, but the ethical transcendent Law. It is most important that we keep in mind this intimate relation between the immanent ethical principle and the vehicle of manifestation. We saw it in the case of *Tao*, the transcendental Moral Law, which is associated with *Ch'i* (器), its manifesting vehicle. We saw it in the case of the Supreme Ultimate, which gives its name to the Primordial Ether. And we see it now in the case of the term Heaven. Heaven, the immaterial Law, has its etherial manifestation in the Empyrean.

The reader is here reminded of the result of our inquiry in Chapter V into the meaning of *Ch'i* (氣), or Ether. Our conclusion was that in its primordial form this *Ch'i* is pure spirit, or the higher synthesis in which both spirit and matter originate. Heaven, therefore, as the Empyrean, or Primordial Ether, is to be regarded as spirit. *Shên* (神), indeed, the word for spirit, is defined in almost identical terms. " *Shên* is the Ether in its purity and brilliance," [1] and since in the same connexion it is expressly stated that *shên* is not the Five Agents, it must be understood to be the primordial ether in the same sense as *T'ien* is said to be. Finally *Shên* is definitely stated to be Law just as *T'ien* is Law.[2] *Shên*

---

[1] 全 書, bk. xlix, f. 41.

[2] 大 全, pt. ii, f. 35.

thus naturally acquires the meaning of " God ", but God in His operation, as *T'ien* is God in His essence. In the *Yi Ching* it is said : " When we speak of Spirit (*Shên*) we mean the subtle presence and operation of God with all things " ; [1] and the commentator explains that " spirit " refers to the mysterious all-powerful operations of the unseen Presence— " not present yet present everywhere, doing nothing yet doing all things." [2]

> And I have felt
> A presence that disturbs me with the joy
> Of elevated thoughts ; a sense sublime
> Of something far more deeply interfused,
> Whose dwelling is in the light of setting suns,
> And the round ocean and the living air,
> And the blue sky, and in the mind of man :
> A motion and a spirit, that impels
> All thinking things, all objects of all thought,
> And rolls through all things.

The Empyrean, therefore, as referred to in the passage quoted above, is not the visible sky, but Heaven the Supreme Being as manifested in the primordial or spirit form of the Ether, from which the visible sky and all other material existences are evolved. Where, then, does the Azure Vault come in ? There is unquestionably in the ancient religious thought of China an intimate connexion between the visible sky and the Supreme Ruler. This connexion, doubtless, is due to the fact that the visible Heaven, in its infinite expanse of azure blue, formless, mysterious, and intangible, was regarded as the purest and most subtle form of the supernal ether accessible to man's cognizance, and was therefore reverenced as symbolical of the invisible Supreme Being.

[1] *Yi Ching*, p. 427.   [2] 易 經 體 註, pt. iv, f. 3.

And just as the First Cause has given its name of Supreme Ultimate to the Primordial Ether in which it is inherent, so, conversely, the Azure Vault has given its name of Empyrean to the First Cause, as Heaven the Supreme Being.

THE SUPREME RULER

The Empyrean is Heaven as manifested in the primordial or spirit form of the Ether. When Chu Hsi, however, contended that the idea of the Empyrean, which scholars of that day were eliminating from the term Heaven, must not be eliminated, he had in mind, not only the content of the word " Empyrean " in itself, but also the meaning attached to it in the ancient Classics, in which the word is repeatedly coupled with the term Heaven as the title of the Supreme Ruler. This consideration brings us to the second of the three senses, in which Chu Hsi tells us the word Heaven is used in these writings ; that is the Ruling Power.

In the *Odes*, where the expression Empyrean most frequently occurs, the word " azure " is found mainly in two combinations—" Azure Heaven " and " Azure Vault ". The latter expression occurs in the Ode " Sang Jou ", in the Decade of *T'ang*, of which the seventh stanza is thus translated by Legge :—

> Heaven is sending down death and disorder,
> And has put an end to our king,
> It is sending down those devourers of the grain,
> So that husbandry is all in evil case.
> All is in peril and going to ruin ;
> I have no strength to do anything,
> And think of (the Power in) the Azure Vault.[1]

[1] *Odes*, p. 523.

The words in parentheses are not in the original, but that the expression " Azure Vault " is rightly interpreted by the translator is obvious.

In the first of the " Odes of the Royal Domain " each stanza concludes with the refrain :—

> O distant and Azure Heaven !
> By what man was this brought about ? [1]

Similarly, in the sixth of the " Odes of Ts'in " occurs the refrain :—

> Thou Azure Heaven there !
> Thou art destroying our good men. [2]

And once more, in the sixth ode of the " Decade of Hsiao Min " the fifth stanza reads :—

> The proud are delighted,
> And the troubled are in sorrow,
> O Azure Heaven ! O Azure Heaven !
> Look on those proud men,
> Pity those troubled. [3]

In reading these passages we cannot escape the conviction that the writers are appealing to a " Power above the sky ", as indicated by Dr. Legge in his notes, and that they " did not rest in the thought of the material heavens " ; and, at least in one instance, to which Dr. Legge calls our attention, this interpretation is supported by the peculiar mode of expression adopted in the original. [4] There can be little doubt that this conception was present to Chu Hsi's thought when he said that in our interpretation of the term Heaven the Empyrean must not be left out of account.

---

[1] Ibid., p. 110.   [2] Ibid., p. 198.
[3] Ibid., p. 348.   [4] Ibid., pp. 112, 200, 348.

It must not be forgotten that it was Chu Hsi's aim, not to depart from, but to confirm and transmit the teaching of the Classics, and these undoubtedly contain the conception of a Personal Ruler. " The term Heaven," says Dr. Legge, " is used everywhere in the Chinese Classics for the Supreme Power, ruling and governing all the affairs of men with an omnipotent and omniscient righteousness and goodness, and this vague term is constantly interchanged in the same paragraph, not to say the same sentence, with the personal names *Ti* and *Shang Ti* . . . According to the oldest Chinese dictionary, the *Shuo Wên* (A.D. 100), the ideograph *T'ien* (天) is formed, ' by association of ideas,' from *yi* (– –) ' one ', and *ta* (大) ' great', meaning what is one and undivided, and great." [1] We may go further. In an interesting work by Dr. F. H. Chalfant, entitled *Early Chinese Writing*, the ideograph 天 is traced through several intervening forms to what is the probable original, 𝍫 which is obviously anthropomorphic in conception, and so includes the idea of personality. Even in the seal form 天 which dates from A.D. 100, about the same time as the *Shuo Wên*, there is still some resemblance to the anthropomorphic similitude of the older form.[2]

When we come to the two terms used for God, *Ti* and *Shang Ti*, which, as Dr. Legge says, are constantly interchanged with *T'ien*, we cannot fail to recognize that the conception that they contain is equally personal. To mention only one or two instances :—

[1] *Sacred Books of the East*, vol. iii, p. xxiv.
[2] *Memoirs of the Carnegie Museum*, vol. iv, No. 1, pl. vi.

The Great Yü in his advice to the Emperor Shun, urging upon him the necessity for care in his choice of men, and the need for attention to " the springs of things ", assures him that thus he will receive the favour of God and the renewal of his appointment by Heaven.[1] The famous T'ang, in his address to the people justifying his action in overthrowing the ruler of Hsia, says : " For the many crimes of the sovereign of Hsia Heaven has given the charge to destroy him . . . As I fear God, I dare not but punish him." And T'ang calls upon the people to assist him to carry out the punishment appointed by Heaven.[2]

In other passages also we find that God, or Heaven, is presented to us as the Supreme Moral Ruler. Calamities are His righteous punishments, and prosperity is the sign of His approval. The Emperor is His vice-gerent, whose appointment is contingent upon his governing the people righteously.

That the bearing of such passages on the question of personality in the Divine Being was recognized by Chu Hsi was shown on more than one occasion. " In the passage," he says, " in which it is said ' The great God conferred upon the people below a moral sense ', the very words ' conferred upon ' carry with them the idea of One who exercises authority." In the *Odes* and *Records*, the personality of the Supreme Ruler, he urges, is implied in such passages as speak of the wrath of God ; and, in the same connexion, he insists that this Supreme Ruler is Law.[3]

---

[1] *Shu Ching*, p. 79.
[2] Ibid., pp. 135–7.
[3] 全 書, bk. xliii, ff. 34–5 (*P.H.N.*, p. 147).

The God of the Classics, then, whether under the title of Empyrean or Supreme Ruler, of Heaven or God, was accepted by Chu Hsi as a personal and righteous Being, ruling and judging in the affairs of men ; and as identical with that Law which Chu Hsi himself regarded as the fundamental element in the universe.

PERSONALITY AND ANTHROPOMORPHISM

The third of the three senses in which, according to Chu Hsi, the term Heaven is used in the Classics is Law. The statement "Heaven is Law" (天 即 理 也) occurs frequently in Chu Hsi's commentaries ; and this fact, perhaps more than any other, has given rise to the impression that Chu Hsi's philosophy was materialistic and anti-theistic. It is necessary, therefore, to ask : What does Chu Hsi mean by this statement ? The answer is not far to seek. In the first place, as we have before noted, the statement in itself embodies a conception farthest removed from materialism. What Chu Hsi asserts is the ethical purity of *T'ien* ; for *Li* is Love, Righteousness, Reverence, and Wisdom, four rays harmoniously co-ordinated in the white light of perfect goodness. These, according to Chu Hsi, are the attributes of the First Cause and Supreme Ruler of the universe. *Li* has been defined as the abstract principle of right. It would be a truer interpretation to say, that it is what the late Dr. Dale termed the Eternal Law of Righteousness ; which, be it noted, like Chu Hsi, Dr. Dale identified with the Divine Being. "What," asks that writer, "is the relation between God and the Eternal Law of Righteousness ? " And his answer is that the relation is a relation of identity. "In God the Law is alive." "In Him its authority is actively asserted." [1] Chu Hsi's *Li* is the Eternal Law of Righteousness ; and, he tells us, *T'ien* is *Li*.

In the second place, so far from teaching a materialistic philosophy, Chu Hsi in this very statement identified *T'ien* with the immaterial element in the universe in contrast to the material, and so was combating what he regarded as the materialistic and anthropomorphic tendencies of his time. It was in opposition to such tendencies that, in his commentary on Chou Tzŭ's monograph on the Supreme Ultimate, he insisted that that philosopher in his opening sentence intended to assert the spirituality of the First Cause, which in the same connexion Chu Hsi identifies with High Heaven and the Empyrean.[2] Indeed, it is in the anthropomorphic conceptions which were then prevalent that we must seek for the explanation of much of Chu Hsi's argument. In the course of a discussion on the life after death and kindred topics Chu Hsi said to one of his pupils : "It is said, 'King Wên ascended and descended at the right and left hand of God.' Now to interpret that statement, as many do in these days, as meaning that King Wên is literally at the right and left hand of God, and that there really is a god like the graven images made by men in the world around us, is clearly incorrect ; nevertheless, there is a sense in which what the sacred writer says is true." [3] In like manner many of his statements were a protest against the prevailing image worship ; and in consequence, in common with his Masters the Brothers Ch'êng he was charged

---

[1] *The Atonement*, by R. W. Dale, pp. 370, 372.

[2] 精 義, pt. i, f. 14.

[3] 語 類, pt. iii, f. 15.

with atheism. But the charge was no less unjust than was
the same charge made against the early Christians, when, in
their passionate insistence that God is spirit, they refused
to worship the gods of the Pantheon. Chu Hsi was a
philosopher, not a religious martyr, but, none the less, his
assertion that Heaven is Law was an assertion of the
spirituality of Heaven, the First Cause and Supreme Ruler
of the universe.

In the statement " Heaven is Law " then, Chu Hsi affirms
the spirituality and ethical perfection of the Divine Being.
In the next chapter we shall see that the statement goes
even further, and carries with it as one of its implications the
personality of the Divine Being as well. But that aspect of
it will be more conveniently discussed in connexion with
Chu Hsi's interpretation of the expression, " The Mind of the
Universe."

In addition to the passages above cited, there are three
other passages of special importance in which Chu Hsi
endeavours to combat the crude conceptions of his time, while
retaining the spiritual and even personal conception of the
Supreme Ruler contained in the Classics. The first of these
has already been quoted in part. The whole passage reads :
" The Empyrean is what is termed Heaven. It is that which
rotates in endless revolution. It is true that it is wrong to say,
as is said in these days, that there is a man in the heavens
judging sin, but it is also wrong to say that there is no Ruler
at all." [1] In this statement we have the Philosopher's position
expressed in explicit terms. On the one hand the term

---

[1] 全 書, bk. xlix, f. 25.

Empyrean, or Heaven, carries with it the conception of a personal Ruler ; but, on the other hand, he rebuts the anthropomorphic conception of that Ruler which was prevalent in his day.

In the second passage he makes a statement which appears to be still more explicit as asserting personality in the Divine Being. Referring to certain extracts which he quotes from the Classics, he says : " These passages indicate that there is a man, as it were, ruling in it all." [1] It will be noted that, while in the passage cited in the preceding paragraph he rebuts the idea that there is " *a man* in the heavens judging sin ", in the one here quoted he asserts that there is " *a man, as it were*, ruling in it all ". In the one case he denies anthropomorphism, and in the other he affirms personality.

In the third passage there is the same fine point of distinction between " a man " and " a man, as it were ". In this case, however, the emphasis is on the assertion of personality in opposition to tendencies at the other extreme from anthropomorphism. One of Chu Hsi's questioners, with a strong leaning in this direction, asked the question—referring to various natural phenomena : " Is it that in all these the Empyrean truly possesses the power which controls the creative and transforming processes, or is it simply that the Supreme Ultimate is the Pivot on which all transformations turn, and therefore that the universe is what it is by a process of self-evolution ? " And again—referring to the Decree of Heaven : " When we consider the inequalities of the Decree, does it not seem as if there is not really one by

---

[1] 全 書, bk. xliii, f. 34 (*P.H.N.*, p. 146 and n. 4).

whose act it is imparted to the creature, but rather that the two ethers, in their intricate complexity and inequality, follow wherever they happen to strike, and, knowing that these inequalities do not proceed from man's own powers, people speak of them as decreed by Heaven?" To both which questions the Philosopher gave one reply: "They simply flow from the Great Source. The phenomena may be such as would lead one to think, namely, that there is not really One by whose act the Decree is imparted to the creature—how could there be a man above us commanding these things to come to pass? But that there is a man, as it were, above us acting in this way, is taught by the *Odes* and *Records*—in such passages, for example, as speak of the wrath of the Supreme Ruler. But still, this Ruler is none other than Law. In the whole universe there is nothing higher than Law: hence the term Ruler. In the passage which says, 'The great God has conferred upon the people below a moral sense,' the very words 'conferred upon' convey the idea of One who exercises authority." [1]

[1] Ibid., bk. xliii, ff. 34–5 (*P.H.N.*, pp. 146–8). The Chinese text reads:—

曰。只是從大原中流出來。模樣似恁地。不是眞有爲之賦子者。那得箇人在上面。分付這箇。詩書所說。便似有箇人在上恁地。如帝乃震怒之類。然這箇亦只是理如此。天下莫尊於理故以帝名之。惟皇上帝。降衷于下民。降。便是有主宰意。 N.B.—The words translated "Supreme Ruler" and "Ruler" are the words which in Legge's translation of the *Odes* and *Records* are uniformly translated "God", as in the quotation given in this context.

It would hardly be possible for the personality of the Supreme Ruler to be more clearly asserted than it is in these passages. The universe is what it is, not by a process of self-evolution, not by a fortuitous conjunction, intricate and complex, of the two ethers; but all things flow from the Great Source : their inequalities come to pass by the command of a Supreme Ruler, who has conferred on men a moral sense which renders them responsible to Himself for the rightness or otherwise of all their actions. In short, Chu Hsi complained of two opposite tendencies in his contemporaries : in some the extreme of anthropomorphism, and in others the error of denying altogether the existence of a Supreme Ruler, and the passages quoted were designed to correct both.

The Philosopher's argument, based upon the word " confer " in the Classics, is not without interest in this connexion. Chu Hsi was too acute a thinker not to know that the same argument could be applied to his own frequent use of this and similar words. Again and again he speaks of the Decree as " imparted " by Heaven, and so becoming man's nature. His favourite illustration of the Decree of Heaven is that of letters patent " conferred " by the Sovereign. He speaks of man's nature as consisting of innumerable principles with which he is " endowed " by Heaven. These expressions, and, indeed, the whole tenor of his discussions of these and similar themes, imply personality. The underlying conception in his mind of the Being concerning whom he naturally thought and spoke and wrote in such terms could not be other than personal.

The charges, therefore, which have been brought against Chu Hsi of materialism and antitheism would alike appear to be without sufficient foundation. In the statement that Heaven is Law, on which those charges have been largely based, he does not deny personality, but asserts the spirituality and ethical perfection of the Divine Being; and in the passages quoted above, in which he gave explicit answers to explicit questions, his assertion of personality in the Supreme Ruler is unequivocal and complete.

CHAPTER XIII

THE MIND OF THE UNIVERSE

A phrase of frequent occurrence in the writings of the Sung School is *T'ien Ti Chih Hsin* (天 地 之 心), which may be rendered " The Mind of the Universe ", or, more literally, " The Mind of Heaven and Earth." The phrase is important in connexion with our study of Chu Hsi's theistic position.

In Chapter VI we had under consideration the expression " Heaven and Earth " as used by this school and found that it has two meanings. It is the common expression for the material universe, and it is also used for the dual intermediary powers *Ch'ien* and *K'un*. There is a third meaning which is its special significance in the phrase " The Mind of Heaven and Earth ". In this third sense it is used interchangeably with the single term " Heaven ", and refers to the Supreme Being elsewhere designated by that term. For example, in a passage in the *Philosophy of Human Nature*, the phrase " the Nature of Heaven and Earth " obviously refers to the same thing as in the immediate context is spoken of as the Nature imparted by Heaven.[1] Again, in another passage referring to the Divine power creating men, the expression " Heaven and Earth " is used interchangeably with " Heaven ", and evidently in the same sense. Similarly, what is true of the phrase " Heaven and Earth " is true of the phrase " The Mind of Heaven and Earth ". It is used

---

[1] 全 書, bk. xlii, f. 4 (*P.H.N.*, pp. 12–13).

interchangeably with the phrase " The Mind of Heaven " [1]; it refers to the same Being as the terms " Great God " and " Heaven " [2]; and the Mind of Heaven and Earth is distinctly stated to be the " source of the whole world ", following which statement is the assertion that " there are not two sources ", and that " the transformations of *Ch'ien* and *K'un* all proceed from this one source ".[3] The expression " The Mind of Heaven and Earth ", therefore, must be interpreted as equivalent to " The Mind of Heaven ".

MIND AND PERSONALITY

In order to understand the full import of the phrase " The Mind of the Universe " we must remember that, while rebounding from the extreme of crude anthropomorphic conceptions, the essence of Chu Hsi's philosophy was that the principles of man's being are also to be found in the Source from which man came ; that, indeed, the constitution of our own being is the only ground of knowledge that we have of the Supreme Being or of the constitution of the Universe.

> I know that He is there as I am here,
> By the same proof, which seems no proof at all,
> It so exceeds familiar forms of proof.

In our analysis of Chu Hsi's doctrine of human nature in the preceding chapters we found that combined with the physical element there is the ethical Nature, or Law, which is inherent in Mind, the organ of its operation. Similarly, the Divine Being is Law as Ruler—Law inherent in Mind,

---

[1] Ibid., bk. xliv, ff. 13–14 (*P.H.N.*, pp. 182–3).
[2] Ibid., bk. xliii, f. 34 (*P.H.N.*, p. 146).
[3] Ibid., bk. xlvi, f. 8 (*P.H.N.*, p. 282).

the organ of His infinite operations in the universe. Chu Hsi expresses this idea in a remarkable sentence: "The Pilot of the Universe is the Mind of the Universe, in which Law is inherent," [1] which is but another way of saying,

"Conscious Law is King of Kings."

In an earlier section the statement was quoted that Love is "the principle of affection and the virtue of the mind". The phrase "the virtue of the mind" might also be rendered "attribute" or "property of the mind". It is the virtue of the mind, we are told, in the same sense as humidity is of water or heat is of fire.[2] It is the characteristic property of mind without which mind would not be mind. In the same sense all four virtues are said to be virtues or attributes of mind.[3] A little reflection will show the importance of this. For what are these virtues or attributes? They are the four principles, Love, Righteousness, Reverence, and Wisdom. Of these, Love is the parent of the other three. What then are the other three? Righteousness is right willing, Reverence—in a special sense the development of Love—is right feeling, and Wisdom is right knowing. In short, to use the phraseology of Western psychologists, these four principles are the three phases of mind conceived in terms of the ethical. In other words, Mind is the seat of personality. Now these principles are the component principles of *Li*, or Law, the ultimate element in the universe, and it will not surprise us to find that the Mind of the Universe is identified with the Law of the Universe. The question was asked:

---

[1] Ibid., bk. xlii, f. 22 (*P.H.N.*, p. 48).
[2] Ibid., bk. xlvii, f. 37 (*P.H.N.*, p. 379).
[3] Ibid., f. 9 (*P.H.N.*, p. 326).

" In the expressions ' the Mind of the Universe ' and ' the Law of the Universe ', is the word ' Law ' used in the sense of a principle and the word ' Mind ' in the sense of ruler ? " " Mind certainly means ruler," was the reply, " but the ruler spoken of is Law. It is not that apart from Mind there is another entity, Law, or that apart from Law there is another entity, Mind." [1]

For Chu Hsi, then, Law is conscious. It does not, and cannot exist, apart from Mind. Its component principles are the attributes both of mind and of personality. When, therefore, he asserts that Heaven is Law he not only affirms the spirituality and ethical purity of the Divine Being ; he predicates personality as well. The statement in itself means that Heaven is a conscious being who feels and knows and wills, and that these faculties are co-ordinated in an ethically perfect and harmonious relation. In the absence of the abstract term " personality " how else could the meaning connoted by that term be more definitely expressed ?

These considerations are confirmed by our study of Chu Hsi's doctrine of Mind in Chapter X, in which we found that mind is regarded as the seat of unity in man's complex organism, that it is the spirit portion of the Ether and as such is the organ of consciousness, and that it is the ruler of man's entire being ; all which implies that mind is the seat of personality. On this interpretation of mind, the phrase " The Mind of the Universe " can have only one meaning : Heaven, the Absolute, possesses both consciousness and personality.

[1] 語 類, bk. i, f. 3.

The reader may object that it is conceivable that the phrase "The Mind of the Universe" was used by Chu Hsi with a different connotation for the word "mind" from that which it has when applied to man. In short, it might be used in a Buddhistic or pantheistic sense, and exclude the idea of personality. Chu Hsi, however, leaves us no room for doubt. In the passage already cited he insists that the term Mind means ruler, which is the Philosopher's way of expressing the idea of personality. Moreover, immediately following this question and answer, the further question is asked : " Does the term mind (that is, in man) correspond to *Ti* (God) ? " And Chu Hsi replied : " The term man corresponds to *T'ien* (Heaven), and the term mind to *Ti* (God)." [1] *Ti*, we have previously explained, is the term used in the Classics as the personal name for God, and in his commentary on the *Yi Ching* is defined by Chu Hsi as meaning Heaven's ruler ; that is, as is expressed in this very statement, the term " *Ti* " stands in the same relation to " *T'ien* " as " mind " does to " man " ; it is the term which, like " mind ", expresses personality.

Pantheistic as well as anthropomorphic tendencies, however, were prevalent in Chu Hsi's day, and he had to meet them. Ch'êng Tzŭ, in his characteristic fashion, had enunciated the paradox : " It is the unchanging law of Heaven and Earth that their mind is imparted without exception to all things in the universe, and that (in this communication of their mind) they are without mind." [2] What Ch'êng Tzŭ referred to was the self-communication, in an ethical sense, of the

[1] Ibid., ff. 3–4.   [2] Ibid., f. 4.

Mind of Heaven and Earth to all things in the universe, impartially and without deliberation as to choice between this or that. One of Chu Hsi's pupils, however, after pondering the riddle, confided to Chu Hsi that, while he was prepared to accept the statement that Heaven and Earth in their cosmic operations are without mind, he was not prepared to accept the other branch of Ch'êng Tzŭ's paradox. "To say that Heaven and Earth possess mind," he contends, "implies thought and action, and how can Heaven and Earth exercise thought? What takes place is no more than that the progress of the seasons and the production of all things come to pass simply because by their constitution they are bound to do so. Where is there room for thought?" Chu Hsi's answer, it must be confessed, was somewhat crushing. "If that be so," he said, "what becomes of the statement in the *Yi*, 'Do we not see in *Fu* the Mind of Heaven and Earth?' According to your statement, we can only say that Heaven and Earth are without mind. But if it were really so, then cows would produce horses, and peach-trees would bear plum blossoms!"[1] Crushing as the reply was, however, it has the merit of clearness from the point of view of our present inquiry. The phrase "The Mind of the Universe" was used by Chu Hsi, not in the Buddhistic or pantheistic sense, but in the sense of a personal ruler. The Mind of the Universe is the Pilot of the Universe, consciously directing the course of the seasons and the production of all things in the universe.

The expression, then, "The Mind of Heaven and Earth" or "The Mind of Heaven", or, if we will, "The Mind of the

[1] Ibid.

Universe," represents the organ of conscious personality in the Divine Being; its attributes are Love, Righteousness, Reverence, and Wisdom—the attributes of man's mind; and it is identified with *Ti*, the God of the ancient Classics, the personal Supreme Ruler to whom the sage-emperor appealed as the God whose vicegerent he was.

> This is the glory—that in all conceived,
> Or felt or known, I recognize a mind
> Not mine but like mine.

LOVE, THE VITAL IMPULSE

In the preceding section our subject was the Mind of the Universe in relation to personality, and our attention was specially called to the psychological significance of Chu Hsi's statement that Love, Righteousness, Reverence, and Wisdom are the essential attributes of mind. In the present section we shall be concerned with this same Mind of the Universe, but in relation to creative evolution—to borrow Bergson's phrase—and with Love as its most distinctive attribute.

To return once more to Ch'êng Tzǔ's definition of Love. "Love," he says, "is the principle of affection and the virtue of the mind." The first part of the definition, as already noted, applies to Love in the narrow sense of one of the four virtues; the second part applies to Love in its comprehensive sense as the parent of all the virtues. While all four virtues are virtues or attributes of mind, "Love," says Chu Hsi, "is the ruling virtue." [1] So characteristic is it of man's mind that it is said, "Love is man's mind," [2]

---

[1] 全 書, bk. xlvii, f. 9 (*P.H.N.*, p. 326).

[2] A statement by Mencius (*Mencius*, p. 290) frequently cited by Chu Hsi; see 全 書, bk. xlvii, ff. 4, 6, etc. (*P.H.N.*, pp. 317, 320, etc.).

much in the same sense as in the *Doctrine of the Mean* it is said, " Love is man " [1] ; on which Legge's comment, quoting from the *Li Chi*, is : " This virtue is called man, because loving, feeling, and the forbearing nature belong to man as he is born. They are that whereby man is man."

In Chu Hsi's system, then, Love is the all-inclusive attribute of mind ; without it mind would not be mind ; and it is even said that Love is mind. In this comprehensive sense Love not only includes, but is the source of, all the virtues. Righteousness, Reverence, and Wisdom are all evolved from Love.[2] " If a man have not Love," it is asked, " how can he have Righteousness, Reverence, and Wisdom ? " [3] What is received from Heaven at the beginning is simply Love, and is therefore the complete substance of the mind. But Love branches out into four divisions ; the first is Love issuing in Love, the second is Love issuing in Righteousness, the third is Love issuing in Reverence, and the fourth is Love issuing in Wisdom—one body with four members united under the headship of Love.[4] The phrase which specially expresses this aspect of Love is " Vital Impulse ". " Love is the vital impulse," says Chu Hsi. " It is after we have received this vital impulse, and thereby are in possession of life, that we have Righteousness, Reverence, Wisdom, and Sincerity. From the point of view of priority Love is first ; from the point of view of greatness Love is greatest." [5]

---

[1] *D.M.*, p. 269.

[2] 全 書, bk. xlviii, f. 7 (*P.H.N.*, p. 389).

[3] Ibid., bk. xlvii, f. 11 (*P.H.N.*, p. 336).

[4] Cf. ibid., f. 5 (*P.H.N.*, p. 318).

[5] Ibid., f. 1 (*P.H.N.*, p. 311).

The Chinese expression which is here rendered vital impulse is *shêng i* (生 意). The first character, *shêng*, is " life " ; and the second, *i*, is " thought " or " purpose ". The expression is similar in meaning to *shêng li* (生 理), which means the principle of life, such as exists in the dry grain of wheat, or in peach and apricot kernels, although to all appearance they are dead.[1] It is because of this latent principle of life in the kernel that its common name is *jên*, love,[2] for to be without love is to be dead.[3] Just as in the case of a block of stone you can neither sow seed in it nor reap fruit from it, so with the hard-hearted man, all that you can say to him is without result.[4]

The expression *shêng i*, however, means more than the principle of life. It refers to the same thing as *shêng li*, but tells us more about it. The principle of vitality latent in the seed or kernel, given the proper conditions, will burst into movement and effort, and this is called *shêng i*, the vital impulse. Its most typical manifestation is in the budding life of spring, with its " new-born burst of glory ", when all nature is surging into life.[5] But it is seen in all four seasons : " Spring is the birth of the vital impulse, summer is its development, autumn is its consummation, and winter is the storing up of the vital impulse." [6] And, finally, the vital impulse is the creative principle running through every stage

[1] Ibid., f. 3 (*P.H.N.*, p. 314).
[2] Ibid.
[3] Ibid., f. 9 (*P.H.N.*, p. 326).
[4] Ibid., f. 5 (*P.H.N.*, p. 319).
[5] Ibid., f. 2 (*P.H.N.*, p. 314).
[6] Ibid., bk. xlviii, f. 8 (*P.H.N.*, p. 401).

in the production of all things in the universe. There is not a single thing which is not the outcome of it.[1] All things possess it as the latent principle of their development.[2]

This vital impulse, this creative mind, whether in man or in the universe, Chu Hsi tells us is Love. In the Creator, it is the creative impulse, the delight in producing things, in giving birth to the creature.[3] In the creature, it is the love of life and the impulse to preserve it, such as Chou Tzŭ recognized in the grass in front of his window which he refused to allow to be cut.[4] In moral beings it is " the gentle mind which loves men and is kind to other creatures ",[5] recognizing the universe as of one substance with itself, the creative mind as its own mind, and the distress of others as its own distress.[6] It is seen in solicitude, the operation of Love : when a man sees a child about to fall into a well the vital impulse within him is wounded and the feeling of solicitude is evoked.[7]

It is an interesting coincidence that almost the very phrase which has recently become current in the philosophy of the West should have been used by Chinese philosophers in the eleventh and twelfth centuries. And, although it would be absurd to suggest that Chu Hsi's " vital impulse " represents in all respects the same idea as Bergson's " *élan vital* ", the coincidence is more than in the mere phrase. Bergson postulates " an original impetus of life "[8]; this " original

[1] Ibid., bk. xlvii, f. 36 (*P.H.N.*, p. 377).
[2] Ibid., f. 3 (*P.H.N.*, pp. 314–15).
[3] Ibid., ff. 22, 23, 36 (*P.H.N.*, pp. 351, 353, 376).
[4] Ibid., f. 15 (*P.H.N*, p. 338).
[5] Ibid., f. 23 (*P.H.N.*, p. 353).
[6] Ibid., f. 36 (*P.H.N.*, p. 378).
[7] Ibid., f. 14 ; cf. ff. 8, 17 (*P.H.N.*, p. 336 ; cf. pp. 325, 341).
[8] *Creative Evolution*, by Henri Bergson, p. 92.

impetus is a common impetus ",[1] each individual retains
a certain impetus from the universal vital impulsion,[2] and
the impetus which results in the instinct of bees and ants, for
example, is the same as that which produces human
consciousness.[3] All this accords with Chu Hsi's philosophy.
Yüan, the principle of Origin pervading the universe, is Love
the vital impulse,[4] and from this one source flow its divergent
streams, in the instinct of sovereignty in bees and ants,[5] in
the growth of grass in front of Chou Tzŭ's window, or in the
solicitude of a man's heart when he sees a child in danger.
What Chu Hsi, however, insists upon is that, whether in man
or in the universe, in its Great Source or in its Flow, this
Vital Impulse is Love.

In considering the Four Ultimata which constitute the
Moral Order of the Universe, we found that they are identified
with the cardinal virtues in man ; and, in particular, that
Yüan, the principle of Origin, is identified with Love as the
vital impulse which runs through all stages of creative
evolution. The same idea is expressed with special reference
to the Mind of the Universe. " Love is the creative mind of
Heaven and Earth which is received by all men as their
mind. Its substance pervades heaven and earth and unites
all things in the universe ; its principle includes the Four
Terminals and unifies all goodness. . . . It is what is
called the Principle of Origin of *Ch'ien* and *K'un.* . . .

---

[1] Ibid., p. 53.
[2] Ibid.
[3] Ibid., pp. 105–6.
[4] 全 書, bk. xlvii, f. 14 (*P.H.N.*, p. 336).
[5] Ibid., bk. xlii, f. 27 (*P.H.N.*, p. 64).

From its transforming and nurturing influence, its mildness
and purity, its simplicity and liberality, its reproductive life
and deathlessness, it is termed Love." [1]   Again, we are told
that the place of Love in the Moral Order is as the creative
mind of Heaven and Earth present in everything.[2]   It is
the source of all laws, the ground of all phenomena.[3]   It is
the beginning of all goodness, the root of every virtue.[4]

Let the reader now recall the argument of the last section.
We found that the Mind of the Universe is the Mind of
Heaven, that the four virtues of which Love is the source and
sum are the attributes of this Mind of Heaven, and that
while rejecting all anthropomorphic conceptions of a crude
materialistic nature, Chu Hsi recognizes this Mind of Heaven
as the personal Ruler and Governor of the universe, the
One Source to whose conscious agency the physical and
moral order of the universe are due.   We now find that the
essential and all-inclusive attribute of this Mind of Heaven,
the One Source of the physical and moral order, is Love as
the Vital Impulse putting forth its Divine energy in all
phases of creative evolution.

We may note here also the added force which the argument
of the preceding section receives from these considerations.
Chu Hsi tells us that if heaven and earth and all things
ceased to be, Love would not be lessened thereby.[5]   Theolo-
gians are not unfamiliar with the argument that Love in the

[1] Ibid., bk. xlvii, f. 39 (*P.H.N.*, pp. 382–3).
[2] Ibid., f. 23 (*P.H.N.*, p. 352).
[3] Ibid., f. 4 (*P.H.N.*, p. 317).
[4] Ibid., f. 23 (*P.H.N.*, p. 352).
[5] Ibid., f. 29 (*P.H.N.*, p. 366).

Divine Being presupposes a triune mode of existence; for the simple reason that Love implies fellowship, and if Love be an essential attribute of deity it must remain, together with the fellowship which it implies, a part of the Divine existence, though all else cease to be. However that may be, at least we may say that Love implies a personal existence; and if it is conceived further that the one thing that abides when all things else have passed away is Love, we must surely conclude that the author of such a conception attributed to the Being, whose imperishable attribute Love is, all that we mean by the abstract term personality. And this Love, the all-inclusive attribute of the Divine Mind, is not some far-away existence having no relation to human existence, but the same Love as that which is spoken of when we are told that Love is man's mind. Creative Love, rejoicing in the life it has created, is the same love as the love of the ideal ruler for his people, or of the father for his child.

That this conception of Divine Love, noble as it is, differs immeasurably from the Christian conception it is hardly necessary to say. The note is a different note from that of Browning, for example, when he writes:

> " The very God! Think, Abib; dost thou think?
> So the All-Great, were the All-Loving, too—
> So, through the thunder comes a human voice!
> Saying: " O heart I made, a heart beats here!
> Face, my hands fashioned, see it in myself!
> Thou hast no power nor may'st conceive of mine!
> But love I gave thee, with myself to love,
> And thou must love me who have died for thee!"

But, though Chu Hsi could not have adopted these lines in the fullness of their meaning as a true expression of his own

thought, he could have adopted them in part. It is true
that in his conception there is little of the " heart-beat ",
still less of that fellowship of love, and least of all of that
Divine self-sacrifice which we find expressed in the poet's
last two lines. How could there be ? The philosopher had
not the poet's data, and could not have the experience. But
that Love, as pure and lofty altruism, is to be found alike in
the Maker's " heart " and in the " heart He made " is the
thesis on which Chu Hsi's whole philosophy is based. Love
is the vital impulse which lies at the heart of the universe, the
source and sum of all that is. To use the Philosopher's own
words: " The Mind of the Universe is Love." [1]

[1] Ibid., bk. xliv, f. 13 (*P.H.N.*, p. 182).

CHAPTER XIV

CONCLUSION

We have now reached the conclusion of our task, and we end on the same note as that on which we began. For the two key-words of all that has preceded are those to which the reader's attention was called at the very outset of our inquiry—Law and Love : Law, the component principles of which are Love, Righteousness, Reverence, and Wisdom ; and Love, the source and sum of all the rest.

Perhaps at this point a personal reference may be permitted. Much of what has been said in these pages, and particularly in the last two chapters, the present writer is fully aware, runs counter to the prevailing impression with regard to Chu Hsi's philosophy. The writer himself, indeed, shared that impression, and regarded the Philosopher's teaching as both materialistic and atheistic, until he began to study the writings of this school at first hand. His studies, extending over several years, convinced him of his error. At a comparatively early stage the idea that this school could be fairly labelled materialistic had to be abandoned, and later the charge of atheism also.

Lest, however, a false impression should have been created as to the place of emphasis in Chu Hsi's philosophy, it should be added that, though the theistic implications of his system he himself saw clearly enough, and though when challenged his answers were explicit, theism did not receive the prominence in his teaching that other doctrines did. If it be asked : What was the reason of this ? The answer is in part to be found in the tendencies of his time. In his rebound from extreme anthropomorphism and transcendentalism he emphasized the spirituality rather than the personality of God. But the chief reason lay in the temperament of the man himself. Chu Hsi was a philosopher, not a preacher. The predominant element in his character was intellectual rather than emotional. If the reader will recall the record of his life as given in an earlier chapter, he will remember that the picture there presented to us is not that of a sage-emperor, who, with his heart wrung by the sufferings of his people, cries out to the pitying Azure Heaven. With such, the realization of the personality of the God to whom he appealed would be manifest in every utterance. Nor is it that of the sage-reformer, who, with intense consciousness of his Divine mission, denounces with burning indignation the misgovernment of petty kings. Chu Hsi was a seeker after truth, fearless though cautious, and as such was loved and reverenced by many like-minded fellow-seekers ; but the atmosphere he breathed was such as would be found in the peaceful groves of the Academy, not such as would be breathed by the prophet of the hills. Wherever he might be in office, though conscientious in administration, zealous in promoting reforms, and sympathetic towards suffering, we find him nevertheless restive and ill at ease until he could return to the seclusion of some lonely temple, and there pursue his studies in peace. In the case of such a man it was hardly likely that we should find the same emphasis or tone in his theistic utterances as we find in, say, the *Odes* and *Records*, or in the writings of Confucius and Mencius.

But if, in our appreciation of Chu Hsi's philosophy, the emphasis is not to be placed on its theistic import, where is it to be placed ? The answer is clear. In any true interpretation of Chu Hsi prominence must be given to the ethical in its relation to his conception of the universe, and most of all to Love as the foundation of the physical and moral order. It is here that the Philosopher himself places the emphasis. For him, Love is the source and sum of all things : animate and inanimate, physical and psychical, material and moral. In the endless procession of worlds Love is the beginning and Love the final goal.

In an eloquent paragraph at the close of his Gifford Lectures, Professor James Ward writes : " We have been contemplating the universe as a realm of ends. . . . Within it we have distinguished the One and the Many, and we have approached it from the standpoint of the latter. In so doing we are liable to a bias, so to say, in favour of the Many : led to the idea of God as ontologically and teleologically essential to their completion, we are apt to speak as if he were a means for them. Those who attempt to start from the standpoint of the One betray a bias towards the opposite extreme. The world, in their view, is for the glory of God ; its ultimate *raison d'être* is to be the means to this divine end. Can we not transcend these one-sided extremes and find some sublimer idea which shall unify them both ? We can indeed ; and that idea is Love. . . . In such a realm of ends we trust ' that God is Love indeed, and Love creation's final law '." [1]

---

[1] *The Realm of Ends*, by James Ward, pp. 452-3.

For Chu Hsi, too, the ever present problem was that of the One and the Many, and in his efforts to solve that problem he reached the same goal as the philosopher of the West. Not, indeed, by the same road, nor possibly with the same content of the word Love. But it is in Love, as the principle of altruism, that he finds the true union of subject and object, of the ego and the universe, of the One and the Many.[1] He begins, as the most modern philosopher begins, with the constitution of his own being ; for what else is there that we really know ? He finds that not Intellect, as the nineteenth century Idealist found ; nor Will, as the present day Pragmatist finds ; but Love, is the fundamental element in human nature. He finds that man's faculties are gathered up in four elemental principles, Love, Righteousness, Reverence, and Wisdom, which are but phases of the one principle, Love ; and that these principles are the Law of his being.

From this starting-point he looks out upon the universe around him. He sees these principles running through all nature, and constituting the moral order of the universe, the Eternal Constants of heaven and earth. He traces them through every stage in the evolution of the cosmos. He sees them in the beast of the forest, in the flying hawk, in the leaping fish. He comes back again to man, and sees these same principles, alike in the sage, in whom they resemble the pearl in clear water shining with the beauty and lustre of unclouded purity ; and in the moral reprobate, in whom they resemble that same pearl submerged in the muddy pool. And, finally, not only does he recognize these principles as

[1] 全 書, bk. xlvii, f. 39 (*P.H.N.*, pp. 382–3).

attributes of the human mind; they are also attributes of the Divine mind.

And for Chu Hsi the greatest of these is Love. Love is the foundation of the universe and " creation's final law ". Love is the source of all things physical, the vital impulse sending forth its creative energy in all stages of cosmic evolution, in things animate and in things inanimate. Love is the foundation of all goodness, the root of every virtue, the basis of that moral order which pervades all things. Love is the all-inclusive attribute of God Himself, the one imperishable and undying existence. LOVE IS ALL, and LOVE IS IN ALL!

scrutiny. If the human mind, then, are also attributes of
the Divine mind.

But for God the intelligence of Reason flows, here is
a condensation of the universe and which has mind left.
Loved the pattern of all this, pattern, the and so has
tending forth the pattern? In all aspect of man's
conditions? Thus amazing and true the informatic. Here
is the condition of all mankind, the sum of man's connection,
form of that of mind, but which partakes all God's image
has a right and a happens of God Himself the and type of
able and all the existence.

INDEX